Sam Smith—Star-Spangled Hero:

The Unsung Patriot who Saved Baltimore

and Helped Win the War of 1812

Special Edition

with Lessons in Leadership

---

by

Marc De Simone, Ph.D.

and

Robert Dudley, M.S., MBA

with

Special Military History Contributor,

Lt. Col. Guy Berry, USMC

2014

See the Website

SamSmithBook.com

To Contact the Authors:

for Speaking Engagements,

for Leadership Training,

to Send a Message

———

To Follow the Blog

———

To Follow Us on Social Media

———

To Order the Original EBook:

with over 300 hyperlinks

and over 100 illustrations

Table of Contents

Section I

Moment of Destiny

Section II

Hero of the War of 1812

by Lt. Col. Guy Berry, USMC

Edited with Contributions by Marc De Simone and

Robert Dudley

Section III

A Full Life

Acknowledgements

This is a story about one of America's great unsung heroes. Little has been written on Sam Smith in the 200 years since his heroic days of defending Baltimore from the British in 1814. His is largely a story of rediscovery.

Two important books on Sam Smith, now out of print, were particularly helpful in our research. *Merchant Congressman in the Young Republic: Samuel Smith of Maryland 1752-1839* was published by Frank Cassell in 1971. John Pancake published *Samuel Smith and the Politics of Business* in 1972. We hope this new book adds fresh insight and dimension to the Sam Smith story.

We wish to thank the staff members at the Maryland Historical Society, especially Debbie Harner, for assistance in our research at the archives in Baltimore. We also applaud the society's museum display on the War of 1812 and President of the Society as well as Burt Kummerow's involvement in the Star Spangled 200 events of Baltimore.

S pecial thanks go to Jim Cheevers, Associate Director and Senior Curator of the United States Naval Academy Museum, for information on the exhibit "Seas, Lakes & Bay; The Naval War of 1812" that was open to the public from April 1 to November 3, 2013. Jennifer Bryan,

Archivist at the Nimitz Library, also provided valuable assistance.

Our thanks also go out to those at the National Headquarters of the Society of the Cincinnati in Washington, DC. Emily Schulz, Director and Curator, and librarians Ellen Clark and Rachel Jirka of the Anderson House graciously allowed us special access to their archives and library.

We want to offer thanks to our friends at the Maryland State Archives in Annapolis for their help and direction. Dr. Papenfuse has been particularly helpful and supportive of our research. Also, our thanks to Dr. Schoeberlein at the Baltimore City Archives for his assistance on this project. We thank the U.S. Senate Historical Office, especially historian Donald A. Ritchie for his help on the history of Sam Smith as a U.S. Senator. Also, our thanks to the Library of Congress Manuscript Division in Washington DC where the Smith Papers are archived.

We wish to thank Lt. Colonel Guy Berry for his work on Chapter 9: the Battle of Baltimore. His instincts as a historian combined with his active duty career in the United States Marine Corps brought a unique perspective to seeing the Battle of Baltimore from the viewpoint of a military commander. He did this work amidst his busy schedule as a squadron commander of Harrier Jet pilots. *Semper Fidelis*, Colonel Berry.

We offer special thanks to our editor Jackie Cheves for her professional work on and contributions to this manuscript. Thank you, Jackie!

Finally, we sincerely thank our wives for their enduring support during such a project. As researchers and writers, we cannot say thanks enough to them for their constant patience and love.

Marc A. De Simone, Sr., Ph.D., Baltimore, MD

Robert Dudley, M.S., MBA, Frederick, MD

October 2014

Dedication

We dedicate this book to American patriots—past, present and future. May great leaders continue to emerge and help preserve our freedoms by defending us from all enemies, foreign and domestic.

About the Authors

Marc A. De Simone, Sr., Ph.D.

Dr. Marc A. De Simone, Sr., is a native Baltimorean and teaches leadership, theories, models, and practical applications at the University of Maryland University College and at Johns Hopkins University. He also provides consulting on leadership to private and public sector entities. Marc holds a Bachelor's in History, which he has taught at both middle school and college levels. He is passionate about lessons learned from our past. He was selected as the *Benjamin Quarles University Honors Scholar in History*, studied under Dr. Benjamin Quarles at Morgan State University, and was inducted into the *Phi Alpha Theta International Honors Society for Historical Studies*, of which he was the President of the *Eta Omega Chapter* in 1976. He holds a Master's degree from St. Mary's Seminary and University, and a Ph.D. from the University of Maryland College Park, where his focus of study was on applied behavioral science in organizational settings and organization leadership. Marc is a master trainer and senior consultant with more than 35 years' experience in teaching, human resource development, and training. At present he is the City of Baltimore's Director of Training and Education in the Mayor's Office of Emergency Management. Married with four children, Marc is also an accomplished musician and volunteer museum docent at Homewood House on the grounds of Johns Hopkins University. He is co-author of the book *Empowering the Leader Within: Four Essential Virtues.*

Robert Dudley

Mr. Robert Dudley is passionate about making history come alive. He recently completed a screenplay about Francis Scott Key. Robert has traveled widely across America and other continents. While living in Europe for more than five years he traveled to twenty-five countries, which helped in the background for this book. He holds a Bachelor's in Liberal Arts (magna cum laude), a Master's in Environmental Biology, and an MBA. He lives in Maryland and enjoys sailing and scuba diving with his wife.

Special Military History Contributor

Lt. Col. Guy Berry, USMC

Colonel Guy Berry is an active duty Marine with nearly 20 years of distinguished service. He is a Harrier jet pilot, and has commanded Harrier Squadrons. A graduate of the Virginia Military Institute, he has also earned a Master's from Villanova University. Colonel Berry has taught history for three years at the U.S. Naval Academy in Annapolis. He has contributed his expertise here by writing

Chapter 9 on the Battle of Baltimore, presenting the battle from the perspective of the American Commanding Officer, Major General Sam Smith, as well as his own professional military perspective on the unique role of the US Navy and Marines upon this pivotal moment in American history.

Introduction

"The advancement and diffusion of knowledge

is the only guardian of true liberty."

James Madison

The War of 1812 has been called America's "Second War of Independence." With the commemoration of the 200th anniversary of the Battle of Baltimore in September 2014, a resurgence of interest in this sometimes "forgotten war" has taken place. We will explore just how close America came to losing that war, and the key role that Sam Smith played in preserving our independence.

How this book came about is a story within a story. One hot and humid summer afternoon in 2013, the authors looked out across the landscape from an elevated vantage point in Baltimore's Patterson Park over the area where the largest convergence of combatants in the War of 1812 had taken place. The ground on which they stood had once been known as Hampstead Hill. Dr. DeSimone spoke of the singularly important role played by Sam Smith in the outcome of those critical days in American history. Mr. Dudley, who was completing a screenplay on the life of Francis Scott Key, was surprised. In all of his research on Key, he had encountered very little on the importance of this unsung hero. Thus began a mutually enjoyable collaborative project to further make known the life, leadership abilities, and accomplishments of Sam Smith. For future leaders and lovers of freedom, here is Sam Smith's bold story.

Section I.

Moment of Destiny

"O thus be it ever when freemen shall stand between their lov'd home and the war's desolation!"

Francis Scott Key

Chapter 1

A Crisis of Leadership

"A leader is best

when people barely know he exists.

Of a good leader, who talks little,

when his work is done, his aim fulfilled,

they will say, "We did this ourselves."

Lao Tzu (604 B.C.)

Imagine this: Washington, DC has been invaded by foreign troops. The White House, the Capitol with the Library of Congress and other public buildings are burning to the ground. The President of the United States has barely escaped capture and is missing, having ridden off into the night[1]. The ominous glow of the smoldering city is visible far and wide in the night sky... Do you think that could never happen? Well, it already has![2]

It was August 1814, and a restless sense of foreboding was raising tensions in nearby Baltimore. The War of 1812 had been going for two years[3], advancing slowly toward the harbor city. On the heels of a humiliating defeat at the Battle of Bladensburg, American soldiers rode terrified and exhausted into Baltimore the night of August 24 to report on the disastrous events, just a few miles northeast of Washington, DC.

The news was devastating. American forces led by 39-year-old Brigadier General William Henry Winder, a Baltimore lawyer with no military training or experience and nephew of the Maryland governor—had been easily routed[4] by well-trained British troops nearly 5,000 strong, who had recently beaten Napoleon Bonaparte in Europe. The rout outside of Washington City was so severe that the British derisively named it the "Bladensburg Races" due to the haste in which the largely untrained American citizen-soldier militia departed. Also exiting the scene were President Madison, Secretary of War John Armstrong, Secretary of State James Monroe, and other Cabinet members who had met with General Winder[5] earlier in the day. Due to the effects of heat exhaustion brought on by stifling daytime temperatures in excess of 100 degrees, the British relented from doggedly pursuing the scattering Americans and waited until later in the day to turn their focus on the burning of Washington that night.[6]

In addition to the extreme summer heat and several days of marching that had exhausted the British troops, a very rare occurrence of a tornado and severe thunderstorm in

Washington on August 25 —attributed by some to have been sent by Divine Providence—wounded and killed more British soldiers than enemy gunfire and helped to douse the flames. Hastily the remaining troops retreated some 45 miles back to the safety of their ships anchored near Benedict, Maryland to embark and recover from their several exhausting days on shore. When rumors reached Baltimore that an impending British arrival was certain, those in charge had to quickly decide whether or not to attempt to defend the city and its people.

As the evening progressed in Baltimore, the menacing orange glow of America's devastated young capital city, less than 40 miles to the southwest, further fueled anxieties. An emergency meeting of the Committee for Vigilance and Safety was called for the next day. Baltimore was now gripped by a crisis of leadership[7].

The meeting came to order at the Baltimore City Council chambers on August 25. Of urgent importance were two questions: should they simply capitulate to the British to save its 50,000 inhabitants, or should Baltimore be defended?

Many prominent citizens, including Charles Carroll of Carrollton (a wealthy Maryland planter and a signer of the Declaration of Independence), believed that opposition to the superior British forces was sheer folly, even madness. Although Carroll had long supported American independence from Britain, he and many others did not support the War of 1812. Unaware of other circumstances now delaying the British troops, that evening Carroll wrote to his son Charles Jr.:

> It is said the enemy are on their march from Washington to Baltimore through the country, which they will probably reach in a day or two; it is probable that a deputation from the city will meet them before they enter the town and capitulate on the best terms they can; resistance will be fruitless, and if made, will only cost the lives of some valuable citizens. It is probable the shipping will be destroyed.[8]

On the other hand, if a defense were to be the choice, who should command all forces in Baltimore? Whom would they choose to save the city, which the British called a "Nest of Pirates," from suffering the same fate as Washington, DC, or worse? If Baltimore were to be defeated, what would stop the British from taking back all of America? Meanwhile, the country appeared leaderless as President Madison was on the run.

Carroll's reticence was not without merit. Baltimore, a leading port city with a lucrative shipping industry, was the third largest city in the United States at that time. A large number of notoriously fast schooner ships known as Baltimore Clippers were produced there, and maritime trade was vital to the early American economy, The issue of American "free trade and sailors' rights" was also one of the major points of contention underlying this war. [9]

America had a very small standing navy, in contrast to Britain, which had the largest and most powerful navy in the world. A method of fighting known as privateering legitimately allowed American captains of civilian merchant ships fitted with small guns to attack British merchant ships on the high seas, take command of the vessels, and profit from their booty. American schooners were fast and inflicted severe economic losses on British shipping. Privateering placed a dangerous target on the city of Baltimore. The British Royal Navy set out to eradicate the schooner ships of the privateers by burning the city and its shipbuilding docks to the ground.

With the threat of the formidable British army possibly reaching Baltimore on foot within the next 36 hours, there was little time to prepare a defense. Baltimore's city leaders continued an intense debate: capitulate or fight!

Maryland's politics at the time were dominated by the Federalist Party. Federalists, including Charles Carroll of Carrollton, did not want war with Britain. In fact, not one Federalist in the U.S. Congress cast a vote in favor of the war in June of 1812. The Governor of Maryland, Levin Winder, was a Federalist. The City of Baltimore was politically split between Federalists and Republicans. Some of the city leaders included veterans from the American Revolution. Several were heroes of that war and were not at all willing to capitulate to the British and forfeit their hard-won American independence.[10]

Federalists argued that America was no military match for the British Empire and should avoid great losses of life. Following the British defeat of Napoleon after a ten-year war on the continent of Europe [11], large reinforcements of veteran soldiers were redirected into American waters in the summer of 1814 (estimates are around 20,000), bolstering the British advantage. Some Americans believed that by capitulation, they could sooner negotiate a new relationship with Britain, resume trade, and get on with their lives.

One account of events reads as follows:

> For Brig. General William Henry Winder, nephew of the federalist governor of Maryland, the wind-swept stormy night of August 25, 1814 is one of apprehension and decision for his next military move as he rode towards Baltimore. A severe thunderstorm augmented the retreating passage from one of the darkest days of the War of 1812 as the U.S. capitol lay in smoldering ruins and national humiliation following Winder's defeat at Bladensburg, Maryland.
>
> At Montgomery County Courthouse, General Winder dashes off a letter to Brig. Gen. John Stricker at Baltimore; *'There remains no doubt but the enemy*

are on the advance to Baltimore.... Are the people animated there? Have you any reinforcements from Pennsylvania?' In the immediate crises, Baltimore seemed next as unfounded rumors spread that the British army was heading directly overland to attack the port city next.

On August 25, a Committee of Safety and Vigilance was organized to coordinate Baltimore's defense (consisting of some 30 community members). A delegation of military and naval officers presented themselves; Commodore John Rodgers[12], Commodore Oliver Hazard Perry, Major George Armistead of Fort McHenry, Commandant Robert Spence and Brig. Gen. John Stricker. These military officers unanimously agreed with three committee members (Robert Stewart, Col. John Edgar Howard and Richard Frisby) that Major General Sam Smith *'take the command of the Forces which may be called into federal service.'* Civilian and military confidence in General Winder had diminished over his defeat at Bladensburg.[13]

Outside the City Council Chambers, Samuel Smith is waiting, to be summoned, like Washington on his day of appointment to command the Continental army in 1775. General Smith informed the newly appointed U.S. Secretary of War, James Monroe, on August 27 that he had been *'appointed by his*

Excellency Gov. Winder to the command of the quota of Maryland under the general order of the 4th July 1814 and that I have assumed command conformably to my rank. ...' As a major general in the Maryland militia and now being called into active federal service, Sam Smith outranked Brig. General Winder as commander of Baltimore's defenses.

Smith's experience as a Revolutionary officer, his leadership in the U.S. Senate, and ability as a successful merchant, provided the necessary qualifications. That August 25, when the Committee of Vigilance and Safety gathered in the Council Chambers, a committee member, Richard Frisby, remembered the critical conversation that took place in the council chambers when Colonel John E. Howard entered the chamber and rose to speak.[14]

Native Baltimorean John Eager Howard, a Colonel who had fought in many battles and was a hero of the American Revolution[15], was now 62 years old.[16] He had received a silver medal from Congress for his valiant command of the 3rd Maryland Regiment of the Continental Army at the pivotal Battle of Cowpens, South Carolina. He had been Governor of Maryland and served in the Continental Congress and U.S. Senate. Despite his Federalist stance, he would now rise to take a stand to defend his beloved Baltimore:

Mr. President, I believe that I have as much property at stake as most others and I have four sons in the field of Battle. I had sooner see my sons dead and my property in ashes, than agree to any capitulation with the enemy. No, my friends, never. All my property is here. My Wife, my children, my friends, and all that is nearest to me on earth are here, but I had sooner see them all buried in ruins, and myself along with them, than see Baltimore make a last and disgraceful surrender to the enemies of our beloved Country.[17]

His fellow Baltimoreans and gathered officers with " *'unbounded confidence in his patriotism, judgment, and valor'*" cheerfully rallied around his standard in defense of their homes and firesides.[18] When General Smith was approached with the news, after a moment of pause, and in a most feeling and animated tone of voice he answered:

"My friends, I have but one life to lose, and that, I have at all times been willing to hazard in defense of my beloved country. Tell the members of your convention that I willingly obey their call, and, confidently expect their hearty cooperation in every necessary means of defense".... Soon the General was on horseback "animating" his fellow citizens to buckle on their armor and prepare to defend their homes and all that is dear to freemen.[19]

In the midst of a severe leadership crisis[20], Sam Smith was now propelled onto center stage of the largest and most decisive battle of the War of 1812[21]. The future of the young American Republic stood in the balance[22]. In a very short time, the well-guided decisions and actions of this largely unsung American hero would literally change the course of American history.[23]

Leadership Lesson 1

When Destiny Calls

Few individuals have been called to lead as Sam Smith was called. Ancient Rome had its Cincinnatus, the famed general who left his plough to defeat Rome's enemies, only to decline the position of Dictator for Life when it was offered to him, and instead return to pick up his plough where he left it before the battle. When destiny calls, *all will do whatever it is their habit to do.* Sam Smith was no exception. He had been preparing for this moment of destiny all of his life; when the crisis came, *he did what it was his habit to do – he led others; and led well.*

When fate taps someone on the shoulder, turns them around, and throws that person a sucker punch, they will do what it is their habit to do; people with bad habits will respond badly . . . people with good habits of leading, will lead well.

A Leadership "Primer" . . . We use some words so frequently that we sometimes take their meanings for granted. The definition of a word is found in the dictionary, but the meaning of a word is often much more subjective and prone to a number of meanings due to such things as common usage, ignorance, and/or semantic assumptions based on connotation.

In this first chapter, it is good to examine *some generic elements of the topic of leadership in general and define key words*, compare key words, and explain what a leader is, and what a leader does, in very basic terms. This will give us a shared lexicon to be able to describe and explain the different phenomena that make up this fascinating subject of Sam Smith as a paragon of leadership virtue. This examination will also assist us as it helps to compares and contrasts the related concepts of "manager" and "supervisor" to that of "leader."

When referring to the concept of "leader" in this book, we mean "leader" as according to a very specific definition of the word "leader" – It is good to establish a simple definition of the word "leader" and compare and contrast "leader" with "manager" and "supervisor." There are many scholarly definitions of "leader" and "leadership," but for our purposes, let us use this as a common definition:

A leader is someone who helps someone else, or some group, to get somewhere or do something that they could not have gotten to or done without the help

As simple as our definition is, it is full of fine nuances and implied complexities. Let's investigate further by breaking it down section by section.

First, a leader is **someone**, *not their title, their position, their place in the organizational hierarchy, but a person.* Often, we refer to individuals as "leaders" because they hold a high office or high level of managerial responsibility. But being a "leader" does not come automatically with the promotion or with the appellation of "leader." How many of us have had to "salute an empty suit." The stories of folks in high places who are the antithesis of what it means to be a good leader are endless. We all could probably identify two or three such individuals without any trouble. *A leader is a person, not a title – Sam Smith led by the personal virtue (good habits of leadership behaviors) of the strength of his character as a leader, not by of virtue of his title.*

Second, a leader is someone **who helps**. Simple, yes; easy, no! Imagine going up to a "leader" and asking them, "Can you help me?" and their response is "No." Sometimes, those we call "leader" lack the skill, or the will, to help others. Through either incompetence or uncooperativeness, those who would be our leaders are sometimes unable to help. If one cannot help due to *lack of ability (the Skill)*, **or** *will not help for some egocentric or socio-centric reason (the Will),* then they are not a leader. They may be a supervisor or manager, they may hold the position of leadership, *but they are not a leader. Sam Smith had the skill and the will to lead those in need to victory in September of 1814.*

Third, a leader is someone who helps **someone else, or some group**. Being a "leader," in its essence, implies that one has "followers." Many self-appointed would-be leaders clamor for a following but have no followers. Real leaders have followers. There is a relationship that is established between the leader and the followers that is mutually beneficial. *Beware of self-professed "leaders" who do not have anyone following. Sam Smith's "followers" – even those who did not particularly care for him personally, nor share the same political beliefs as he professed – chose him above all others to be the one man that they would follow as the supreme commander of the forces at the Defense of Baltimore.*

Next, a leader is someone who helps someone else, or some group, **to get some place or do something**. *The object of leadership is to bring about some sort of improved change of state, some sort of desirable outcome, output, problem solved, destination reached, or benefit gained. For Sam Smith, it was the Defense of Baltimore.* For Moses and the Children of Israel, it was getting to the Promised Land, for Harriett Tubman, it was following the Drinking Gourd to freedom, for George Washington, it was helping to establish the *Novus ordo seclorum* (new order of things) we call the United States of America. For Lee Iacocca, it was saving Chrysler Motor Company, for a corporate executive, it's probably return on investment and double digit profitability for the fourth quarter of the fiscal year. For the people in mission-critical professions, it may be successfully accomplishing the mission while maintaining good morale. *Whatever it is, the leader assists by doing something or leading in a special direction; and is the catalyst for, and the causing of, this desirable change for the better.*

Lastly, a leader is someone who helps someone else, or some group, to get some place or do **something that they could not have gotten to or done without the help**, because if the followers don't need the help, then they don't need the leader. Sometimes, a "leader" may actually be an impediment to the followers. A truly *good leader is someone, like Cincinnatus, like George Washington, like Sam Smith; someone who is constantly trying to work him/herself, out of a job. If the leader does not add value, then there is no reason for them attempting to lead.*

Now that we've defined what a leader is, it is necessary to point out the distinction between a leader and a manger. This difference is implied in the following definition for the term Manager:

A manager is someone who manages things, programs, or projects, and/or, for all practical purposes in some organizations, someone who supervises supervisors.

In most modern organizations, managers are those people who "supervise" others, who in turn are themselves first-line *supervisors*. Indeed, in some organizations a manger is someone who signs the time sheet of a person who, in turn, signs somebody else's time sheet. Although, in other organizations, it is possible that one can be a manger and have no "direct reports" at all; so it is with certain *project managers* or those who manage *cross-functionally in a matrix organization*. Usually, *managers are in leadership positions, but that does not necessarily mean that they are leaders*. Managers can be policy makers and administrators of large programs and in high leadership positions in organizations and not actually be real leaders according to our definition. In a perfect world, all mangers would be good leaders as well, but in the real world, *there are no guarantees that the ability to lead others comes with the promotion to a position of management in an organization. Sam Smith possessed leadership and management knowledge, attitude, and skills.*

The word "supervisor" comes directly from the combination of the two Latin words "super" (over), and "visor" (seer) – or "Overseer" as it is known in the Angelo-Saxon-derived English language. Therefore, a good definition for the word supervisor is:

A Supervisor is someone who oversees the work and oversees the workers.

The common folk of the agrarian past used the word "Overseer" when referring to the person with oversight responsibilities on the farm, but in the more gentile environs of the modern workplace we use the more ostentatious Latin-root word, "Supervisor," to describe the one who performs the same function. Either way, the effect is the same – watch over the work to make sure things are getting done to accomplish the mission, and watch over the workers to make sure they're all in their places with bright smiling faces.

As it is with managers, so it is with supervisors - one can be in a position of supervision without necessarily being a good leader. All three terms, *Leader, Manager, and Supervisor,* contain mutually exclusive elements which render it difficult to exclusively use any of the three terms to define any of the other individual terms. In other words, one can be a manager without being a leader or a supervisor, etc. and vice versa. Indeed, one can be a leader without being a manger or supervisor, though it is always best for organizations when managers and supervisors are true leaders in the sense of the definition given above. *Sam Smith could perform all three functions.*

Regarding "Nature vs. Nurture" . . .

There is a profound lesson in the life of Sam Smith as a leader; a lesson regarding the effects of "Nature vs. Nurture" which is best illustrated in two great books - *"Tarzan of the Apes"* by Edgar Rice Burroughs, and *"The Prince and the Pauper,"* by Mark Twain. Both classics clearly represent differing and paradoxical "myths" that seem to depict two diametrically opposed points of view as to why and how people behave - *the so-called "Nature vs. Nurture" debate* - in literature. Both myths inspire each of the opposing camps in the controversy separately, and give protagonists and antagonists a deep sense of well-being as they proceed to attempt to trounce each other's' flaws in logic and reasoning by *appealing to the emotions* through various logical fallacies and polemical rhetoric. In fact, empiricism is preferred by scientists for investigating these sorts of things for this very reason.

In the *Tarzan* myth, a baby boy, who is by birth an English Lord and Earl of Greystoke, is raised by a she-ape to become "Lord of the Jungle." This myth portrays to us that he is a *"natural born leader."* Even the direst of environmental factors cannot keep him from rising to the top of the food chain; *he was born to rule – either in England, or wherever he may find himself.* The real question is this: "What might one expect to happen to a baby picked up and raised by a she-ape in the jungle?" *Did* being *"blue-blooded"* English aristocracy really compel Tarzan, by virtue of his DNA, to become a leader?

The Prince and the Pauper myth tells the story of two almost identical boys who trade identities – one is the crown prince who only wants to be carefree like a "real boy", and the other is an beggar urchin who only wants a taste of the life of luxury. They trade places and eventually, after many twists and interesting adventures, they resume their rightful places, with the prince resuming his rightful royal status, and the pauper getting a fine position that acknowledges his abilities and cleverness. The point is: *"If you had been born in a castle, you would be king – regardless as to whom your daddy may be . . ." A great story, but a myth.*

That's the point – these stories live on through the generations precisely because they speak to this tension between the contributions of Nature and Nurture in the development of leaders. After over 100 years of debating and studying the question, the verdict is still not in – most thoughtful folks see it as a false dichotomy. *It is not a question of "either/or," but **Yes/And.** Nature plays a part, but so does Nurture!*

Just remember; both of these wonderful stories are myths. *Myths represent societal thinking as a sort of "mental shorthand" which can portray deep realities in a concise manner at best, or can over simplify complex realities and cause critical thinking to take a break and enjoy the fantasy at worst.* The difference between fantasy and an illusion is that a fantasy is purely in the mind of the dreamer, whereas an illusion may be based on some perceived reality which is not quite what it seems to be in truth. The Truth is usually a bit more complicated, less romantic, and somewhere in between the extremes.

Sam Smith is a great example of the combination of nature and nurture in producing a great leader. When destiny called, he answered.

[1] Howard, H. (2012). *Mr. and Mrs. Madison's War: America's First Couple and the Second War of Independence.* NY, NY: Bloomsbury Press.

[2] Pitch, A. (1998). *The Burning of Washington: The British Invasion of 1812.* Annapolis, MD: Naval Institute Press.

[3] Borneman, W. (2004). *1812: The War That Forged a Nation.* NY, NY: Harper Collins.

[4] Winder later experienced a military court martial but escaped conviction and returned to practicing law in Baltimore.

[5] William H. Winder Letter Book, 1814, MS 918; and Papers, MS 919: Maryland Historical Society.

[6] Eshelman, R. (2011). *A Travel Guide to the War of 1812 in the Chesapeake.* Baltimore, MD: The Johns Hopkins University Press.

[7] Cohen, E. (2002). *Supreme Command: Soldiers, Statesmen and Leadership in Wartime.* NY, NY: The Free Press.

[8] Letter No. 150, 26 August, 1814 to his son Charles Carroll Jr., Letters of Charles Carroll of Carrollton, Maryland Historical Society

[9] Perkins, B. (Editor) (1962). *The Causes of the War of 1812.* Hinsdale, IL: The Dryden Press.

[10] Langguth, A. (2006). *Union 1812: The Americans Who Fought the Second War of Independence.* NY, NY: Simon & Schuster.

[11] Harvey, R. (2007). *The War of Wars: The Epic Struggle Between Britain and France 1789 to 1815.* NY, NY: Carroll & Graf Publishers.

[12] Paullin, C. (1910). *Commodore John Rodgers.* Cleveland, OH: The Arthur H. Clark Company.

Schroeder, J. (2006). *Commodore John Rodgers: Paragon of the Early American Navy.* University Press of Florida.

[13] Hansen, M. (2010). *Collaboration: How Leaders Avoid the Traps, Build Common Ground, and Reap Big Results.* Boston, MA: Harvard Business School Publishing.

[14] *Samuel Smith Papers,* MSS 18974, Reel 5, Cont. 7-8, Library of Congress. Dated 1839; Secretary Theodore Bland to the Committee Aug. 25, 1814.

FROM:
http://maryland1812.wordpress.com/2011/04/11/decision-at-baltimore-august-25-1814/Written by Scott Sheads

[15] Piecuch, J. and Beakes, J. (2009). *John Eager Howard in the American Revolution.* Nautical & Aviation Press: Charleston, NC.

[16] MacDonald, J. (1997). *Tale of Two Soldiers: JE Howard & Samuel Smith and the New Nation.* Thesis for Masters Degree. Maryland Historical Society MF 179.H848 M135.

[17] Irwin, T. (2014). *Impact: Great Leadership Changes Everything.* Dallas, TX: BenBella Books.

[18] Leavitt, M. and McKeown, R. (2013). *Finding Allies, Building Alliances: 8 Elements that Bring and Keep People Together.* San Francisco, CA: Jossey-Bass Publishing.

[19] *Samuel Smith Papers,* MSS 18974, Reel 5, Cont. 7-8, Library of Congress. Dated 1839; Secretary Theodore Bland to the Committee Aug. 25, 1814.

FROM:
http://maryland1812.wordpress.com/2011/04/11/decision-at-baltimore-august-25-1814/Written by Scott Sheads

[20] Cassell, F. (1971). "Response to Crisis: Baltimore in 1814." *Maryland Historical Magazine 66: pg. 261-287.*

[21] Useem and Bennis (1999). *The Leadership Moment.* NY, NY: Random House.

[22] Williams, D. (2005). *Real Leadership: Helping People and Organizations Face Their Toughest Challenges.* San Francisco, CA: Berrett-Koehler Publishing.

[23] Cassell, F. (1971). *Merchant Congressman in the Young Republic: Sam Smith of Maryland, 1752-1839.* Madison, WI: University of Wisconsin Press.

Pancake, J.(1972). *Samuel Smith and the Politics of Business.* University of Alabama Press.

Cohen, W. (2001). *The Stuff of Heroes: The Eight Universal Laws of Leadership.* Longstreet Press.

Kolenda, C. (2001). *Leadership: The Warrior's Art.* Carlisle, PA: The Army War College Foundation Press.

Schwartz, R. (2013). *Smart Leaders, Smarter Teams.* San Francisco, CA: Jossey-Bass Publishing.

Sinek, S. (2011). *Start With Why: How Great Leaders Inspire Everyone to Take Action.* NY, NY: Penguin Group.

Snyder, S. and George, B. (2013). *Leadership and the Art of Struggle: How Great Leaders Grow Through Challenge and Adversity.* San Francisco, CA: Berrett-Koehler Publishers.

Wills, G. (1994). *Certain Trumpets: The Nature of Leadership.* NY, NY: Touchstone.

Chapter 2

A Life of Preparation

"Leadership development is a

lifetime journey, not a brief trip."

John Maxwell

The Smith family hailed from County Tyrone, in what today is Northern Ireland. The patriarch of the family, the elder Samuel Smith (grandfather of Sam Smith) emigrated at the age of 35 from the land of the Scots-Irish to the American Colonies in 1728, settling in Lancaster County, Pennsylvania with his wife and six-year-old son, John. The Smiths emigrated with three other Church of Scotland/Presbyterian families—the Buchanan, the Sterret, and the Spear—four families whose relationships would be intertwined for generations to come.

These new colonists were entrepreneurial and industrious.[1] In time the elder Sam Smith owned land, a flour mill, and held a minor job in the colonial government. For several years he was Sheriff of Lancaster County. In 1750 as the elder Sam Smith was aging, his son John took the lead in the family affairs. John sold the family assets in Lancaster and moved westward, with the three aforementioned families, to Carlisle, Pennsylvania.[2]

John Smith purchased land around Carlisle and opened a general store. He supplied local farmers with manufactured goods and accepted payment in grains which he then shipped to Baltimore. Grains warehoused in Baltimore were then shipped around the British Empire. Selling grain was a source of great wealth in the early colonial period as the demand was high. The mid-Atlantic colonies had good conditions for growing grains, particularly wheat. The Smith family prospered.

John Smith married Mary Buchanan in 1750 in Carlisle. The first of their five children was born July 27, 1752. They named him Samuel, after his grandfather.

Located in the Susquehanna River Valley, Carlisle was gateway to the frontier of the Allegheny Mountains and a good place for John Smith's growing business. Supplying farmers with necessary goods was very lucrative. Due to conflicts with the local Indians and the French traders in the area, the British built a fort in Carlisle. Young Sam

Smith grew up observing military activities there. In fact, his home was used as the headquarters for a British General.

At age six, young Sam Smith was enrolled in a local school, but only for one year. In 1759, the Smith, Buchanan, Sterret, and Spear families sold everything and moved together to Baltimore. The dangers of the French and Indian War and fighting in the Carlisle area had been bad for business. Wheat production dropped as farmers were recruited for militia duty. Indian raids that had resulted in the brutal deaths of whole families and sometimes included the kidnapping of young women were particularly feared by the Colonists.[3]

Fewer than 1,000 people lived in the town of Baltimore by 1760 when the Smiths and the other three families arrived from Carlisle. Located on the Patapsco River, west of the Chesapeake Bay, Baltimore showed promise of becoming a growing port, where finished goods from Europe could be sent to the expanding colonies, and agricultural goods from the American frontier could be shipped to England, Europe, the Caribbean, South America and beyond. In time, grains from central Pennsylvania, Maryland, and northern Virginia would be traded through this strategic port.

John Smith arrived in Baltimore with 40,000 pounds sterling. The other three families had also arrived with capital. John Smith formed a new business partnership with his brother-in-law, William Buchanan. They built a wharf, warehouses, and invested in ships. *Smith & Buchanan* flew a white and blue flag and exported grains to Europe, South America, and the West Indies. They prospered and built mansions in town. Within a decade Smith and Buchanan became leading businessmen in Baltimore. The Smiths, Buchanans, Sterrets, and Spears all became financially successful in this young city and together, they helped found the First Presbyterian Church of Baltimore in 1764.[4]

For the first few years in Baltimore, young Sam Smith returned to private schools. At age 14 he went to work for his father's firm as a clerk, becoming a proficient bookkeeper. In 1771, at age 19, he sailed to France on a Smith & Buchanan ship named the *Carlisle,* which was carrying a shipment of American flour. He then made his way to London where he served as a representative of Smith & Buchanan, developing business relationships with London mercantile companies that were at the center of world trade.[5]

Smith then contracted to ship a load of lead from Bristol, England to Venice, Italy. Through no fault of his own, the ship sank in the harbor of Venice. He spent the next two months there taking care of the insurance and salvage operation, and observing business opportunities there for future use. He traveled on to Naples and Rome, combining tourism with business and learning.

By the spring of 1773, Smith sailed to Marseilles, France, and then to Barcelona, Spain, seeking commercial opportunities for the family business in the western Mediterranean region. He visited various ports in Spain, as well as inland cities such as Valencia and Granada. At the British fortress of Gibraltar, he arranged a tour of the fortifications. These experiences and observations would serve him well in the years to come.

Smith sailed to Lisbon, Portugal, and eventually made his way back to London to spend the winter. He chose not to go to Paris, having determined that it was not of sufficient value to his shipping interests. In London he received a letter from his Father making him a partner in the family shipping business. His travels had proved he was ready to join his father. In the spring of 1774, he toured England, visiting key manufacturing centers and making purchases of goods to ship back to America for resale.

Although this would be Smith's only trip to Europe in the course of his lifetime, he had learned much about European economics, politics, and history. The strategic business contacts he developed also benefitted the Smiths' shipping interests. Furthermore, Smith's travels had helped develop an additional quality that would serve him well over the years ahead: leadership.[6]

By the time Smith arrived in Philadelphia in 1774, the First Continental Congress was meeting there.[7] He boarded a coach for Baltimore, where he looked forward to a happy family reunion. But circumstances would soon change. At the age of 22, Sam Smith was about to answer the call of his country for American Independence.[8]

Leadership Lesson 2

Empowering the Leader within by Becoming a Lifetime Learner – Sam Smith and the Four Cardinal Virtues

Sam Smith's family history and early development had a large part in making him the man he would become in later life. This developmental process empowered Sam Smith to lead others when it came his time to lead. As a result of his early experience, his natural leadership tendencies were honed and refined. The concept of *empowering the leader within the individual* (in order to become the sort of leader that one wants, or needs to be) is exemplified in the Life of Sam Smith. So, just what is the correct understanding and use of *the concept of empowerment*? What made Sam Smith the leader he would become?

Empowerment is a developmental process; it is a subheading of the concept of "developing others," as it were. *The basic responsibility which supervision, management, and leadership all have in common is to develop others, while ensuring that the work of the organization is still being done.* That is precisely why the three terms seem to be used interchangeably in common parlance.

The military best understands and employs the concept of empowerment in their rank structure. As it was in the time of Sam Smith, so it is today; as soon as one attains a certain rank, they immediately begin being "developed" or "empowered" for the next one. Smart leaders may intuitively or intentionally engage in this process with their subordinates. If the supervisor is busy working toward their own advancement to the next career level, then, by default, they will need to develop subordinate team leaders, individuals in charge, acting supervisors, and other so-designated employees that can be groomed to act in their capacity as replacements on day. *If you are engaged in the process of developing subordinates these individuals will be at-the-ready when opportunity presents itself. And opportunity is always waiting. Sam Smith's father sent him on his European trip to help Sam develop into the man of action he would become through the developmental process of the journey.*

For the record, "Empowerment" is not "power to the people" – that's a recipe for anarchy. Empowerment, rather, is here defined as:

Assisting others in acquiring the necessary *Knowledge*, appropriate *Attitude,* sufficient *Skills*, and providing followers with the requisite *Resources* necessary to

accomplish their part of the organizational Mission, is true "Empowerment".

Like the definition of leadership in chapter 1, *this is a simple idea, but complex in its understanding.* Elaborating on this idea, one sees that the *first three: Knowledge, Attitude, and Skills – are internal to the follower* and best developed through training, coaching, mentoring, and experience. The *fourth element, Resources, is external to the empowering leader and the receptive follower*, and must be provided by the organization through the proactive efforts of the leader, if necessary. *Sam Smith's early years and his father's leadership and "investment" in young Sam's European adventure would help to empower the leader within Sam, so that, when the time came, Sam Smith could empower the leader in others. By being a lifelong learner, Sam Smith became a lifelong leader, and was able to teach others how to empower the leader within themselves.*

---

[1] Boorstein, D. (1958). *The Americans: The Colonial Experience.* NY, NY: Vintage Books.

[2] Cassell, F. (1971). *Merchant Congressman in the Young Republic: Sam Smith of Maryland, 1752-183; Chapter 1.* Madison, WI: University of Wisconsin Press.

[3] Borneman, W. (2006). *The French and Indian War: Deciding the Fate of North America.* NY, NY: Harper Collins.

Fowler, W. (2005). *Empires at War: The French and Indian War and the Struggle for North America, 1754 to 1763.*Ny, NY: Walker & Company.

[4] Boulden, J. (1875). *The Presbyterians of Baltimore: Their Churches and Historic Graveyards.* Baltimore: Boyle & Son. This was the first Presbyterian Church in Baltimore and became the parent church of some sixteen more Presbyterian churches to follow in Baltimore.

[5] Smith gives his personal account of these early years in a biographical sketch which is in the archives of the Library of Congress: Samuel Smith Family Papers.

[6] Blanchard and Miller (2012). *Great Leaders Grow: Becoming a Leader for Life.* San Francisco, CA: Berrett-Koehler Publishing.

Cashman, K. (2008). *Leadership from the Inside Out: Becoming a Leader for Life.* San Francisco, CA: Berrett-Koehler Publishing.

Kaplan, R. (2013). *What You're Really Meant to Do: A Road Map for Reaching Your Unique Potential.* Boston, MA: Harvard Business School Publishing.

[7] Pancake, J. (1972). *Samuel Smith and the Politics of Business, pg.6.* University of Alabama Press.

[8] Cress, L. (1982). *Citizens in Arms: The Army and the Militia in American Society to 1812.* UNC Press.

Chapter 3

Revolutionary War Hero

"Success is not final, failure is not fatal: it is

the courage to continue that counts."

Attributed to Winston Churchill

The country that 22-year-old Sam Smith returned home to in 1774 had changed dramatically during his travels in Europe. Tensions between England and the Colonies continued to rise.

By the end of 1773, while Smith was still in England, the overbearing taxes that the British had imposed on the American Colonies had led to the Boston Tea Party and resulted in a British military government in the city of Boston. By September 1774, the First Continental Congress had agreed that trade restrictions on goods from England were the best immediate response. The restrictions, in due course, drastically affected the shipping business of Smith & Buchanan, leading John Smith to seek trade with new markets.

The newly reorganized company of John Smith & Sons adapted to the crisis by increasing grain sales to merchants in the Mediterranean and the West Indies. The Smith family's commitment to American independence was evident early on as they began trading milled flour shipments in exchange for arms and ammunition, which were then supplied to the Maryland Committee of Safety. At that time, John Smith (Sam's father) was himself an active member of the Baltimore Committee of Safety.

As the drumbeat of revolution intensified, the young Sam Smith took the first steps in what would become a lifetime military career. He joined a local militia in Baltimore called the Baltimore Independent Cadets, the first uniformed military company in Maryland. Eventually he became a captain in Colonel William Smallwood's First Maryland Regiment. It was in this capacity that Smith was ordered to go to Annapolis and arrest the British Colonial Governor, Sir Robert Eden. Smith was unsuccessful in his attempt. Governor Eden, at the age of 34, was admired in Maryland and allowed to depart safely to England in June of 1776.

Meanwhile, beginning in April 1775, untrained citizens known as "Continentals" in the New England colony of Massachusetts were banding together to take their stand against British occupation. In March of 1776, under the command of George Washington[1], the culminating battle in the nearly year-long Siege of Boston resulted in the British departure to Nova Scotia. On July 4, 1776, a statement that

36

came to be known as America's Declaration of Independence was issued by the Continental Congress[2] in Philadelphia. [3]

Just five days later on July 9th, General Washington called once again upon the militia to assemble at the current site of the City Hall in Manhattan to hear a public reading of a copy of the Declaration of Independence, which had just arrived from Philadelphia by special courier.[4] Afterward, local Sons of Liberty ran down to the Bowling Green to topple the gilded lead equestrian statue of King George III. Within a month the assembled American soldiers faced veteran British troops across the East River, in Brooklyn and Long Island.

The British Navy filled the harbor with more than 100 warships and 32,000 red coat soldiers who were preparing to end the war in one conclusive battle.[5] They took on the 10,000 American soldiers under Washington's command in the largest single battle of the war, the Battle of Long Island which began on August 27, 1776.[6]

Arriving from Maryland was Smallwood's Regiment that included 23-year-old Sam Smith and 22-year-old John Ross Key, a young man from Frederick, Maryland (who three years later would become the father of Francis Scott Key).

The Americans were outnumbered three-to-one and quickly became surrounded, but Washington's subordinate, Major

General William Alexander, ordered the men of "The Maryland 400" from the 1st Maryland Regiment to stand their ground and hold off the British for several hours until sunset while the bulk of the American forces retreated to temporary safety.[7] Losses for Maryland were heavy, with 256 soldiers of the Maryland 400 either killed, wounded or captured.

After sunset, General Washington organized a silent all-night orderly American retreat across the East River back to Manhattan.[8] Small boats were used to ferry the soldiers at the point where the Brooklyn Bridge stands today. With great secrecy, cunning, and determination, Washington managed to evacuate nearly 10,000 men. Sam Smith was on one of the last boats to escape along with General Washington. An early morning fog helped hide them amidst the first light of dawn as British soldiers fired shots at them into the mist. General Washington would never forget the bold Marylanders who helped save the revolution at Brooklyn Heights.[9]

The Americans retreated north to fight at Harlem, then further at White Plains. Welcomed reinforcements came in from Maryland and other states, but by late October, the British continued pursuing the Continental Army. General Washington utilized the proven Marylanders as a rear guard unit. In the Battle for Chatterton's Hill, Smith commanded a 1,600-man force from a high point overlooking the Bronx River to slow the British attack as long as possible. Although outnumbered and nearly surrounded, Smith and his men escaped. They had endured the major part of the fighting.

Washington again led a strategic retreat across New Jersey, towards Philadelphia. Along the way, the Marylanders continued to defend the rear, seeking all means to delay the British advance in order to give Washington more time for his slow-moving troops to escape. On December 10,1776 Smith was promoted to Major.[10]

That winter of 1776-77, Smith was sent back to Baltimore to help recruit new men to rebuild the Maryland Regiment. He was promoted to Lieutenant Colonel February 2, 1777.[11] That winter he helped train his new recruits.

By this time the war was taking a severe toll on John Smith's shipping business and the Smith family finances. The British blockade of the Chesapeake Bay had shut off American shipping trade out of Baltimore. Inflation caused by the war was eating away at their savings. That same winter, the 24-year-old Sam Smith became engaged to Margaret Spear. While they were still engaged, Sam Smith was off to fight again with his Maryland Regiment.

In 1777, British General Howe transported 17,000 troops from New York to the Chesapeake Bay with the goal of capturing America's capital city of Philadelphia from the south. In late August, British ships arrived at the Northern end of the Chesapeake Bay, at modern day Elkton. The first round of this campaign was fought at Brandywine Creek, and ended in disaster for the Americans. Sam Smith, however, survived the day and rallied stragglers to a defensive hill until he had a force of over 1,000 men. In the dark of night, he led them to safety to fight another day.

While it looked probable that the British Army would take Philadelphia, General Washington ordered a defensive action on the Delaware River just south of Philadelphia to cut off the British Navy from coming up the river and supplying the British Army. If the Americans could stop the British Navy long enough for the river to freeze, they would force the British Army to leave Philadelphia due to lack of supplies for the winter. Washington chose Lt. Col. Sam Smith to be the senior American officer to defend Fort Mifflin, located on Mud Island in the Delaware River.[12]

In early October, 1777, Smith went to work to prepare Fort Mifflin's defenses. With winter nearing, he requested food, clothes, ammunition, and artillery officers. He had only one week before the British Navy sailed into the Delaware Bay with over 80 warships. Once the fight for control of the river began, Smith endured a six-week non-stop artillery duel with the British. In the end, overwhelming naval cannon fire finally drove the Americans from their defenses. Smith was injured and evacuated, and the British fleet eventually reached Philadelphia and took control of the city. American patriots evacuated the city while the

American army retreated to Valley Forge. It would be the lowest point of the war for Washington and his men.[13]

Smith was ordered to return to Baltimore for the winter to recruit more soldiers for the coming year. By January of 1778, he returned to Valley Forge with fresh recruits from Baltimore. The British retreated from Philadelphia in June and began marching across New Jersey back to New York City with the Americans in pursuit.

The Battle of Monmouth in June, 1778, proved to be the last fighting engagement in the revolution for Smith. The British made it to New York City and remained there for the rest of the year. The war had come to a temporary stalemate. That summer, Smith was invited to join George Washington's staff but he declined, preferring instead to stay in the field with his men.

Smith returned to Baltimore in the winter of 1778, again to supervise recruiting. This time he asked to resign his commission due mainly to the deterioration of his family's finances. In those days, officers served largely at their own expense, and the Smith family business was running out of money due to the naval blockade and economic inflation. While Smith was still very committed to the cause of the revolution, he was also needed at home to bolster the family's income and business.[14]

At the age of 26, on the last day of the year, December 31, 1778, Smith married his fiancée of two years, Margaret

Spear, at the First Presbyterian Church of Baltimore . In the spring of 1779, Smith wrote an emotional and apologetic letter to General Washington informing the General that he needed to resign his commission due to his financial situation, but he wished to retain his rank, so as to continue assisting the revolution in other official capacities.[15] Washington wrote back commending Smith for his valiant service.[16] That summer, Smith was named Colonel in the Maryland Militia and given command of the Baltimore Town Battalion, charged with protecting Baltimore from British attack. This began his 35-year role in his capacity as the protector and defender of his beloved Baltimore. Meanwhile, Sam Smith looked to new creative ways to help both his family and the revolution: privateering and government contracting.[17]

Leadership Lesson 3

Everything Prepares One for Leadership

As was noted before, when fate taps you on the shoulder and swings you around and throws you a "sucker punch," you will do what it is your habit to do - you either block the blow, or you get hit. This is true because we are all creatures of habit. When fate placed Sam Smith in the thick of the struggle for independence, the experienced taught him several valuable lessons of a lifetime which prepared him for the events that transpired at Baltimore in 1814. Let's *review some of these habits Sam develop, so as to learn vicariously from his experience some great behavioral traits we may want to emulate to build our own "muscle memory tool chest of leadership automatic response dispositions:"*

1. The Habit of Being Faithful to Friends and Family – Sam Smith was true to his father's business and his friends in Baltimore. He would not desert either in a crisis or hour of need. Those who would lead should practice the habit of being faithful to others, so that they will do the right thing in a crisis.

2. The Habit of Volunteerism – The Latin word, *"Adsum"* summarizes Sam Smith's habit of volunteerism. *Adsum* has several meanings which apply directly to Sam Smith: to be present, be near, be in attendance, to have to do, and to assist. Sam never shrunk from a challenge. When others would fall or falter, he did his duty. He was one of the first to step up during the revolution, and continued to shout "Adsum!" every time he saw an opportunity to help by leading those who did not know what to do. *Those who would lead others should practice volunteering for the hard tasks, so that in times of duty they will heed the call to service and leadership.*

43

3. The Habit of Knowing when to Stand Firm, and when to Yield to Fight Another Day – Under the tutelage of none other than George Washington, Sam Smith learned "when to hold them, and when to fold them." Again and again, when asked to defend the rear, Sam Smith delivered for his beloved General Washington. Repeatedly standing firm, and escaping to fight another day. *Those who would lead others must practice the habit of capturing this "alternating current" of firmness and flexibility – the great oxymoronic combination - which helps the leader to be faithful to the mission, while simultaneously being faithful to looking after the morale of those who follow, and their needs in the leadership equation.*

---

[1] Aikman, L. (1983). *Rider with Destiny: George Washington.* McLean, VA: Link Press.

[2] Antal, J. (2013). *7 Leadership Lessons of the American Revolution: The Founding Fathers, Liberty and the Struggle for Independence.* Havertown, PA: Casemate Publishers.

[3] McCulough, D. (2005). *1776.* NY, NY: Simon & Schuster.

[4] Flexner, J. (1974). *Washington: The Indispensable Man.* NY, NY: A Bay Back Book.

[5] Johnston, H. (1878). *The Campaign of 1776 around New York and Brooklyn.* Brooklyn, NY: The Long Island Historical Society.

[6] Gladwell, M. (2013). *David and Goliath: Underdogs, Misfits and the Art of Battling Giants.* Little Brown & Company.

[7] Von Schell, A. et. al. (2013). *Battle Leadership.* Echo Point Books.

[8] Snyder, S. and George, B. (2013). *Leadership and the Art of Struggle: How Great Leaders Grow Through Challenge and Adversity.* San Francisco, CA: Berrett-Koehler Publishers.

[9] Cohen, W. (2001). *The Stuff of Heroes: The Eight Universal Laws of Leadership.* Longstreet Press.

[10] Maryland Historical Society, Sam Smith papers

[11] Ibid

[12] Jackson, J. (1986). *Fort Mifflin, Valiant Defender of the Delaware.* James & Sons: Norristown, PA.

[13] Hybels, B. (2012) *Courageous Leadership.* Grand Rapids, MI: Zondervan Press.

[14] Blanchard and Miller (2012). *Great Leaders Grow: Becoming A Leader for Life.* San Francisco, CA: Berrett-Koehler Publishing.

[15] Smith and Washington correspondence, September 1777 to May 1778: Maryland Historical Society, Sam Smith Papers

[16] Phillips, D. (1997). *The Founding Fathers on Leadership.* NY, NY: Warner Books.

[17] Creveld, M. (1977). *Supplying War: Logistics.* NY, NY: Cambridge University Press.

Chapter 4

Successful Baltimore Businessman

"Timing, perseverance, and ten years of trying

will eventually make you look like an overnight success."

Biz Stone, Twitter co-founder

Entrepreneurship was a hallmark of the Smith family through several generations. The impact of the Revolution had devastating effects on American merchants, requiring trade companies like Smith & Sons to come up with creative solutions to remain profitable.[1]

In early 1779, 26-year-old Smith resigned from the Continental Army and returned to the Maryland Militia in Baltimore to rebuild the family business while continuing to support the revolution. He engaged in the risky business of privateering, which was basically a legally sanctioned form of piracy on enemy shipping interests. The new American government condoned the attack of British merchant ships on the high seas as a means of crippling the

British economy during wartime. Many American shippers rebuilt their fortunes through privateering, which also included blockade running past the British war ships.

Smith & Sons eventually captured about a dozen new vessels by such activity. An expanded fleet made possible more trade, especially with the West Indies. Commodities like wheat and flour were sold at premium prices due to the wartime risks involved.

Smith also served as a broker for government contracts to provide bread, flour, and wheat produced in Maryland for the colony of Virginia. He negotiated contracts directly with Thomas Jefferson, who was then Governor of Virginia, thereby establishing a life-long friendship.[2] In Maryland, Smith became the exclusive purchasing agent for wheat and flour purchases, at a five percent commission, which was largely used to supply Maryland troops serving in the Continental Army. This expanded to include the supply and repair of gunboats to fight in the Chesapeake Bay. Smith & Sons became a provider of general military supplies as well.[3]

During the American Revolution, those who remained loyal to Britain and opposed American independence came to be known as loyalists or "Tories." In Maryland, loyalist properties were seized by the state and sold at bargain rates. Proceeds were used to fund the revolution. Sam Smith purchased such bargain properties, including several lots of land in the town of Baltimore as well as some acreage in what was then Baltimore County. He also built a distillery in Baltimore during the war.

In September 1781, General Washington and the Continental Army, augmented by Royal French troops under the command of Comte de Rochambeau, arrived in Baltimore on their way south to engage the British.[4] They camped north of town for several weeks in preparation for their march. This southern move was risky yet bold. Smith was able to aid in providing hospitality and supplies for the troops, resulting in an army refreshed and energized to confront Cornwallis in the battle that would ultimately win the war for the Americans.[5]

The British sought to defeat the Americans in the south but had suffered a severe loss at the Battle of Cowpens, South Carolina. This led to a series of events resulting in Cornwallis camping at Yorktown near the sea in expectation of British naval reinforcements. When the French navy arrived and blocked the British navy, Cornwallis was trapped by the American and French land forces and forced to surrender, ending the war and finally yielding American independence.[6]

By the time the hostilities ended in the fall of 1781 (the actual Treaty of Paris was signed at the end of 1783), Sam Smith had helped his family regain its prosperity.[7] The business would soon be renamed Samuel & John Smith Company.

As citizen soldiers returned to farming, grain supplies increased and the Smiths' export-import business grew. Lumber, wheat and flour was shipped to Sam Smith's old contacts in Spain, and Italy; in turn, their wines were imported to America. Large amounts of tobacco were shipped to England, and Smith subcontracted the shipment of tobacco to France under Robert Morris of Philadelphia, who was the exclusive purchasing agent for France in America.

In December of 1783, the Treaty of Paris was ratified in the temporary national capital of Annapolis, Maryland. General Washington traveled from New York, stopping in Baltimore, entering the city with a military escort. A victory parade and banquets were held in celebration, Sam Smith hosting. The next day General Washington resigned his commission at the Maryland State House in the Old Senate Chamber. Artist John Trumbull commemorated the event in his famous painting, *General George Washington Resigning His Commission*. The following day Washington departed for Mount Vernon, his Virginia estate, to resume civilian life.[8]

The following year, Sam Smith's grandfather died in Baltimore at the age of 91. He had lived to see his family become well established in America. He also saw America win its independence in the American Revolution. His aspirations for a legacy of freedom would be passed on, especially to his grandson and namesake, Sam Smith.[9]

Sam Smith eventually became involved in banking. He purchased shares in the Bank of Maryland and sat as a member of its first board. He also owned a retail store in Baltimore which sold his imported goods. By 1790 he owned approximately 20 ships, had expanded the company warehouses, and invested in a local Baltimore ironworks business. To help run and manage these many enterprises, Smith eventually took on a younger business partner, his cousin James Buchanan. The new company was renamed S. Smith & Buchanan.[10]

In mid-April 1789, the newly elected first president of the United States, George Washington, was escorted through the town of Baltimore on his way to New York, for the first presidential inauguration. The ceremonial procession included local militia regiments, officials and bands. Smith was among those proud to celebrate the new president's election and visit to Baltimore. A banquet and toasts were enjoyed at the famous Fountain Inn.

Smith was eventually appointed by a Maryland governor to the rank of Brigadier General of the Maryland Militia,[11] the highest military post in the state. He was then promoted to the rank of Major General on April 8, 1795 by Maryland Governor J.H. Stone.[12] He would hold this rank for the next nineteen years, and in spite of his many accomplishments, Smith enjoyed most of all being addressed as "General Sam Smith" in social circles. At this time, the Smiths lived in a two-story brick mansion on Gay Street in Baltimore.

By 1790 the population of Baltimore Town was just over 15,000. Of all the sea ports on the East Coast, it was the least expensive port of entry for merchants who were shipping goods to the American West.[13] American trade with Europe, South America and Asia grew dramatically. This included shipments of tea, coffee, chinaware, spices, silk, and opium (which was legal at the time). Such trade carried by American ships would arrive in American ports – especially the port of Baltimore, arriving on its world famous Baltimore Clipper ships. A portion of these goods would be further shipped on to ports in Europe. Manufactured and finished goods from Europe would then be shipped on American ships back to America, and from there on to the West Indies and South America. American merchants involved in this growing global and Atlantic triangular trade network took great risks, but often made great fortunes. America soon became the largest neutral carrier of goods in the world.

In 1790, American ships like the Baltimore Clipper ships carried about 40% of all American trade; by 1807 this had grown to 92%—from $43 million in 1790, to $246 million in 1807. Smith's family profited immensely from this boom in American trade.

John Smith, father of Sam, died in Baltimore on January 9, 1794 at age 72. He had served as a Representative at the Convention which formed the Maryland State Constitution in 1776, and served two terms in the Maryland State Senate. Sam Smith, carrying on the traditions of his grandfather and father, continued their involvement in political and business affairs as the young nation grew.

Sam Smith believed that a standing American navy was critical to the protection of a robust maritime trade on the high seas. In 1797 Baltimore Town subsumed Jones Town (Old Town) and Fells Point, and was incorporated as the City of Baltimore. On September 7 of that year, the U.S. Frigate *Constellation,* the second warship for the new U.S. Navy, was launched from Baltimore. This swift and agile ship, built in the Sterrett Shipyard, would later be nicknamed the "Yankee Racehorse" by the French. Five additional frigates made up the original Navy fleet, all built in ports along the eastern seaboard.[14] The *United States* was launched May 10, 1797, from Philadelphia; the *Constitution,* "Old Ironsides," was launched October 21, 1797, from Boston; the *Congress* was launched August 15, 1799, from Portsmouth, New Hampshire; the *Chesapeake* was launched December 2, 1799, from Gosport, Virginia (near Norfolk); the *President* was launched April 10, 1800, from New York, New York. These ships would play various roles in the coming conflicts with France, Britain, and the Barbary Pirates of North Africa. Sam Smith was deeply involved in the policies surrounding the principle of free trade that motivated the building of these ships.

In 1801, newly elected third President Thomas Jefferson, offered Smith the full-time cabinet position of Secretary of the Navy. Smith turned down the offer, but did agree to temporarily run the Navy Department without pay while keeping his House of Representatives seat in Congress. Eventually, Smith's brother, Robert, took the position, with Sam remaining influential in naval affairs from his role in Congress. The Smith brothers would serve together in Washington exerting great influence during the next ten years.

By 1800, Smith had designed and built his country home on a 600-acre estate about three miles outside of the city. He called it Montebello—meaning 'beautiful mount' in Italian, named in honor of a French victory over Austria that same year. The white, two-story mansion faced southwest, with a grand columned porch that overlooked the city and harbor of Baltimore and the Patapsco River. It was lavishly furnished with goods from around the world.[15] Smith enjoyed a dark-paneled study filled with books, especially those by Greek and Roman authors.[16] Smith's wife, Margaret, gave birth to 12 children in all, but only six lived to adulthood. There were many grandchildren, and the Smiths loved to see Montebello filled with them. In 1803 Smith also built a home in the area of Capitol Hill in

Washington, DC, where they often entertained on a grand scale and at great expense.[17]

In 1819, at the age of 66, Sam Smith endured a reversal of fortune that shook him deeply. He lost his business and personal fortune due to a surprising turn of events related to his business partner of some 30 years. Smith's cousin, James A. Buchanan, had been running *S. Smith & Buchanan* for many years during the time Smith was involved with his political career. After the War of 1812, the second Bank of the United States was chartered in 1816, with James Buchanan appointed as the president of the Baltimore branch. Buchanan secretly began to engage in wild speculation with the stock of the bank. Along with several other insiders, he loaned himself uncollateralized funds to buy bank stock on margin, anticipating it would rise quickly in value and allow him to cash in on a fortune. Instead there was a bank panic, and the scheme came crashing down, taking Sam Smith's fortune with it since the bank loans were in the name of *S. Smith & Buchanan Company*. Smith was suddenly served with liens on Montebello, along with his Baltimore townhouse and other assets. The once-affluent Smiths were suddenly in debt over $300,000. Smith was stunned and became deeply depressed. The resulting social stigma affected him deeply.

Over time, however, Sam Smith slowly began to rebuild his finances. His family and friends helped and eventually, after seven years of frugality and hard work, he was able to pay off all his debts. In spite of fortunes made, lost, and regained, Smith continued to be respected by all who knew him.

Leadership Lesson 4

Leadership – In Good Times, and in Bad, the Focus is on Mission and Morale

An effective leader, such as Sam Smith, is someone with the Knowledge, Attitude, Skills, Competencies, Desire, and Resources (readily available) who is truly "empowered" and is able to get things done with and through the efforts of others. The two essential ingredients for this alchemic process to take place are attention to the **"Mission"** of the organization, or what we shall refer to as "M-1," and attention to **"Morale,"** or "M-2." If a leader can't help someone get the tasks achieved (M-1), then that so-call leader is, *ipso facto*, NOT a leader at all. Also per example, if a leader does not ensure the maintenance of good working relationships on the part of the workers, *between everyone concerned*, and *the effect of that bad Morale (M-2) on achieving the goals of the organization (M-1), then the Mission (M-1) cannot be accomplished.* The direct result of most M-1 failures is due precisely because of the M-2 problems. There are those in authority in organizations who are better at M-1 issues (taking care of business) than M-2 issues (taking care of each other), or vise-versa; but it is not an "either/or" proposition – that would be a false dichotomy. *It is the hallmark of a great* *leader, such as Sam Smith, to be able to successfully address both M-1 and M-2.* See the illustration below:

Figure 1. The Mission/Morale Grid

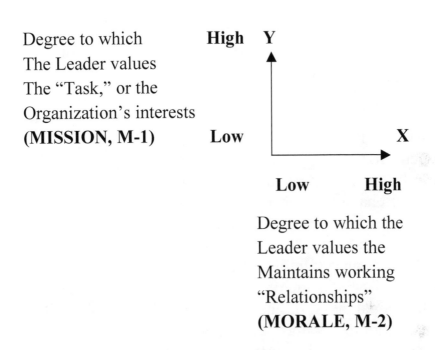

Degree to which
The Leader values
The "Task," or the
Organization's interests
(MISSION, M-1)

High Y

Low

X

Low   High

Degree to which the
Leader values the
Maintains working
"Relationships"
(MORALE, M-2)

Ultimately, a leader's effectiveness to the organization will be judged by how well the leader helps the followers to *achieve the organizational Mission,* which can be measure by the scale on the "Y" axis above; and, as to how well the leader maintains good *esprit de corps*, or maintains good working relationships that assist the organization in accomplishing its Mission *through good Morale* – as measured on the scale on the "X" axis above. Both M-1 and M-2 can be measured to indicate the overall effectiveness of a particular leader by identifying the intersection of these two quantifiable variables on the two scales, as indicated on the resulting grid in the figure above, and noting their co-relationship, one to the other, or "correlation."

The most effective leaders will be measured as "High"/"High," or upper right-hand quadrant of the resulting grid that is drawn from these two scales. This grid is derivative from, and has its origins in, the Ohio State University Leadership Studies, in the 1950's. Forms of these two critical elements (M-1 and M-2) were reported independent of each another per the results of questionnaire research on leaders and their subordinates. Thus, the "Leader Behavior Description Questionnaire" (LDBQ), and the "Supervisor Behavior Description Questionnaire" (SDBQ) came into being to study the phenomenon of leadership from an empirical perspective. "Mission" was studied under the name of "Initiating Structure" around the organizational tasks, or goals, and "Morale" was studied as "Consideration," or the degree to which leaders act in a friendly and supportive way with subordinates or followers. This famous study methodology is often referred to as a standard way of measuring leadership's effect on the organization. Around the same time period, the "people-task" distinction was also developed in other research (Blake and Mouton, McGregor, et al). Initiating Structure (Mission) is another way of designating the task orientation on the part of leaders, and Consideration (Morale) is the people-orientation aspect of the corroborating research. Additionally, the Michigan Leadership Studies, which also investigated the variables of "task" and "people," were also conducted in this period and further established variations of these two constructs (M-1 and M-2) as being of the essence of effective leadership (Fleishman, 1953), (Halpin & Winer, 1957), (Stodgill, 1962).

The modern empirical research on leadership indicates exactly what we have been considering in the life of Sam Smith all along; *taking care of business (M-1) and taking care of each other (M-2) were standard operating procedures for Sam Smith – in good times and in bad, for richer, or poorer, throughout his career in business, the military, and politics.* Regarding Sam Smith's leadership "style" at the Defense of Baltimore in 1814, whomever he couldn't convince with logical argument, he beseeched. Whomever was unaffected by his requests, he directed toward action. Whoever did not respond to direction, he ordered, or if necessary, used pressure until they did *their* duty, *his* way. As a successful businessman, general, and politician, Sam Smith adapted his leadership "style" to the situation at hand, in good times and bad, to accomplish the mission while maintaining good morale. There is a profound lesson in leadership here to follow.

---

[1] Cassell, F. (1971). *Merchant Congressman in the Young Republic: Sam Smith of Maryland, 1752-1839; pg. 38.* Madison, WI: University of Wisconsin Press.

[2] Cassell, Ibid pg 39

[3] Creveld, M. (1977). *Supplying War: Logistics*. NY, NY: Cambridge University Press.

[4] Heath, C. and D (2013). *Decisive: How to Make Better Choices in Life and Work*. NY, NY: Crown Publishing.

[5] Heifetz, R. (2009). *The Practice of Adaptive Leadership*. Boston, MA: Harvard Business School Publishing.

[6] Cameron, K. (2012). *Positive Leadership: Strategies for Extraordinary Performance*. San Francisco, CA: Berrett-Koehler Publishing.

[7] Mahler, M. (2011). *Live Life Aggressively*.

[8] Ellis, J. (2004). *His Excellency: George Washington*. NY, NY: First Vintage Books.

[9] Schwartz, P. (1996). *The Art of the Long View: Planning for the Future in an Uncertain World*. NY, NY: Doubleday Press.

[10] Pancake, J. (1972). *Samuel Smith and the Politics of Business; pg. 37*. University of Alabama Press.

[11] This painting hangs today in the City of Baltimore Council Chambers.

[12] See Appendix I for the Commission Document

[13] Browne, G. (1980). *Baltimore in the New Nation 1789-1861. Chapel Hill, NC:* UNC Press.

[14] Toll, I. (2006). *Six Frigates: The Epic History of the Founding of the U.S. Navy.* NY, NY: W.W. Norton.

[15] Items included a French Clock, French candelabras, a large French "Looking Glass", imported busts of Washington and Franklin, a Piano Forte, Tea sets, Carpets, Glassware, Silverware, and China. These are listed in the Smith papers at the Baltimore Historical Society.

[16] His library also included books such as Fielding's Works, Charles V by Robertson, History of America, Spanish Dictionary and Grammar, Homer, Travels by Coxe, Hume's History of England, Locke's Works, British Theatre, Study of Nature, History of Greece, Rousseau's Works, Moliere Works, etc. These are listed in the Baltimore City Archives with the Sam Smith Collection.

[17] Carson, B. (1990). *Ambitious Appetites: Dining, Behavior and Patterns of Consumption in Federal Washington.* Washington DC: American Institute of Architects Press.

Chapter 5

Political Service

1790 to 1800

"Public service must be more than

doing a job efficiently and

honestly. It must be a complete

dedication to the people and to

the nation."

Margaret Chase Smith, Senator from Maine

As a prominent and successful merchant in Baltimore, Sam Smith naturally became involved in community affairs and participated on various local committees. In 1783, he was appointed as one of the important wardens of the Port of Baltimore who were tasked with keeping the waterways clear, collecting duties from incoming vessels, and building wharves. Smith was also appointed by the governor to head the state militia. In 1790, he ran unopposed and won a seat in the Maryland House of Delegates where he served for two years. His public service continued as he went on to serve in the U.S. House of Representatives.[1]

As the first two-party system[2] evolved in America, Marylanders sided with either Federalists or Democrat-Republicans. The politics within Baltimore was split as well, and the polarization between the two parties grew. Smith, a conservative businessman who favored free trade, low taxes and low debts, also favored a strong military, while preferring to avoid unnecessary wars. He spent most of his political career functioning as an independent "gentleman statesman". At times, however, hardball politics were his only recourse.

At the age of 40, Smith traveled to Philadelphia as a freshman for the 3rd United States Congress to take his place as a Federalist in the red brick building called Congress Hall. Based on the 1790 Census, the first in American history, there were 105 seats in the House of Representatives. Eight seats were from Maryland, four from each party. A total of 50 Federalists were offset by a majority of 55 Democrat-Republicans. Early in his national political career, Smith had become acquainted with Congressman James Madison of Virginia. Spring of 1793 was the beginning of President Washington's second term and Smith enjoyed reconnecting with his former military commander. The U.S. Capital had just moved from New York City to Philadelphia. Both men were members of the Society of the Cincinnati, an exclusive society for former military officers who had served at least three years in the Continental Army or Navy. James McHenry,[3] also a member of the Society of the Cincinnati, was a Federalist from Baltimore, was well known to Sam Smith as they lived together in Baltimore and attended the same church. He was later appointed Secretary of War by President Washington in January, 1796. [4]

Smith's unique qualifications as both an owner of a substantial shipping company and a Revolutionary War hero, in addition to being in command of a state militia brought him high regard in Congress in two main areas of public policy: commercial trade and military affairs. Most of his legislative contributions would focus on trade policy and national defense.[5]

In 1789, the French Revolution began to rip Europe apart. The French monarchy was violently overthrown, and in January of 1793, King Louis XVI was executed by guillotine. This threatened other monarchies as the disturbing news spread. France spiraled out of control. The French militarized their society, drafting a million-man army and launching multiple wars across Europe. In 1793, France declared war on Britain resulting in a series of conflicts that lasted until 1815. America was caught in the middle.[6]

In April of 1793, President Washington had issued his Neutrality Proclamation as an attempt to keep America from being drawn into the European wars. This policy became so controversial that by the end of the year it led to the resignation of Secretary of State Thomas Jefferson, who wanted to support the French. It contributed to a major political divide resulting in the first American two-party system.

Sam Smith favored neutrality as a means to keep the American shipping trade flowing smoothly. France and England, however, would interfere with American shipping regularly over the next two decades as a result of their ongoing European wars. To add to this, North African pirates were impeding American free trade in the Mediterranean. This eventually led to the Barbary Wars. [7]

In March of 1794, Sam Smith voted to build the first six navy frigates for the purpose of protecting American trade on the high seas[8], primarily in defense against the Barbary pirates. James Madison led the House argument against this, and the vote was 43 to 41. The naval measure passed by a narrow margin; a victory for Smith. Later, in 1798, Smith helped create the U.S. Department of the Navy.

Meanwhile, in the fall of 1794, there was a serious revolt in parts of Western Pennsylvania and Western Maryland over the new taxation of whisky. General Smith was activated to lead 300 men of the Maryland State Militia to march to Frederick, Maryland to protect the state arsenal there. President Washington and Alexander Hamilton rode to

Western Pennsylvania with more than 10,000 militiamen to put down the rebellion. Smith returned to Congress and argued against increases in such excise taxes. He felt that good maritime trade policy would result in increased import duties which were a better way to pay down the federal debt. He argued that raising internal taxes would discourage capital investment in the future of American manufacturing.

In 1794, America had no real standing national military. Its only way to deal effectively with the belligerent French and British superpowers was through trade policies. This resulted in various trade wars involving the imposition of duties and tariffs, embargoes or boycotts, seizure of foreign assets, eventually shutting down all trade completely. Such measures could easily escalate into war, so President Washington decided to send a fellow Virginian, the Chief Justice of the Supreme Court, John Jay, to London, to negotiate a treaty to avoid worsening relations. The resulting Jay Treaty (largely drafted by Alexander Hamilton) became very controversial and divisive in American politics. Smith originally supported the treaty because he hoped it would end the harassment of American ocean-going commerce. Later, however, he came to oppose the treaty when it failed to achieve its main objective, free trade.

On May 1, 1796, the funding bill for the Jay Treaty passed the House by a close vote of 51 to 48. Smith ended up voting for it, believing that some treaty was better than no treaty. His strong support of open trade was in spite of party affiliation.

President Washington declined to run for a third term, desiring to retire from public life after more than 40 years of service. In September of 1796, he published his famous Farewell Address. He warned against divisive party politics and asked Americans to remain united above all. He emphasized the importance of morality and religion in society, and encouraged free and stable trade by defending the rights of American merchants.[9]

Vice President John Adams, a Federalist from Boston, was elected President in the fall of 1796. Thomas Jefferson, a Democrat-Republican from Virginia, became the next Vice-President. By that time Smith was siding with the Jeffersonian Democrat-Republicans.

As party strife in Baltimore continued to increase after 1796, Smith was often politically opposed by prominent local Federalists and friends like James McHenry, John Eager Howard (who entered the U.S. Senate that year), and Judge Joseph Hopper Nicholson. Nevertheless, through his broader connections, Smith became the most powerful politician in Baltimore with the strong support of Republican businessmen, the militia, and his prominent relatives.[10]

John Adams was inaugurated in Philadelphia as the second president of the United States in March, 1797. The major focus of his presidency was the threat of war with France. The Jay Treaty with England had offended Revolutionary France to the point that she now viewed America as an enemy. In addition, America was in debt to France financially for its help during the American Revolution. After the French Revolution, however, Americans balked at sending payments to the new revolutionary French government.

The seizure of large numbers of American ships and crews by France brought the young country to the brink of war once again. Smith and others continued to rally for strengthening the army as well as improving American port and harbor fortifications. This resulted in two years of improvements on the fort to protect Baltimore. This new upgraded fort was named Fort McHenry.

The debate over military spending created an ongoing political strain between Smith and Albert Gallatin, a Swiss immigrant who lived in Pennsylvania. Gallatin, a staunch Federalist, became a Congressman in 1795. Gallatin and the Federalists were opposed to heavy spending on defense. Their preference was to pay down past debts by raising taxes and keep the military to a minimum. Smith, on the other hand, felt it was every American's duty to provide for a common defense and that the protection of sea commerce was justified since it was the main source of America's

68

revenues (collected from import duties). The six largest cities on the American coastline—Boston, New York, Philadelphia, Baltimore, Charleston and New Orleans—were booming port cities. Furthermore, Smith argued that the recent massive loss in American property due to ship seizures far outweighed any cost for improving the navy to protect American shipping and sailors.[11]

Meanwhile, in France, American diplomats had been poorly treated by the revolutionary French government (the so called X,Y,Z Affair), adding to the threat of war. Smith concluded that it was now essential to make rapid military preparations.

By the summer of 1798, Smith actively supported bills that were passed in Congress to improve the army, launch a new Department of the Navy, and create the U.S. Marine Corps, which was established on July 11, 1798. President Adams quickly signed all these measures into law.

Paying for military spending was another matter. The proposed solution was to have a national property tax. It was approved, but only for one year. Smith wanted it to be permanent in order to provide long-term military strength for the country.

The most controversial political move of the Adams administration was the enactment of the Alien and Sedition Acts. Designed to promote safety and security during the threat of war, the laws were used more to threaten and potentially destroy political enemies. Smith strongly opposed these acts. The Federalists were heavily criticized for passing these laws, and the Acts expired after a few years. Subsequent administrations avoided such heavy-handed laws, even during times of war.

During this period, America was straining over opposing viewpoints regarding Britain and France, best illustrated by stances between Federalists and Democrat-Republicans. In the congressional election of 1798, Smith was targeted by the Federalists who raised money from well beyond Maryland in order to defeat his campaign. Nevertheless, largely due to Smith's support from the local militia, he was reelected. Under his leadership Baltimore became a stronghold for the Democrat-Republican Party. This made Smith the key to winning the state of Maryland in the upcoming presidential election of 1800.

The undeclared Quasi-War with France escalated from 1798 to 1800. America lost as many as 2,000 ships during this conflict. Insurance rates for ship owners soared. In Baltimore, there was a severe recession as shipping was impeded by this war. President Adams lost a second term due to the unpopularity of his handling of these events.

The presidential election of 1800 was a pivotal moment that ushered in 24 years of Democrat-Republican presidents (the "Virginia Dynasty") and marked the beginning of the downfall of the Federalist Party in

America. Federalist John Adams was easily defeated, but there was a tie vote between Aaron Burr and Thomas Jefferson. This tie meant that the election would be decided by the House of Representatives, which was meeting in Washington, DC for the first time. Each state was given one vote. There were 16 states at this time, so nine states' votes were needed to win the presidency. Jefferson had eight states on his side. He needed only one more.

Smith's friendships with both Burr and Jefferson led to him working as a behind-the-scenes negotiator over several months as both candidates jockeyed to win the presidency. Interestingly, Jefferson and Smith were both living in the same boarding house in DC at the time, and spoke regularly as this showdown played out. The swing states of Maryland and Vermont were teetering. But in the end, it was Delaware that changed its position by casting a blank ballot and thereby, tilted the election. It is still a bit of a mystery as to what actually caused this change, but after 35 ballots, on February 17, 1801, the election finally went to Jefferson. The era of Jeffersonian Democracy was about to begin and Sam Smith was at its center.

Leadership Lesson 5

Leaders and Politics

(Based on Principles taught in: Heifetz, R., Linsky, M., (2002). Leadership on the line: staying alive through the dangers of leading. Boston, MA: Harvard Business School Press. ISBN No. 1-57851-437-1)

Has anyone from an organization ever reached out to you and given you the subtle "warning" thing? You know how things go . . . sometimes they give you an oblique warning (or implied threat) before they pounce. Then again, sometimes they just mess with you to let you know they're watching you and that they are not happy, and then – if you do the right thing politically speaking - you may get "rehabilitated" and back in everyone's good graces. This could be a sign that you are in trouble, politically, as an aspiring leader in your organization. *Sam Smith faced these sorts of situations throughout his career and left us a valuable lesson about how to survive as an effective leader in a highly politicized environment.*

Usually, if the "powers that be" are really out to get you, they do these four things, sometimes in this pattern *(similar to the Use of Force Continuum taught in Law Enforcement, only this is used to politically neutralizing somebody "in-house" who is highly visible, well liked, and is perceived to be a threat to the established political status quo in the organization):*

1. First, they try to **Marginalize** you to make you irrelevant and let you know (ever so subtly) they're unhappy with your behavior and induce you to get with the "program;"

2. If you don't "get the message," and that doesn't work, they will try to **Distract** you from your goal to keep you off your game in the hopes you'll be rendered ineffectual;

3. Going up the continuum of force, if you are still perceived as a threat, your detractors and enemies may try to **Seduce** you - not necessarily with sexual lures (although it sometimes goes down that way) but with a promotion, or cushy job, or one of the *"Three P's" - Power, Profit, or Pleasure"* - this is a very effective strategy, and most folks on the "hit list" politically "get the memo" about this time and roll over and assume compliant and acceptable behavior;

4. Finally, if all else fails, they may choose to **Attack** you . . . at first it may be indirectly (stab you in the back), but if that doesn't do the trick, then they may even attack you directly . . . either figuratively, or in some cases, even literally and physically. (Heifetz and Linsky)

Be careful in a highly politicized environment - watch your six o'clock . . . things are not always as they seem. The higher you get up the flagpole, the more people can see

73

your backside. Sometimes they're just jealous and trying to clip your wings a little - if not, you could be in for the treatment described above. Ask yourself: *"WWSSD – What would Sam Smith do?"* Or, ask: "Is the *juice worth the squeeze?*" – In other words, "Am I willing to risk these things to continue with my course of action?" If so, then do the right thing, do the best you can, and treat others as you would have them treat you if the situation were reversed.

"Politics" has an evil connotation to some in modern society – *it did in Sam Smith's day as well.* Some politicians see the word as pejorative and prefer to be referred to as "civil servants" or "public officials;" they take umbrage when referred to as "politicians." It has jokingly been quipped that "Politics comes from two Greek words – 'Poly' which means` many,' and 'tics,' which are blood sucking parasites!" The word "Politics" actually does indeed come from the Greeks. The root-word, "polis," means "city," and the word was used to describe the machinations of the original democracies of Greek city-states. All organizations are political to one degree or another. The concept of "politics" in organizations is not necessarily always a bad thing. Sometimes, though, not being able to navigate the political straits can have dire consequences for would-be leaders.

The challenge for leaders is to learn how to become politically astute, or savvy, without becoming too political. As it was with Sam Smith, so it is with us today. When one crosses the line between knowing how to survive in a political environment and becoming part of the vested interests of the political process, one has ceased to be a leader and has become a "politico." Once that happens, not only is the leader's effectiveness potentially compromised, but the politico is now subject to the law of the political jungle – "eat or be eaten." Most people go into various leadership positions because they want to be part of the solution to societal problems – to improve the status quo - not to become part of the system of potential back-door compromises that sometimes requires selling out to the *status quo* for the questionable *quid pro quo.*

An analogy is in order to better describe the dynamics of what happens when a leader becomes too political. Common thinking is that organized crime groups usually do not target police officers for retribution because this is bad for their business and would draw too much negative attention and retribution to their operations. The thinking is that if, let's say, a police officer is sought out and killed by someone in organized crime, then that officer must have been "dirty" – someone who participated in organized crime activities or benefited from the activities of the criminals.

This, of course, is not always the case and is a gross generalization of the prevailing popular opinion for illustrative purposes only. The story goes like this: if one becomes part of the organized crime "system" by being "on the take," then one passes from the rule of law and into the realm of organized crime and the criminals' "laws" that apply there apply to such an individual who benefits from the life of crime. In other words, even a wayward police officer who "plays the gangster's' game," must understand that they "play by the gangster's rules," and is subject to the same treatment as any other participant. So, if a police officer is on the take and violates the "rules" of organized crime, he or she is given the same treatment by the criminals that any other criminal would receive, or so it is believed. *The same sort of thing is analogous to the leader who becomes too politically "involved."*

Once one crosses the line and becomes a *politico,* the rules or the organizational politicians apply. As the political landscape changes, the new political forces begin to take action against those political factions (and individuals) whom they perceive as a threat to their hegemony. Therefore, by becoming too specifically aligned with the politics of the organization, the leader may risk exposure to becoming a target for political factions contrary to the ones supported by the leader. This is a controversial analogy about a complicated subject, but anecdotal evidence exists to prove the validity of the concept. *How many times has a leader who has stepped over the line and become a political functionary of a specific political faction, been summarily fired by the new regime once it comes to power?*

Leaders cannot control all of the elements of the political environment in which they find themselves; *not even Sam Smith was immune to this reality.* The only behavior which one can control is one's own behavior. On a good day, and with a lot of effort, one may be able to control one's own behavioral response to the vicissitudes of the polis. *That is why this lesson is so important. The leader cannot control the politics of the organization, but, with herculean effort, can attempt to control his, or her, own heart. Strengthen the heart, and you strengthen the leader.* The leader with a strengthened heart is thus better prepared to deal with the inherent dangers of the political environment in which he or she finds themselves. *This is the lesson of how Sam Smith, the politician, rose above partisan politics for the common good of the polis.*

---

[1] Wood, G. (2009). *Empire of Liberty: A History of the Early Republic, 1789 - 1815.* NY, NY: Oxford University Press.

[2] Bowers, C. (1936). *Jefferson in Power: The Death Struggle of the Federalists.* Cambridge, MA: Riverside Press.

[3] Robbins, K. (2013). *James McHenry: Forgotten Federalist.* Atlanta, GA: University of Georgia Press.

[4] Myers, J. (2010). *Liberty Without Anarchy: A History of the Society of the Cincinnati.* Charlottesville, VA: University of Virginia Press.

[5] Cassell, F. (1971). *Merchant Congressman in the Young Republic: Sam Smith of Maryland, 1752-1839.* Madison, WI: University of Wisconsin Press.

[6] Harvey, R. (2007). *The War of Wars: The Epic Struggle Between Britain and France 1789 to 1815.* NY, NY: Carroll & Graf Publishers.

[7] Harding and Harding (1999). *Seapower and Naval Warfare, 1650 to 1830.* London, UK: UCL Press.

[8] Toll, I. (2006). *Six Frigates: The Epic History of the Founding of the U.S. Navy.* NY, NY: W.W. Norton.

[9] Ellis, J. (2004). *His Excellency: George Washington.* NY, NY: First Vintage Books.

[10] Lencioni, P. (2006). *Silos, Politics and Turf Wars.* San Francisco, CA: Jossey-Bass.

[11] Covey (1992). *Principle Centered Leadership.* NY, NY: Simon & Schuster.

Section II.

Hero of the War of 1812

"War is what happens when

language fails."

Margaret Atwood

Chapter 6

Background to the War of 1812

"Wars are, of course, as a rule to be avoided;

but they are far better than

certain kinds of peace."

Theodore Roosevelt

Every war has a back story. The War of 1812, sometimes referred to as the "Forgotten War," or America's "Second War of Independence," [1]was the culmination of an intense rivalry between France and England that had been going on across several continents for more than 100 years.[2]

Early exploration and settlements in North America were part of a global competition among the European powers for building colonial empires. Colonies in North America were mostly Spanish, French, and English. The Spanish controlled what we today know as Florida, Mexico, the American Southwest, and much of California. The French developed an extensive fur trading empire and settled in eastern Canada, as well as in lands along the Mississippi river including the strategically important port city of New Orleans. The French explored much of the Ohio River Valley and the Midwest region, even into the Rocky Mountain region. The British financed settlements along the Atlantic seaboard, as well as the Hudson Bay Company in Northern Canada. They also explored the Northwest coastline of what would eventually become Oregon, Washington, and British Columbia as well as lands in the Pacific, including the Hawaiian Islands. The Russians sought trapping opportunities in Alaska and in northern California around the Russian River just north of present day San Francisco.

Over time, the British became dominant in this European competition for North America, extending their global empire. The Spanish focused more on Central and South America and would eventually sell Florida to the United States in 1821. The French were decisively defeated by the British as a result of the French and Indian War (1754 to 1763) and became mostly limited in North America to the area of French Quebec and New Orleans.

Colonial America's break from Great Britain (as a result of the American Revolutionary War which lasted from 1775 to 1783) dealt a severe blow to the British grand strategy to control all of North America. The French played a major role in the American victory over British forces in that conflict. It was a case of direct blowback following French losses to the British in the French and Indian War. In 1803, the French Emperor Napoleon dealt another harsh blow to the British by selling the vast Louisiana Territory—which stretched from the Mississippi River to the Rocky Mountains, and from New Orleans to Canada—to the United States. Nevertheless, the British did not give up on their grand ambitions for North America. For more than 30 years after the close of the American Revolution, British leaders worked relentlessly towards the day when they would gain control of the vast and valuable North American continent, linking their Atlantic and Pacific trading empires. The global thousand-ship Royal Navy provided dominance at sea and protection for their international system of colonial trade known as mercantilism. [3]

Following the American Revolution, the British implemented a long-range four-part strategy to retake America. They did this by offering Americans lucrative incentives to immigrate to Canada, financing New England trading companies through London banks and influencing public opinion, impeding American westward expansion by supporting and agitating native American Indians, and interfering with American immigration and sea trade. The young United States continued to be pressured by the British Empire both from within and without.[4]

First, by offering immigration incentives, large numbers of American "Tories" who were sympathetic to Britain during the Revolution were drawn by offers of affordable land and low taxes into Canada. A major exodus of more than 40,000 Loyalists from the Colonies eventually resettled in Nova Scotia and Quebec. Even more settled in "Upper Canada" west of modern day Toronto.[5] It is estimated that as many as 500,000 loyalists left the newly founded United States to settle in British territory.

Second, financing from London banks bolstered New England trading companies, creating a strong dependence on trade with and finance from Britain. The Bank of England also owned shares in the National Bank of the United States and exerted financial pressures on the young country from 1791 to 1811 when the first 20 year Bank Charter ended. Continued British financial influence in New England undermined loans for the American war effort in 1812. Political pressure was stepped up. British spies infiltrated the New England states to influence regional politics, newspapers, and public opinion. The Federalist Party dominated New England politically. These Federalists opposed the War of 1812, conducted illegal trade with the British during the war, and some even conspired to urge New Englanders to secede from the United States during the war.[6] By 1814, the British plan was to defeat the American navy on Lake Champlain, then march south to New York City and split New England off from the rest of America. When that failed, a convention was called in November in Hartford, Connecticut further seeking to undermine the American War effort.[7]

Third, continual British agitation of Native American Indian tribes against the United States was part of the systematic British effort to block U.S. westward expansion. In attempts to prevent the Americans from crossing over and settling west of the Appalachian Mountains, the British supplied Indians with firearms and strategic advice. Chief Tecumseh built a powerful 15 nation Indian Confederacy with British help. In the Northwest Territories, this help was provided from the British in Canada who supplied the British-controlled frontier forts on the American side of the border. The British were supposed to vacate these forts in accordance with the 1783 Treaty of Paris that ended the American Revolution, but failed to do so. Similarly, in the Southeast, the British supplied arms and agitated the Creek Indians to fight the Americans to prevent any westward expansion there.[8]

Fourth, the British continued to conduct a trade war against America, which for decades they had used to weaken the American economy in preparation for an eventual military attack.[9] Various trade sanctions were placed on American shipping in an effort to limit economic growth. As France and England continued to face off in one war after another, American shipping and commerce were frequently caught in the crossfire. Thousands of American merchant ships were confiscated by both French and British belligerents, and many American sailors were captured and impressed (forced) to serve in the British navy. Through this often violent method of "recruitment", the British insisted that those born in Britain could never renounce British Sovereignty over their lives as subjects to the Crown, even if they became legitimate naturalized American citizens. About one-third of American sailors were immigrants, valuable targets for the Royal Navy that desperately needed more sailors during these war years.[10]

When President James Madison finally declared war against Britain in 1812, it was out of total exasperation. The Americans had tried to avoid war for decades, yet they were also desperate to defend their recently hard won independence. [11]

Madison had hoped to take Canada easily and quickly. He had several purposes for targeting Canada early in the war. First, he wanted to stop the British from stirring up Indian agitation and supplying them with weapons on America's western frontiers. Second, he wanted to cut off Canadian supplies to the British fleet based in Halifax, Nova Scotia. Third, he intended to stop the British support of spies who were operating underground for the secession of New England.[12]

The tide of the War of 1812 shifted dramatically in the favor of the British when French Emperor Napoleon abdicated in Europe in the spring of 1814. The British could finally concentrate enough of their veteran forces against the Americans. That summer the American states were blockaded from Boston and New York all the way to New Orleans by a massive British naval blockade. This was highly effective and caused a severe economic depression in America. Inflation became rampant and many banks collapsed due to the elimination of the national central bank in 1811. Madison had a difficult time funding the war, and the government actually defaulted economically on its payments by November of 1814— the only time in American history that the government defaulted on its debts.[13]

America's future was at stake and in grave jeopardy. Great Britain was seeking to recapture its former colonies and spread its empire across the North American continent, from the Atlantic to the Pacific, and from the North Pole to the Gulf of Mexico. A British victory in the War of 1812 would inhance their dominance over global trade, their increased wealth from the American continent's natural resources, and a glorious triumph of the monarchy over the American experiment in republican government.[14] News of the bold, young nation—the first to create a unique form of government that moved beyond the predominant European monarchial system—spread to countries around the globe. When the bloody regicidal French Revolution followed the American Revolution, it further shook the monarchies all over Europe. Two and a half decades of intense warfare followed, only to temporarily restore a limited French monarchy. [15]

Sam Smith, like many Americans, sought for many years to avoid war and hoped to negotiate with the British to reach sound resolutions to trade differences. However, as early as 1805, President Jefferson's plenipotentiary to the British Court, James Monroe, wrote to then Senator Sam Smith from London asking confidentially for his trusted and seasoned advice on how best to wage a naval war against Great Britain. Smith knew that America was not militarily prepared to win a war against the British since there would be no help from the French. The American army was small and largely unprofessional. The American navy had only 17 warships compared to the British global fleet of over 1,000. The American economy was young and fragile and the ability to finance a war was very limited.[16] In spite of these factors, over the next few years Smith came to the conclusion that the British were not dealing in good faith. It became painfully obvious that they had no intention of negotiating with America for a peaceful outcome. They were seeking to keep the Americans contained and economically weakened until the Napoleonic Wars could be resolved, at which time they would pivot their imperial energies and unleash all of their might to take back the lost American colonies and more.[17] Once Smith and others arrived at this grim reality[18], they sought to quickly build up America's defenses as best they could and prepare for the inevitable conflict.[19]

In the Spring of 1807, Secretary of State James Madison corresponded with Senator Smith asking for advice on commercial treaties. Madison knew that tensions were mounting that were leading towards eventual conflict. Secretary of the Treasury, Albert Gallatin wrote Smith on July 17 discussing strategies to prepare for war. He wanted advice on how best to raise the money for war (bank loans, tariffs, land sales, lotteries, etc.). Gallatin predicted "the Chesapeake Bay will be blocked by war." He bluntly stated "We must take Halifax 'coute qui coute'. How many troops will be needed to defeat Canada?" He also wanted advice on how best to protect America's China and East India trade. [20]

President Jefferson had closed off all American exports to England for over a year in 1808, hoping to send a message by attempting to hurt the British economy. Instead, this boomeranged and seriously hurt the American economy through the loss of jobs and exports. When Madison became President in 1809, he continued American economic sanctions against Britain with a so called Non-Intercourse Act (1809 to 1811), which again mostly hurt the American economy. These were naive trade policy efforts intended to coerce the British into fair international relations with the young American government, but all to no avail.

Each country resorted to increased privateering. These attacks on each other's merchant fleets resulted in thousands of ships being confiscated along with their cargoes and seamen. Privateering was, in effect, a form of government sanctioned "piracy", which took a major economic toll on both sides and resulted, ultimately, in a declared war. For the Americans, there seemed no way out. The War of 1812 was the result of patriotic Americans standing up for their hard-won independence as the founders had done a generation before. [21]Even when the odds were once again very much against them[22], the young country endured the many challenges and eventually won a second war of independence, further establishing itself as a free and independent country built on republican values. Sam Smith played a major role in the drama of both American wars for independence.[23]

Leadership Lesson 6

Clear Strategic Thinking and Organizational Empowerment

Sam Smith the Organizer and *"Strategoi"*

Our very concept of the "Organization" comes to us from the Ancient Greeks (Greek Root: οργανον or transliterated as *"Organon,"* a verb which means *"to implement,"* or literally, *"that with which one works")*. Aristotle taught that an organization – any organization - even such as the fledgling United States - possesses certain identifiable and essential attributes, or what have come to be known as "The Four Marks of an Organization" – those four elemental things which together in their presence constitute the *conditio sine qua non* of any organization's existence:

1. A group of PEOPLE (the essential *Material Cause - "that out of which a thing comes to be, and which persists"*);

2. With some identified form of LEADERSHIP (*Formal Cause - "the essence," "the account of what-it-is- to-be, and the parts of the account"*);

3. With the MEANS (resources, or *Efficient Cause - "the primary source of change"*) to produce;

4. An END (outcomes or outputs, or *Final Cause - "the end, or "telos," that reason, for the sake of which, a thing is done"*).

The Athenian Greeks addressed the need for *organizational leadership* by developing a unique class of individuals. These leaders in Ancient Greece were known as *Strategoi. Sam Smith, in addition to being an American Cincinnatus, was also one of the first **American Strategoi.***

The **Strategoi** (Greek: στρατηγός = literally *"army leader,"* and from whence we get our English word, "Strategy") were an elite group of Philosopher/Warriors who provided the ancient equivalent of "boots-on-the-ground" leadership to those who followed them into battle.

90

They were trained to be "a healthy mind in a healthy body." Their mental prowess was to be as keen as their physical abilities. Thus, the *Strategoi* did not have to wait for orders from the politically sensitive "high command" or from some potentate who fancied himself a general and who was not directly involved in the battle (as was the case with most of the Greek's enemies), but were empowered to assess, decide, and act out the strategy on the tactical and operational level for optimal success in achieving the Mission. This concept of empowering "hands-on" leaders would eventually help to make the Greek army of Alexander the Great a force with which to be reckoned in the Ancient World.

There is another important lesson to be learned here: *Empowerment works;* especially if it is correctly understood and correctly employed. So just what is the correct understanding and use of the concept of empowerment? *How did Sam Smith "empower" those who followed him to the point of defeating the greatest military power of his day, the British war machine that had just defeated Napoleon Bonaparte?*

The Answer (again) is Empowerment . . .

Empowerment (as defined previously) is best understood as a developmental process; it is a subheading of the concept of "developing others." The basic responsibility of supervision, management, and especially leadership, is to develop others, while ensuring that the work is being done. Sam Smith used his background in business to master the logistics necessary to ensure that everyone had what they needed to succeed.

The concept of empowerment is exemplified and illustrated through the following familiar (if archaic) proverb: *"You can't make a silk purse out of a sow's ear."* Contrary to a more modern and intuitive understanding of the expression, one can indeed make an excellent purse out of the supple pig skin leather of a sow's ear – in bygone days excellent purses were thus made - that required only a drawstring at the top, since there was no need to stitch the sides of the inside of the naturally conical shaped severed appendage – and, in former times, sow's ear purses were highly prized by the rich and well-to-do, as opposed to the linen purses of the commoners which were always tearing at the seams and wearing out after little use.

Even into the time of Sam Smith, country folk and frontiersmen used sow's ears purses. So, according to a proper understanding of the expression, *if an artisan had the necessary Knowledge, appropriate Attitude, sufficient Skills, he or she could make an excellent purse – but not a silk purse.* Before the 1800's, silk was the sole proprietary commodity of the Chinese, and the journey across the Silk Road through Europe, all the way from one end of Asia to the other to China, took years to complete through dangerous and exotic lands. Only kings could afford silk purses.

The moral of the story, today, is that the leader must see to it that the followers have internalized the first three elements (Knowledge, Attitude, and Skills) through the leader's good example, training, coaching, mentoring, and experience. Perhaps more importantly, leaders also must also ensure the quality and sufficiency of the requite Resources necessary to help the followers do their part in accomplishing the organization's Mission.

Imagine the frustration of followers who want to do a good job, but are denied access to the things necessary to accomplish the task according to expectations and standards. No matter how good their Knowledge, Attitude, and Skills may be, without the Resources that the organization provides through the efforts of the effective leader, followers just can't be "empowered" to make a Silk Purse out of a Sow's Ear. *Sam Smith used his life experience to ensure that those who followed him were truly empowered.*

Today, it seems so many organizations operate under the thinking that empowerment is just telling people to do the best they can, and hoping they'll do it – without ensuring that leadership provides the requisite resources to folks who have been trained, coached, mentored, and with the experience necessary, to accomplish the task!

[1] Borneman, W. (2004). *1812: The War That Forged A Nation*. NY, NY: Harper Collins.

[2] When France declared war against Britain in 1793, President George Washington quickly pronounced America to be neutral. The two countries again went to war in 1803, beginning a series of wars that would last for the next 12 years. The Napoleonic Wars became epochal in the history of warfare. A naval turning point occurred in 1805 when the combined Spanish and French navies were defeated by Admiral Nelson and the British Royal Navy at the Battle of Trafalgar off the southwest coast of Spain. This eliminated the threat of a French invasion of England across the English Channel, and assured British naval dominance at sea for the next 100 years.

[3] Harding and Harding (1999). *Seapower and Naval Warfare, 1650 to 1830*. London, UK: UCL Press.

[4] Taylor, A. (2010). *The Civil War of 1812: American Citizens, British Subjects, Irish Rebels, and Indian Allies.* NY, NY: Alfred Knopf Publishers.

[5] Ryerson, E. (1970). *The Loyalists of America and Their Times: From 1620 to 1816.* NY, NY: Haskell House Publishers.

[6] Adams, H. (1877). *Documents Relating to New-England Federalism.* Boston, MA: Brown & Company.

[7] Dwight, T. (1833). *History of the Hartford Convention: with a Review of the Policy of the United States Government which Led to the War of 1812.* NY, NY: N. & J. White.

[8] Nugent, W. (2008). *Habits of Empire: A History of American Expansion.* NY, NY: Vintage Books.

[9] All wars are underwritten by economic factors. See *The Rise and Fall of the Great Powers* by Paul Kennedy.

[10] Perkins, B. (Editor) (1962). *The Causes of the War of 1812.* Hinsdale, IL: The Dryden Press.

[11] Rutland, R. (1981). *James Madison and the Search for Nationhood.* Washington, DC: U.S. Government Printing Office.

[12] Dobelli, R. (2013). *The Art of Thinking Clearly.* NY, NY: Harper Collins.

[13] Lafley and Martin (2013). *Playing to Win: How Strategy Really Works.* Boston, MA: Harvard University Press.

[14] Handel, M. (2001). *Masters of War: Classical Strategic Thought.* Portland, OR: Frank Cass Publishers.

[15] Harvey, R. (2007). *The War of Wars: The Epic Struggle between Britain and France 1789 to 1815.* NY, NY: Carroll & Graf Publishers.

[16] Goleman, G. (2011). *Leadership: The Power of Emotional Intelligence.* Northampton, MA: More than Sound.

[17] Bell, D. (2007). *The First Total War: Napoleon's Europe and the Birth of Warfare as We Know It.* NY, NY: Houghton Mifflin Company.

[18] Neustadt and May (1988). *Thinking In-Time: The Uses of History for Decision Makers.* NY, NY: A Free Press.

[19] Correspondence with James Monroe, 1805: Sam Smith Collection, MS 1790, Maryland Historical Society.

[20] Correspondence with James Madison & Albert Gallatin, 1807: Sam Smith Collection, MS 1790, Maryland Historical Society.

[21] Hickey, D. (Editor) (2013). *The War of 1812: Writings from the Second War of Independence.* NY, NY: Literary Classics.

[22] Gladwell, M. (2013). *David and Goliath: Underdogs, Misfits and the Art of Battling Giants.* Little Brown & Company.

[23] Klein, G. (2014). *Seeing What Others Don't: The Remarkable Ways We Gain Insights.* NY, NY: Public Affairs.

Chapter 7

Political Service

1801 to 1812

"The supreme art of war is to subdue the enemy

without fighting."

Sun Tzu, *The Art of War*

The consecutive terms of presidents Thomas Jefferson, James Madison, and James Monroe (that ran from 1801 to 1825) are known as the "Virginia Dynasty". This period marked a major shift in American politics, giving rise to the dominance of the "Jeffersonian" Democrat-Republican Party and the slow demise of the Federalist Party. As demonstrated by the various positions to which he was appointed, Sam Smith played significant roles in each of these "Virginia" administrations. [1]

The transfer of power after the election of 1800 was the first change in governing party control in American history, and the beginning of the end for the Federalist Party. Smith's pivotal role helped tilt the outcome in one of the closest elections the country would ever experience. [2] The majority control of the House of Representatives shifted, with 103 seats held by Democrat-Republicans and 39 seats held by Federalists. There was a new small majority of Democrat-Republicans in the U.S. Senate. President Jefferson enjoyed the cooperation of both houses of Congress as he began to take the country in a new direction.

In addition to penning the Declaration of Independence in 1776, Thomas Jefferson had served two years as Governor of Virginia (1779–1781) during the American Revolution. He had been Minister to France for four years (1785–1789) and then returned to America to serve as Washington's Secretary of State for four years (1790–1793). He also served four years as Vice President under John Adams (1797–1801).

Jefferson was a classic Francophile who did not like, nor trust, the British. He was the founder of the new Democrat-Republican Party and became the first President inaugurated in America's new capital, Washington, DC. Smith was present at Jefferson's inauguration as this new era in American politics was ushered in.

As previously mentioned, during the American Revolution Sam Smith had been the designated exclusive agent for Maryland, and in that capacity had negotiated the sales of food supplies to Virginia through Thomas Jefferson, who was governor at that time. Later, Smith became a member of Congress in Philadelphia when Jefferson was Secretary of State. It was largely due to Jefferson's influence that Smith shifted away from the Federalist Party during those years. When Jefferson became Vice President under John Adams, Smith's support for Jefferson's positions on foreign policy grew. In 1800, Smith played a critical role in getting Jefferson elected as President.[3]

President Jefferson appointed James Madison as Secretary of State for eight years. Smith had worked with Madison in Congress in Philadelphia and dealt with Madison on foreign policy during the Jefferson years. He continued to provide seasoned advice through the following two-term Madison Presidency years as well. When James Monroe was appointed by Jefferson as Minister to London for eight years, Smith corresponded with him often regarding trade policy. This continued into the successive years when Monroe became Secretary of State under Madison. Albert Gallatin was appointed by Jefferson as Secretary of Treasury for eight years. When it came to budgetary policies that conflicted with American military preparedness, Gallatin and Smith locked horns.

In the spring of 1801, President Jefferson offered the cabinet position of Secretary of the Navy to Smith. This demonstrated Jefferson's appreciation for Smith's political support and the respect Jefferson had for Smith's expertise on matters of seagoing commerce and naval defense. As noted previously, Smith only accepted the position on a temporary basis as he wanted to keep his seat in Congress. He latter lobbied for a position as a foreign minister, but Jefferson felt that since Smith lacked formal legal training he was unqualified for negotiating and drafting foreign agreements. However, six months later, Jefferson appointed Smith's brother, Robert, as the full-time Secretary of the Navy for eight years, a political move to keep Sam Smith close to Navy matters. Robert Smith was a prominent maritime lawyer in Baltimore, but was not nearly as knowledgeable about the operational side of the shipping trade or military affairs as his older brother, Sam. Robert was subsequently appointed by President Madison as Secretary of State in 1809, keeping the Smith brothers close to the center of power.

The first test of the Jefferson Administration was the result of Jefferson refusing to pay tribute to the pasha of Tripoli who was committing acts of piracy against American shipping in the Mediterranean. Sam Smith backed Jefferson's firm stance since American trade was being hurt and American sailors were being captured and put into Muslim slavery or held for ransom. This conflict began the Barbary Wars of 1801 to 1805, with a later finale in 1815. This conflict was a test of the young country's resolve. Robert Smith oversaw the first US Navy squadron to sail across the Atlantic. The American Navy and Marines ultimately defeated the Barbary pirates, a fact that is forever immortalized in the words of the Marine Corps Hymn "to the shores of Tripoli."

On July 4, 1802, President Jefferson launched the U.S. Military Academy, at West Point, NY. As an army officer in the American Revolution, Sam Smith knew personally the importance of having professionally trained officers to lead the army. He advised and supported Jefferson's actions to create the academy.

During Jefferson's first presidential term, Napoleon declared war on Britain, which began a decade of warfare known as the Napoleonic Wars across Europe and around the world from 1803 to 1815. To raise money for his war chest, Napoleon sold the Louisiana Territory to the United States in 1803 for $15 million dollars, making it one of the largest land deals in American history. With the stroke of a pen, the size of America doubled, and as mentioned in Chapter 6, the hopes of the British to take control of the majority of the North American continent were thwarted. This was a pivotal moment which painted an even larger target on the back of the young American Republic. This large payment to Napoleon would help finance the Napoleonic Wars for the next decade as well as open the doors for American westward expansion. Britain would now chart a course for total war on America. That same year Sam Smith was elected U.S. Senator from Maryland. The Lewis and Clark expedition was prepared for its launch in the following year and for the rest of his life Sam

Smith would be a long-term supporter of the expanding America West. It was mostly politicians from southern and western states who wanted this expansion. For this reason the so-called "War Hawks" would later vote in 1812 in favor of war against Britain. They reasoned it was the British who had for decades attempted to block Americans from any westward movement beyond the Appalachian Mountains. War with Britain opened the possibility for future westward development, if the British could successfully be removed from most of North America. [4]

Meanwhile, the ongoing strain between Federalists and Democrat-Republicans was growing, spreading even to the churches. The First Presbyterian Church of Baltimore, of which the Smith family was among the founders, split along the lines of the views of the two national political parties in 1803. A new church, called the Second Presbyterian Church, was started by Reverend John Glendy who was a staunch Democrat-Republican and personal friend of Thomas Jefferson. Glendy came from the same area of Northern Ireland from which the Smith ancestors had come. He had fled to America and originally settled in Virginia as the result of the Irish war for independence from the British, the so-called Irish Rebellion of 1798. Sam Smith remained a lifetime member of the First Presbyterian Church in spite of the deep divisions within his church community. [5] Years later, Reverend Glendy would strongly and publically support Sam Smith in the defense of

Baltimore against the British attack in 1814. The following year Reverend Glendy would become Chaplin for the U.S. Senate.

In 1803, Sam Smith entered the U.S. Senate. Later that year Smith's niece, "Betsy" Patterson was married in Baltimore by the Catholic Bishop John Carroll to Jerome Bonaparte, the younger brother of Napoleon Bonaparte. This caused a stir as people began to wonder what such a close connection to the warring future Emperor of France might mean for Sam Smith and America. [6]

In the following summer of 1804, Vice President Aaron Burr shot and killed Alexander Hamilton in a famous duel in New Jersey. Duels were outlawed in New Jersey and New York by that time, so Burr was indicted for murder while serving as Vice President of the United States. Hamilton had been Jefferson's major political enemy for fourteen years, and now he was dead. Burr became absent from Washington, DC when he fled south to avoid prosecution for murder and could not, therefore, preside over the U.S. Senate. This was a precarious time for senators such as Sam Smith.

Further adding to this drama, President Jefferson launched a political attack seeking the impeachment of the Federalist Supreme Court Justice Samuel Chase, one of the signers of the Declaration of Independence from Maryland. This was an attempt by Jefferson to diminish Federalist influences in the judiciary. It is the only time in American history that a sitting U.S. Justice of the Supreme Court has been impeached. Senator Sam Smith participated in this dramatic trial. Chase was not convicted, but the event left much dissention in Maryland.

Burr's murder indictment eventually went away but his political career was ended by the close of Jefferson's first term. Burr would later be involved in what appeared to be a bizarre treasonous plot. He was accused of treason by President Jefferson, and stood trial in Federal Court in Richmond, Virginia with the Federalist Chief Justice John Marshall presiding. Burr was acquitted and soon left America for several years. He travelled to Britain and other parts of Europe. In 1805, Sam Smith became President Pro Tempore of the Senate (1805 to 1808) which meant he was now second in the line of succession to the presidency and a powerful force in Jefferson's second term.

In 1807, an event that became known as the Leopard Affair moved America to the edge of war by sparking even further anger against Britain. The British Royal Navy ship HMS *Leopard* had attacked an American Navy ship, the USS *Chesapeake* off the coast of Norfolk, Virginia. The British then boarded to search the American ship for "British sailors." This event so angered Americans that many wanted to go to war with England immediately.

Jefferson, Sam Smith and others knew America was not militarily prepared for war, so Jefferson sought to retaliate by imposing a trade embargo against England. Jefferson's subsequent Embargo Act blocked all British ships from entering American ports and ordered all American ships to only sail between American ports. He hoped the economic impact on England would shake them into respecting American neutrality and cease from confiscating American ships, cargoes and seamen. Nevertheless, from 1807 to 1812, an additional 900 American ships were seized. Sam Smith agreed with this embargo even though it hurt America (including his own shipping company) in the short run. [7] He knew that the British economy was already seriously strained due to the expense of fighting the Napoleonic Wars in Europe. However, the American public suffered to the point that the embargo became extremely unpopular. Jefferson left office on that sour note and Madison became President the day the Embargo Act ended. Smith believed it was a mistake to lift the embargo. He truly hoped that if the Americans had hung on a little longer, the British would have given in due to economic pressure. He hoped they would then negotiate for better relations in disputes over sailor's rights and fair trade[8], thereby avoiding a war. [9]

Sam Smith supported the election of Madison as President. Newly elected President Madison decided to employ a slightly different version of an embargo called the "Non-

Intercourse Act" which only blocked American trade with Britain and France. Again, this mostly hurt the American economy while American ships continued to be seized. Clearly both the British and the French were more focused on their war in Europe than on American free trade and sailor's rights.

As mentioned earlier, Sam Smith's younger brother, Robert, was appointed as President Madison's first Secretary of State, and served for two years from March 1809, to April of 1811. This upset Albert Gallatin who wanted the post. The animosity between the Smith brothers and Gallatin continued to grow with time. Like Madison, Robert Smith had graduated from Princeton University. He was a lawyer who had served as Secretary of the Navy for eight years under President Jefferson. It was hoped that his tenure during those years of maritime troubles would help in his new role as Secretary of State. His brother, Sam, was very influential in the Senate. Therefore, this family arrangement had multiple potential political benefits and advantages for Madison. [10]

Over his two years in this important cabinet position, Robert Smith experienced a major falling out with President Madison. In 1811, there was a crisis over the central bank of the United States. The "Bank of the United States" had been chartered for 20 years in 1791 and was now near its expiration. There was great controversy over the existence of the bank, which had been started under the direction of Alexander Hamilton. There were serious questions as to what private interests controlled this powerful bank. Some said that English banks exerted influence over America's National Bank and this was done through manipulations of surrogates in the Federalist Party. (This may help explain why the Federalists were totally opposed to the war with Britain.) Sam Smith was strongly opposed to a re-charter, and helped kill the bank in the Senate. He was not opposed to the concept of a central bank, but rather to private control and any possible foreign influences or Federalist party political manipulations of a national bank. Therefore, when America went to war in 1812, there was no central bank to help finance the costs. Madison and Gallatin had been in favor of re-chartering the Bank. This was the last straw for Madison. In March of 1811, Madison summarily fired Secretary of State Robert Smith, and replaced him with James Monroe, while keeping Gallatin in the presidential cabinet. [11] The Smith brothers were outraged. Robert Smith's political career was ended. Sam Smith was largely ostracized within the Democrat-Republican Party as well as dropped from Dolley Madison's party guest list – a societal fate worse than death in the nation's capital of that day. [12]

After Robert Smith's removal, President Madison and others made many trumped-up accusations about Robert's alleged misdeeds, disloyalty, and unfitness. Robert countered by publishing an attack on the Madison administration in a Baltimore newspaper. [13]All this caused Madison to alienate Senator Sam Smith as well. After the incidents that surrounded his brother and Madison, Sam Smith became an even more independent-minded politician. [14]

By late 1811, Madison had decided privately that America should declare war on Britain. [15] Smith, too, who for years had sought peaceful policies with England and France, finally became convinced that war was inevitable. [16] Although he had hoped for peace, Smith had sought to warn and advise Jefferson, Madison, Monroe and Gallatin for several years in advance that the time for war was likely to come. Now that time had arrived. [17]

In June of 1812, after brief Congressional debates concerning war with Britain, a vote was finally taken. [18] The Senate count was 19 "yeas" (including Senator Smith's) to 13 "nays." The House count was 79 "yeas" to 49 "nays." No Federalists voted in favor of war.

President Madison announced the first declaration of war in American history on June 19, 1812. This would henceforth be described by the Federalists as "Mr. Madison's War." As a decorated veteran of the first War for Independence, Senator and General Sam Smith was now resolutely determined to win this Second War for American Independence. [19]

Commodore John Rodgers was in New York City on the flagship USS *President* when news arrived of the declaration of war. Within an hour, he set sail with his squadron and on June, 23, he came upon the British frigate HMS *Belvidera*. That afternoon when coming into range, Rodgers himself fired the first shot of the war by his own hand. When firing another shot, his naval gun exploded, breaking his leg and killing 16 of his men. The British ship escaped that day. Nevertheless, the war was now officially on.[20]

Leadership Lesson 7

A Lifetime of Making

Careful Deliberation & Bold Choices

Sam Smith had a keen eye when it came to dealing with the workings of the British Crown in the New World. As a result, America was able to sever the last vestiges of fealty to the Old World and its moribund attacks against this great Republic and the "American Experiment" in representative democracy. In retrospect, Sam Smith's choices seem like a "no brainer." After all, America has proven to be somewhat "exceptional" as a "city on a hill" in the affairs of the world since his time. But during his era, the "smart money" would have bet on the British in both the wars.

Sam Smith's clear eyes led to bold choices; in business, in war, in governance, and in life. Leaders, such as Sam Smith, provide followers with a salvific sense of sight that sees through the clutter of the present crisis to potential rewards of persistence.

It is written: *". . . prepare yourself for trials. Be sincere of heart and steadfast, and do not be impetuous in time of adversity . . . that you may prosper in your last days. Accept whatever happens to you; in periods of humiliation be patient. For in fire gold is tested and worthy men in the crucible of humiliation."* (Sirach 2:1-5). Sam Smith suffered the humiliation of political intrigue and false accusations against himself and his family, yet when the chips were down after the defeat (and disappearance) of James Madison at the Battle of Bladensburg, it was none other than Sam Smith whom the nation called on to save the country from *". . . the war's desolation."*

The lesson in leadership learned by considering the political life of Sam Smith here is simple; the insightfulness of the leader impacts those who follow. Each leader's vision is a complex thing, and will be covered extensively in the leadership lesson of Chapter 9 of this book, but for now, consider that the leader's vision is influenced by three important things:

1. Their personal experience gained through remembrance and deliberation on formative events in the past,

2. Their perception of the strategic opportunities in the current presenting situation, and

3. Being able to process and translate that wisdom gained through personal experience into a communicable vision that is compelling and attractive to those who want (or need) to be led.

Simple? Yes. Easy? No! It is true; one's greatness is tested in the crucible of humiliation. Those who derive wisdom from the experience are generally better prepared to deal with the adversities of leadership in the future. *Sam Smith's entire life was a preparation for his leadership exhibited at the Defense of Baltimore. All would-be leaders should ask themselves this question: "What sort of "leadership" will I exhibit based on my life lessons?"*

---

[1] Williams, D. (2005). *Real Leadership: Helping People and Organizations Face Their Toughest Challenges*. San Francisco, CA: Berrett-Koehler Publishing.

[2] Cassell, F. (1968). *General Smith and the Election of 1800.* Maryland Historical Magazine, December, Vol. 63, No. 4, pg. 341.

[3] Pancake, J. (1972). *Samuel Smith and the Politics of Business, pgs. 53-58.* University of Alabama Press.

[4] Nugent, W. (2008). *Habits of Empire: A History of American Expansion.* NY, NY: Vintage Books.

[5] George et. al., (2007). *True North: Discover Your Authentic Leadership.* San Francisco, CA: Jossey-Bass.

[6] Bell, D. (2007). *The First Total War: Napoleon's Europe and the Birth of Warfare as We Know It.* NY, NY: Houghton Mifflin Company.

[7] Linsky & Heifetz (2002). *Leadership on the Line: Staying Alive through the Dangers of Leading.* Boston, MA: Harvard Business School Publishing.

[8] As Smith had hoped, the British government eventually did reverse the orders in council regarding the impressment of sailors on American ships but it was too late by the time they finally took the step as war had just been declared by Madison. It has been argued by some historians that the British pushed the Americans so far in the hopes that they would declare war so it would look like the British were then simply reacting to American belligerence and aggression.

[9] Hybels, B. (2012) *Courageous Leadership*. Grand Rapids, MI: Zondervan Press.

[10] Rutland, R. (1981). *James Madison and the Search for Nationhood.* Washington, DC: US Government Printing Office.

[11] Original letters from Sam and Robert Smith archived at the Maryland Historical Society indicate that thirty years later, some of these wild accusations resurfaced in a Boston newspaper. These were in the form of comments attributed to John Quincy Adams who supposedly stated at a social gathering that the blame for starting the War of 1812 was due to the actions of Robert Smith when he was Secretary of State. It was inferred that the younger Smith had offended and angered the British Monarch to the point of allegedly being single handedly responsible for causing the war! The publication of John Quincy Adams' alleged remarks led to Robert Smith publishing an open letter in the same Boston newspaper demanding that Adams publicly disavow any such comments. Adams did publish a rather weak disavowal but did not specifically deny the tenor of the remarks attributed to him in the original newspaper article. This whole affair appears to be purely political wrangling but shows how deep the divide ran for decades following the war.

[12] Allgore, C. (2006). *A Perfect Union: Dolley Madison and the Creation of the American Nation.* NY, NY: Henry Holt & Company.

[13] Smith, R. (1811). *Address to the People of Baltimore,* Sun Newspaper, Baltimore; also Baltimore American Newspaper July 6, 1811.

[14] Dotlitch et. al., (2004). *Leadership Passages: The Personal and Professional Transitions that Make or Break a Leader.* San Francisco, CA: Jossey-Bass.

[15] Wills, G. (1994). *Certain Trumpets: The Nature of Leadership.* NY, NY: Touchstone.

[16] McIntosh & Rima (2007). *Overcoming the Dark Side of Leadership.* Grand Rapids, MI: Baker Books.

[17] Heath, C. & D. (2013). *Decisive: How to Make Better Choices in Life and Work.* NY, NY: Crown Publishing.

[18] Useem & Bennis (1999). *The Leadership Moment.* NY, NY: Random House.

[19] Kolenda, C. (2001*). Leadership: The Warrior's Art.* Carlisle, PA: The Army War College Foundation Press.

[20] Schroeder, J. (2006). *Commodore John Rodgers: Paragon of the Early American Navy.* University Press of Florida.

Chapter 8

Preparations for the Battle of Baltimore

"For lack of training, they

lacked knowledge.

For lack of knowledge, they lacked confidence.

For lack of confidence, they

lacked victory."

Gaius Julius Caesar (100 to 44 B.C.)

President Madison submitted his third annual speech to Congress on November 5, 1811, and revealed his expectation of war by calling for improvements and expansion of the army, the militia, and the navy. Senator Sam Smith voted enthusiastically in favor of these defense measures. Smith believed war with Britain had become inevitable and gave his special support to the navy and coastal defenses, knowing that much of the war would pivot on strategic control of the seas, bays, and inlets. [1]

In the spring of 1812, Smith proposed on the Senate floor to declare war on both France and England–both countries had been wreaking havoc on American maritime interests and trade. Ultimately, in June, Congress called for war on England alone. The debate in the House of Representatives over a war declaration was brief. The House voted in favor of war on June 4th. The debate in the Senate, however, lasted for days. The vote was close. Three votes could have blocked the war. Sam Smith voted in favor. On June 18, 1812, the U.S. Congress declared war for the first time in its history. [2]

Baltimore, in 1812, was a dynamic American city–third largest in the nation, a major trading port and shipbuilding center, and home to anti-British privateers[3]. The diverse population included many immigrants such as French, Irish, and Germans who had arrived over the years bringing with them their anti- British sentiments. When war was announced, the nation's reaction was mixed. Baltimore experienced a major riot focused mainly against an anti-war newspaper, *The Federal Republican.* The city was deeply divided politically. Federalists were set against the war, but the majority of Baltimore's citizens were so ready to take on the British that attacks on this Federalist newspaper lasted for days, resulting in the destruction of their offices and printing presses as well as the first war casualty on land.

The publisher, Alexander Contee Hanson Jr., had fled to Georgetown until the dust settled. Upon his return to resume business at 45 S. Charles Street, he and two dozen of his supporters were violently attacked a second time, viewed as treasonous for speaking out against the war. Local militia was called in to protect them from the mob that surrounded the building. After a brief truce, the group of Federalists was taken to the city jail for protection. Late that night, however, the mob broke into the jail, beat Hanson severely, killed General James N. Lingan, and also beat Revolutionary War hero, Henry "Light Horse Harry" Lee, of Virginia (the father of the Civil War Confederate General Robert E. Lee). The violent series of events came to be known as the Great Baltimore Riots of 1812, and earned Baltimore one of its many nicknames,"Mob Town." [4] Nevertheless, later that year, publisher Hanson was elected to the U.S. Congress from Maryland as a Federalist. [5]

With war formally declared, Smith knew Baltimore would become a prime target by the British. As a U.S. Senator from Maryland, he had been concerned for years about adequate military training and protection for the city. As a co-owner of a successful shipping company, he was intimately familiar with the abuses Americans suffered at the hands of the British and the French on the high seas. [6] He also knew that the British considered Baltimore a "nest of pirates" due to the number of privateers that originated from the home of the famous Baltimore Clipper ships. A pragmatic and prescient realist, Smith knew that aggressive preparations would be necessary to meet the unavoidable attack by the British.[7] Others were less wary, particularly Secretary of War Armstrong and Secretary of the Navy Jones.

Smith's advance preparations ranged from building up Fort McHenry and its surrounds–replete with the allocation of larger cannon to keep the attacking British ships farther at bay from the city—to training and developing the Baltimore defenders and Maryland militia, preparing Hampstead Hill with cannon and redoubts, orchestrating a regional intelligence network, devising and refining an overall battle strategy, and surrounding himself with a strong and competent leadership team. [8]

Fort McHenry was originally built in the late 1790s, a time in which concerns of an all-out war with France fueled an urgency to build a modern fort. At that time American ports along the Atlantic coast were always potential targets for naval attacks, so coastal defenses were necessarily prepared. The fort was named in honor of James McHenry, a Revolutionary War hero from Baltimore. He was a signer of the U.S. Constitution, and served as Secretary of War under Presidents Washington and Adams. Then Congressman, Sam Smith lobbied for federal funds to build the new brick fort as an improved defense for the city and port of Baltimore. [9]

Fort McHenry was built on the site of an earlier earthen defense known as Fort Whetstone. From 1798 to 1800, the new fort was reconstructed in a pentagonal shape. Smith's early experience at Fort Mifflin on the Delaware River near Philadelphia during the American Revolution proved to him that the best way to deal with an attack by sea was to keep the city out of reach of powerful naval guns. He took a keen interest in modernizing the protection provided for his home town of Baltimore. [10]

Smith returned to Baltimore from Washington, DC in June, 1812, to begin organizing and overseeing the city's defenses. Money needed to be raised. Smith began by speaking to Baltimore bankers and businessmen. As it turned out, much of the needed finances came from local Baltimoreans themselves. The federal government provided some arms, but was very slow in assisting. The State of Maryland was politically controlled by Federalists, and was also very reluctant to help pay the costs of military preparations. [11]

In January of 1813, Sam Smith received a letter (see Appendix 2 for the entire letter) from an old colleague, Jonathan Dayton. Dayton was a veteran of the American Revolution and the youngest signer of the US Constitution. He had been Speaker of the US House of Representatives and Senator from New Jersey. He had known Smith for over 35 years. He wrote Smith because of his personal distress over the incompetent military leadership of the US

Army and was urging Smith to take command of the Army before there were any additional disasters. The early stages of the war in Canada had been a complete failure. Dayton, a former political enemy, was asking Smith to come to the rescue.

> "You must yourself again come forward, and reassume your military character - take the command of our Armies, or if that be already promised to Mr. Munro, as report says it is - take the command of that important portion of them which will be destined in the spring to invade Canada. You will reinspire all with that all essential in a General, confidence, which under most unhappy auspices has nearly expired and cannot be revived without extraordinary efforts on the part of our Government... Place all this, I entreat, in the debate on the new Army bill, in that strong clear and striking point of view, of which you are so capable, and have the term of enlistment of consequence extended from one to at least two years. Having done this, and whatever else you can towards establishing the military system on a firm and proper basis with a view to the coming crisis and emergency within the few short weeks which remain of the present season, let us then hear of you, and see you on a character in which you are not only more wanted, but can be so much more useful."[12]

By April 1813, the British naval juggernaught suddenly and ominously appeared at Baltimore's front door. Admiral Cockburn and his squadron sailed in close to reconnoiter Baltimore for planning the following summer's operations. He took depth findings, observed Fort McHenry's defenses through his spyglass, and blockaded the city's harbor for three weeks.[13] This alarmed the people of Baltimore and further energized Sam Smith. As the British terrorized the Chesapeake Bay communities in 1813, Smith demanded support from the apathetic Maryland Governor Levin Winder and federal officials in Washington. Fort McHenry had only 50 regular army troops serving to protect it, and its commander at that time, Major Beall, was largely uncooperative with Smith. Smith asked for muskets, ammunition, cannon, and supplies of every kind. The Governor responded weakly with a vague comment for Smith to prepare the militia to defend the city and its port.

As head of the Maryland militia, General Smith began intense training of military units in preparation for defending the city. He rotated units and trained them for short periods of time because there were no funds to pay them. He sent Major William Barney with a cavalry unit to reconnoiter the North Point area in anticipation of a British landing there. They planned ambushes and set up lookouts to signal British naval movements. [14]

In 1813, the Baltimore City Council created a Committee of Public Supply, with some members who were friends of

Smith, to procure necessary goods to prepare for the defense of Baltimore. The committee purchased food and supplies for the militia with the understanding that the federal government would later reimburse the city. This allowed for quicker action and played a large role in the effective preparations of Baltimore. [15]

General Smith added a new force to his defensive plan, the "Marine Fencibles". One hundred and fifty local marine seamen who were landlocked (due to the British blockade) manned guard boats at night and helped prepare the big cannon inside Fort McHenry.[16] These men would prove invaluable.

Repairs and expansion of defenses at the fort began and continued through the summer of 1813. Both civilian and militia work gangs rebuilt large fortifications in front of the fort. The arsenal included 56 large unmounted cannon that had been salvaged from a French ship. Smith ordered carriages to be built so that by the fall, the cannon were operational and ready for action.[17]

Hampstead Hill was a strategic geographic high-point that lay east of the city. Smith fortified the location by posting several hundred troops there. By late summer in 1813, approximately 50 cannon were positioned on the hill; one year later there were more than 100 cannon positioned along a several-mile defensive line running across this hill. Hampstead Hill would become the center of Smith's main line of defense against a potential land attack against the city. He would ultimately place more than 10,000 men behind this defensive line. [18]

By June of 1813, Smith left Brigadier General John Stricker, his Revolutionary War comrade-in-arms, in command at Baltimore and returned to Washington, DC, where he presided as Chairman of the Naval Affairs Committee in the Senate. He continued to lobby for increased resources for defenses on behalf of Baltimore. That summer Smith was successful in his recommendation to remove 61 year old Major Beall as commander of Fort McHenry. The new replacement was 33 year old Major George Armistead.[19] The cooperation between the new Major and the General was much better, allowing improvements at the fort to proceed at a more rapid pace.[20] It was not all positive for Smith though. Judge Joseph Hopper Nicholson, having a commission as a Captain, was second in command at the fort. As a Federalist, he was an ardent political adversary of General Smith. Over time, Nicholson sought to undermine Smith's reputation and smear his ability to lead the defense of Baltimore.[21]

During the summer of 1813, British Admiral Cockburn continued to terrorize Maryland communities up and down the Chesapeake Bay. In Baltimore, Sam Smith stepped up preparations for a British attack, which he was certain would eventually come. The militia underwent more training. Additional major preparations of Fort McHenry took place that summer, including the making of two new American flags for the fort. It is thought that Commodore Joshua Barney and General John Stricker recommended to Major George Armistead that Mrs. Mary Pickersgill make a large garrison flag, one that the British would have no trouble seeing from a distance. Delivered to the fort in late August, 1813, the flag measured 30 feet by 42 feet, the largest battle flag in the world. Each of its eight red and seven white stripes measured two-feet wide. Each of the fifteen white stars measured two-feet across, and represented the thirteen original colonies, plus Kentucky and Vermont which had joined the Union since the Revolutionary War. Since the size of a flag often reflected the number of troops it represented, its purpose was possibly also a ruse to trick the British into believing that the fort was home to a much larger contingent. [22]

That summer, Smith listened carefully to the recommendations of the veteran Commodore Joshua Barney, who provided a plan for building a Chesapeake Flotilla of small gun boats.[23] Smith helped convince the federal government to back and fund this plan. The Chesapeake Flotilla was built by winter, led by Joshua Barney himself. The gun boats were designed to harass the British fleet in the Bay, and were successful in this purpose.[24]

Upon the direction of Smith, additional defenses were added in order to protect the flanks of Fort McHenry on the far side of the Patapsco River.[25] Captain Samuel Babcock was the engineer Smith selected to design a battery located one and a half miles west of Fort McHenry on the shores of the Patapsco Ferry Branch. The federal government was not willing to pay for this battery so the city of Baltimore paid for it from its own resources. The half-moon shaped cannon battery was built from sod and contained six 18-pound French naval guns. In 1813, Battery Babcock was manned by a company of U.S. Sea Fencibles. In 1814, it would be manned by 75 sailors from the land-bound Chesapeake Bay Flotilla.

Fort Covington, located another one-and-a-half miles west of Battery Babcock (today the location of the headquarters of the *Baltimore Sun* newspaper printing facility), was eventually named for Brigadier General Leonard Covington, a Maryland native who was killed in Canada in the fall of 1813. The fort was V-shaped with a 10-foot-high brick wall enclosure. The front of the fort faced the harbor with a 16-foot ditch and a battery of ten 18-pound cannon. It included living quarters for a company and a powder magazine. It was first manned by a naval company of U.S. Sea Fencibles.

Across the harbor from Fort McHenry to the northeast was Lazaretto Point where three cannon were added. The distance between these two points was the narrowest in the harbor, and therefore a critical chokepoint for stopping any British ships from entering the harbor. Smith was working on a plan to completely block the harbor when the time of battle came.

British Admiral Cockburn's squadron returned to Baltimore briefly in August, 1813. Once again, Smith quickly activated the Baltimore militia and stood by for two weeks with the British ships in full view. The British squadron then departed the Chesapeake Bay for the rest of the year and anchored for the winter in Bermuda.

By the spring of 1814, Napoleon had been removed from power in Europe, leading Smith to assume that the British would be returning to America with more army troops and an even larger naval fleet. Indeed, the British sent 12,000 troops to Canada under Sir George Prevost. In August, a large fleet of war ships arrived in the Chesapeake Bay with a force of nearly 5,000 veteran soldiers under Major General Robert Ross. They landed at Benedict, Maryland on August 19. As described in Chapter One, they quickly succeeded in defeating the American defenders at Bladensburg, Maryland, then proceeded to burn Washington, D.C. A poem mocking President Madison was penned to mark the memory of the "Bladensburg Races". Smith now assumed that his beloved Baltimore was next, and as General, he went into full motion. Ironically, earlier that same month, Smith, who was then a sitting U.S. senator, was voted out of the senate by the pro-British Federalist-controlled Maryland legislature. It was, therefore, as a "lame duck" senator whose term in office would end the following March, that Smith led the heroic Defense of Baltimore. [26]

As the man holding the highest military rank, Smith secured official command of all forces in Baltimore from Governor Winder in late August. He then rallied his leadership team of officers, particularly his naval and marine officers with their expertise in placing and operating cannon. Commodore Rodgers, Smith's protégé, arrived by land from Pennsylvania with some 600 of his navy and marine men along with Captain Porter from New York just in time to join with the celebrated Captain Oliver Hazard Perry (who was already in Baltimore overseeing the building of the ship USS *Java*) and help the General strategize and synchronize the final preparations that would make all the difference for Baltimore and America.[27] As Commanding Officer of all American forces in Baltimore, Major General Sam Smith called an emergency meeting of his key officers to take place at Fort McHenry in order to launch plans for the imminent defense of Baltimore. [28]

Leadership Lesson 8

Sam Smith and the Importance of

Being Able to Lead Teams

Sam Smith possessed a unique set of human interaction skills essential for peak leadership performance in high stress situations. Those of us who are not so naturally gifted may want to emulate Sam Smith by developing those abilities in ourselves.

To begin this developmental process, would-be leaders should be asking self-examining questions regarding their own behavior. This is true because each of us can only truly "control" our own behavior, and then do our best to model the sort of behaviors we expect in others, because *those who lead best,* (as it is said) *lead by example.* Here are some soul searching questions, paraphrased liberally from Football Coach Lou Holtz and applied to our current topic, which will help us *to be the kind of leader Sam Smith was* when it comes to building our team:

1.   **Am I, as a leader, doing that which is appropriate to the situation**? Not just morally right or ethically right, but right as in appropriate for the needs of the other persons on the team in this situation, at this time. If yes, fine. If not, then stop doing what is wrong and focus on doing what is appropriate.

2.   **Am I doing all that I possibly can to do, as far as what is necessary to be done in this situation?** People can tell when we're half-stepping - and people know when they see someone really doing the best they can, too! *Always do as Sam Smith would do;* that is, the very best you can as the circumstances present themselves.

3.   **Am I doing my best to live the *Golden Rule* in my dealing with others?** The Golden Rule isn't *"She who has the gold rules,"* or *"He who wears the gold makes the rules,"* or even *"Do unto others IF they do unto me",* or *"Do unto others before they can get a chance to do it unto me,"* but the real Golden Rule – *"Do unto others as you would have them do unto you."* This is the epitome of being proactive, like Sam Smith, and not reactive, because others may not be doing "good" unto you in the present. We need to ask "how would I like to be treated?" and then treat others that way regardless as to how they are treating me here and now.

These questions are important because our lives as leaders, like Sam Smith's life was, are *public lives* - everybody else is watching our every move. In fact, *these leadership questions we ask ourselves correspond directly to another set of questions that others internally are asking of us* as we model appropriate leadership behavior. Their questions asked of us as leaders are:

1.   **Why should I trust you as my leader?** If we are doing what is appropriate we shouldn't have to worry about being seen as trustworthy.

2.   **Where is your commitment to the mission of our team?** We cannot expect others to follow us by sending them ahead where we would not go. We need to do the right things the right way, and lead from the front. Self-sacrifice on the part of the leader for the followers inspires them to do great things. And, finally,

3.   **Do you really care about me, as a person**? How can I show those who follow me that I truly do care about them as an individual person in an appropriate fashion? No one wants to be on a team with someone who couldn't care less about him or her. The morale of those who follow is just as paramount as the accomplishment of the mission. If I'm doing unto others as I would have them do unto me, then that should not be a problem.

So, if one wants to improve one's leadership in order to improve team interactions, one needs to model the behaviors that Sam Smith exhibited in times of crisis. One has to "Walk the Talk" . . .

[1] Utt, R. (2012). *Ships of Oak, Guns of Iron: The War of 1812 and the Forging of the American Navy.* Washington, D.C.: Regnery Publishing.

[2] Langguth, A. J. (2006). *Union 1812: The Americans Who Fought the Second War of Independence.* NY, NY: Simon & Schuster.

[3] Garitee, J. (1977). *The Republic's Private Navy: The American Privateering Business as Practiced by Baltimore during the War of 1812.* Middletown: Wesleyan University Press.

[4] Chew, R. (2009). "The Origins of Mob Town: Social Division and Racial Conflict in the Baltimore Riots of 1812." *Maryland Historical Magazine 104: pgs 272-301.*

[5] Hanson, Alexander Contee (1737-1877). Papers, MS 408, Maryland Historical Society.

[6] For example, on December 10, 1810, Smith lost one of his merchant ships, the Vigilant, taken by the French ship Imperatricia of Calais. He lost 444 hogsheads of tobacco and 50 bales of cotton. The ship was headed for the neutral port of Gothenburg, Sweden but was captured at 54 degrees and 10 minutes north and 3 degrees east longitude. Maryland State Archives SCM 5993 Smith papers.

[7] Weeks, B. (1989). "This Present Time of Alarm: Baltimoreans Prepare for Invasion." *Maryland Historical Magazine 84: pg. 259-266.*

[8] Miller & Blanchard (2011). *The Secret of Teams: What Great Teams Know and Do.* San Francisco, CA: Berrett-Koehler Publishing.

[9] Sheads, S. (1995). *Fort McHenry.* Baltimore, MD: The Nautical and Aviation Publishing Company of America.

[10] Lafley & Martin (2013). *Playing to Win: How Strategy Really Works.* Boston, MA: Harvard University Press.

[11] Creveld, M. (1977). *Supplying War: Logistics.* NY, NY: Cambridge University Press.

[12] Letter to Samuel Smith from Jonathan Dayton, January 26, 1813: Sam Smith Collection, MS 1790, Maryland Historical Society.

[13] George, C. (2000). *Terror on the Chesapeake: The War of 1812 on the Bay.* Shippensburg, PA: White Maine Books.

[14] Rath & Conchie (2009). *Strengths Based Leadership: Great Leaders, Teams, and Why People Follow.* NY, NY: Gallup Press.

[15] Hansen, M. (2010). *Collaboration: How Leaders Avoid the Traps, Build Common Ground, and Reap Big Results.* Boston, MA: Harvard Business School Publishing.

[16] Thomas, J. (2013) *Leadership Embodied: The Secrets to Success of the Most Effective Navy and Marines Corps Leaders*. Annapolis, MD: Naval Institute Press.

[17] Goleman, D. (2013). *Focus: The Hidden Driver of Excellence*. NY, NY: Harper Collins.

[18] Handel, M. (2001). *Masters of War: Classical Strategic Thought*. Portland, OR: Frank Cass Publishers.

[19] Armistead was the brother-in-law to Sam Smith's son-in-law.

[20] Leavitt, M. & McKeown, R. (2013). *Finding Allies, Building Alliances: 8 Elements that Bring and Keep People Together*. San Francisco, CA: Jossey-Bass Publishing.

[21] Eshelman, R. and Sheads, S. (2013). *Chesapeake Legends and Lore from the War of 1812, pg 75.* Charleston, SC: History Press.

[22] The Mary Pickersgill townhouse is a tourist attraction today located at East Pratt and Albemarle Streets in what is now Baltimore's "Little Italy." The original 30-by-42-foot flag is on permanent display (along with a temporary display of Francis Scott Key's handwritten poem) at the American History Museum in Washington, DC. The size of the flag often reflected the number of troops. If so, this primitive form of "PSYOPS" (Psychological Operations) was used to convey selected misinformation to the British

attackers. History is replete with examples of using trickery to fool an advancing enemy. As has often been said, "War is the art of deception." Armistead's statue stands on the grounds of Fort McHenry today.

[23] Schwartz, R. (2013). *Smart Leaders, Smarter Teams*. San Francisco, CA: Jossey-Bass Publishing.

[24] Eshelman, R. & Sheads, S. (2013). *Chesapeake Legends and Lore from the War of 1812*. Charleston, SC: History Press.

[25] Dobelli, R. (2013). *The Art of Thinking Clearly*. NY, NY: Harper Collins.

[26] Puryear, E. (2000). *American Generalship: Character is Everything: The Art of Command*. Presidio Press.

[27] Blanchard, K. et. al. (2013). *Trust Works: 4 Keys to Building Lasting Relationships*. NY, NY: Harper Collins.

[28] Cohen, E. (2002). *Supreme Command: Soldiers, Statesmen and Leadership in Wartime*. NY, NY: The Free Press.

Chapter 9

The Battle of Baltimore

by Lt. Col. Guy Berry, USMC

Edited with Contributions by Marc De Simone and Robert Dudley

"You can have peace. Or you

can have freedom. Don't ever

count on having both at once."

Robert. A. Heinlein

The Battle of Baltimore is one of the most important moments in American history.[1] The scene of the bombardment of Fort McHenry inspired Francis Scott Key, a lawyer born and raised in Maryland, to pen the words to the poem "The Defense of Fort McHenry" from his unconventional vantage point aboard a ship just off of North Point. That very battle, known as the Defense of Baltimore, was critical to the preservation of American independence. [2]

During the first week of September, in 1814, while everyone in Baltimore was bracing for the expected attack, British Vice Admiral Alexander Cochrane had other ideas. Following the burning of America's capital, the large British fleet sailed south from Benedict, Maryland, to their base on Tangier Island in the Chesapeake Bay. Rear Admiral Cockburn was dispatched to Bermuda aboard the HMS *Albion*, sent for repairs. The heat was unbearable and it was the worst time of year in the Chesapeake Bay for mosquito-borne diseases, so Vice Admiral Cochrane wanted to sail out into the Atlantic and move north to attack Rhode Island. Suddenly, the flagship HMS *Tonnant* raised a flag, signaling for Cockburn to turn back. He was about ten miles south of the main fleet when he turned around. A celestial navigator aboard the British flag ship realized that the greatest high tides and strongest tidal currents of the year were converging on the Chesapeake Bay due to the soon new moon (September 13th) combined with the coming Autumn equinox (September 22nd). [3] As a result, it was decided the British fleet would remain in the Chesapeake Bay for the next two weeks and attack Baltimore. The special high tides would work to the British naval advantage, providing increased depth for their large war ships. An excited Cockburn was fully pleased. Ross was slowly persuaded, while the more conservative Cochrane had only reluctantly agreed. On Wednesday, September 7, the fleet began moving north up the Chesapeake Bay, this time towards Baltimore. That same afternoon, southbound   Key and Skinner reached the flagship HMS *Tonnant* and boarded her to negotiate for the release of an American prisoner, the elderly Dr. Beanes.

On Saturday, September 10th, Major George Armistead, Commander of Fort McHenry, wrote a letter to his pregnant wife, Louisa, who was in Gettysburg expecting to give birth any day. He told her that he thought the British were reportedly seen sailing south and leaving the Chesapeake Bay and that he hoped to see her shortly. [4] He said he was eating well and was not going to spend the night at the fort in order to get a better night's sleep. He hoped[5] she would present him with a son soon. [6] Later that evening, word arrived in Baltimore that the British fleet was seen moving north, presumably towards their beloved port city. No one was sure what to think.

Sam Smith served as Commander of all U.S. forces during the pivotal battle that was about to begin. The earlier grand failure of American leadership at Bladensburg resulted in the burning of the nation's capital and Sam Smith was not about to let that happen to Baltimore. [7] His life had prepared him for just such an event, and when the time came, his skilled leadership helped save America from the portentous British attack.[8]

Sunday, September 11, 1814, was the very first "September 11th" that would shake the nation. Much of the Baltimore citizenry was coming out of church about noon on that Sunday as church bells began ringing. Suddenly, a signal

137

cannon located on Federal Hill sounded the warning that the British fleet had just been spotted in the Chesapeake Bay arriving several miles away from Fort McHenry. Reverend Kemp, of St. Paul's Episcopal Church in Baltimore, knowing the seriousness of the danger at hand, wrote the following prayer:

> "O God! The Almighty ruler of nations in whose hands are all power and dominion. While we hold in grateful remembrance the perseverance of our city and our people, on this memorable day, give us grace to receive a continuance of thy protection and of thy favors. Preserve us from the influence of sin and the dangers of impiety. May we ever remember that while righteousness exalts a nation, sin is the ruin and reproach of any people. Make us ascribe our preservation and our happiness to Thy overruling power. Let us ever worship and adore Thee in spirit and truth. Through Jesus Christ our Lord, Amen."[9]

That afternoon, Major General Sam Smith peered down the Patapsco River basin toward the Chesapeake Bay and saw the vanguard of the full force of the intimidating British expeditionary war machine bearing down on the city he loved. [10]A flotilla of more than 50 British war ships were positioned about seven miles downriver as the crow flies from Baltimore City.[11] The entire course of his life now culminated at this moment when his leadership, knowledge, and perseverance would be put to the test against his oldest enemy, the British Empire. [12]

General Smith was not alone in this endeavor, of course. Citizens of the city of Baltimore, at first divided over opposing a British invasion, were now fully behind their leader.[13] At Smith's disposal was a numerically superior, but mostly novice group of regular army, militia, and townspeople. [14] Smith would rely on his few experienced and combat-proven officers to lead this highly motivated but largely inexperienced defense force. This situation changed for the better when one key piece of this puzzle was put in place shortly before the British arrival, which was Commodore John Rodgers, Smith's former protégé (he sailed as an apprentice seaman aboard Smith merchant vessels as a teenager) and now the Navy's preeminent and most influential senior naval officer during America's Age of Sail.[15]

Rodgers had traveled overland from Philadelphia, accompanied by approximately 600 fellow U.S. Navy and Marine combatants along with Captain David Porter from New York, arriving at Baltimore on August 25, 1814, under orders from the Secretary of the Navy, William Jones. It was too late to help at Bladensburg, so Rodgers remained in the city long enough to participate in the meeting at which Sam Smith was selected as Commander of all forces over Baltimore.[16] Rodgers then took command of more than a thousand men in the reorganization of the defense of Washington. Next, he led American forces along the Potomac River, attacking Gordon's British Squadron as it sailed south after sacking the port town of Alexandria. Commodore Rodgers returned to Baltimore on Wednesday, September 7th, after re-raising the flag over the smoldering remnants of Washington City, whose residents remained frightened.[17]

To General Smith and Commodore Rodgers, it must have seemed like the ruins of the American Experiment lay in the ashes of Washington after August 24th; representatives of government had evacuated, the President himself was on the run, the White House and Congressional buildings had been plundered and torched. Were it not for a providential tornado and a torrential thunderstorm that doused the fires, the condition of the city would likely have been much worse.[18] Members of the American militia and regular army who tried to stop the British advance at Bladensburg fired only briefly before fleeing the battlefield. In contrast, however, Commodore Barney[19], along with his Navy and Marine forces, provided the only real resistance, but they were ultimately overrun by superior numbers of veteran British forces. Barney was seriously wounded, being shot in the thigh. He and his men had fought so bravely that General Ross did not take them prisoner but immediately paroled them as a show of respect. The infamous "Bladensburg Races" opened the door to the ultimate psychological prize—America's Capital— and the British took full advantage.

Rodgers' return to Baltimore on September 7th was not a moment too soon. Although he brought alarming news about the condition of Washington, he was a battle-tested and reliable military officer on whom Smith knew he could depend.[20] After all, he had fired the first shots of the war. Smith had a plan for Rodgers, the senior naval officer then in Baltimore, and set him up for an opportunity to avenge the devastation he had witnessed in Washington. [21]

Smith's anticipated "worst case scenario" was now coming to fruition. If the city of Washington had been taken so easily, what would stop the British from exacting a devastating revenge on Baltimore, a city they considered a "nest of pirates" and a constant thorn in the side of British commerce?[22] Angered by having to pay continually higher prices for all imported goods, British sentiments toward the destruction of Baltimore were growing. The higher prices were caused by increased insurance rates and commodity scarcities due to the harassment of British shipping by American privateers and outstanding naval officers in open ocean naval combat. Baltimore, to some, was an even more attractive strategic target than Washington. The London press had exclaimed:

> ...if any towns are to suffer, they should be the objects, in order to crush a large body of privateer shipping in Baltimore, and in Washington to destroy a pretty well supplied arsenal, and thus prevent Congress meeting there again, an event much and

generally wished for by the people of New York, Philadelphia and the Eastern States. [23]

Since the United States declared war on Great Britain in 1812, the British Empire had been fighting a largely defensive naval campaign against the Americans. Their primary enemy, however, was closer at hand, and a much more dangerous foe, in the form of France led by the operationally brilliant Napoleon Bonaparte. The British, wisely, elected to deal with the nearby French before turning their full attention to the American nuisance across the Atlantic Ocean. The British finished their war with Napoleon in the spring of 1814, which freed up 20,000 seasoned British regular troops—Wellington's "Invincibles"— making them available for redeployment to America. The British now had a five-point strategy for defeating the Americans which was remarkably similar to their strategy during the American Revolutionary War more than 30 years earlier:

1. In the North, take New England; invade from Montreal, Canada and sever the New England states from the rest of America on a line from Lake Champlain down the Hudson River to New York City;

2. In the South, capture the valuable port of New Orleans and deny the use of the Mississippi River as a source of commerce and travel to the interior of the

United States; eventually take the Louisiana Territory;

3. In the Mid-Atlantic Region, send a robust expeditionary force to the Mid-Atlantic coastline of America; control major port cities such as Philadelphia, Norfolk and Charleston; enter the Chesapeake Bay to reinforce Admiral Alexander Cockburn (who for the previous year had been harassing, reconnoitering, and blockading Chesapeake ports and towns as best his limited forces allowed), which would relieve the pressure the Americans were putting on British-friendly forces in the Great Lakes region.

4. Continue to supply and agitate the Native American Indians in the northwest and the southeast, and block any future American expansion westward;

And fifth, in 1814, the British Admiralty enforced a massive naval blockade from New England all the way to New Orleans in the Gulf of Mexico.[24] With this aggressive blockade and the destruction of American port cities, it was believed in London that the British Royal Navy, army and marines would force a quick end to the war and likely bring the recalcitrant former Colonial Americans back to the bosom of the British Crown. At least that was the plan.[25]

The small British force allotted to battle the Americans had now been reinforced by some of the most seasoned professional soldiers in the world. Up to that point, the British Empire was in possession of the most impressive expeditionary war machine in history. When Sam Smith hurried to Fort McHenry after church on September 11, 1814, and gazed out beyond Baltimore Harbor at the full measure of the force arrayed against his hometown, he was resolved to stand firm. [26] He proudly wore his Congressional Presentation Sword which honored his bravery in the Revolutionary War. This not only garnered him much respect, but inspired the men he would now lead as their commanding officer. [27]

The British North American Station flotilla, under the command of Vice Admiral Sir Alexander Cochrane, was double the size of the entire American Navy. The British ships approaching Baltimore included seven powerful 2nd and 3rd Rate Ships of the Line: HMS *Tonnant* (80 guns), HMS *Albion* (74), HMS *Madagascar* (74), HMS *Ramillies* (74), HMS *Royal Oak* (74), HMS *Severn* (50) and HMS *Diomede* (50). In contrast, the Americans had *no* Ships of the Line in service. Also accompanying the highly respected Cochrane were the frigates: HMS *Havannah* (42), HMS *Weser* (44), HMS *Brune* (38), HMS *Melpomene* (38), HMS *Seahorse* (38), HMS *Surprize* (38), HMS *Trave* (38) and the HMS *Thames* (32). Those eight frigates alone would have been a match for the entire American Navy at the time, but support didn't end there. Also in the flotilla were the sloops HMS *Rover* (18) and HMS *Wolverine* (18), which escorted three additional troop transport ships carrying approximately 5,000 Royal Marines, soldiers, and artillerymen, led by Major General Robert Ross. Ironically, Ross grew up in the area of Northern Ireland that Sam Smith's family had emigrated from to America. Ross was a seasoned and competent general, intensely loved by his men. In terms of leadership, experience, and professionalism, this force was one of the finest the British could field.[28]

The British expeditionary way of warfare boiled down to simple fire and maneuver, played out on grand scale. Lay down a base of fire, usually with artillery, and then maneuver an element on the fixed and covered enemy. While this time-tested method of tactical and operational advantage had been used by land armies for years, the British used the sea as a maneuver space to land their Royal Marines and support them from their "floating castles". British dominance of the littorals and oceans was unquestioned, dramatically demonstrated nine years earlier when the British Navy had defeated the combined fleets of Spain and France (at that time the second and third largest naval powers in the world) at the famous Battle of Trafalgar off the southwest coast of Spain.

Naval maneuver power was combined with a disciplined, well-trained and highly skilled amphibious force. The British Royal Marines were only part of that force, as almost all British Army troops were trained to quickly transition from ship to shore and conduct operations with the coordinated support of naval gunfire. Using the seas and the littorals as maneuvering space allowed a level of operational flexibility that gave the British Admiralty and leadership the freedom to strike their enemy by surprise. If a battle didn't go as planned, a tactical withdrawal back to the ships could be expeditiously executed and the force moved to a more advantageous position. This ability gave the British an important advantage over a land-based army. Unmatched ship-to-shore power, coordination, and discipline served as the muscle of the enforcement arm of the British Empire, the full might of which was about to be unleashed on Baltimore.[29]

Sam Smith knew well the British way of war. During his days as a young officer at Fort Mifflin outside of Philadelphia, he experienced firsthand six weeks of British naval bombardment. He knew that a formidable display of naval might was pending and that such withering firepower had the potential to scatter and demoralize his inexperienced defense force. He also knew there would be an amphibious landing with a march to Baltimore City, and Smith also correctly anticipated its route. [30]

The British generally preferred to burn a town rather than reduce it by naval fire; this tactic provided a more efficient and thorough use of ammunition. They were bent on making a loud and clear statement that by landing on any American shore and burning any city in their path, they could easily coerce the rest of the country to capitulate to whatever British demands would follow and quickly end the war! [31]

Fortunately for the people of Baltimore, and for the young United States, the American General in charge was a man of tested fortitude, resilience, and grit, whose years of military expertise, political experience, and business acumen left few to doubt his ability to lead during this critical test of American strength and independence.[32] Smith's first layer of defense was strategic placement of the people of Maryland themselves, aided by a robust partisan network that warily apprised him of British plans and movements. His next layer of defense was to place and sink a series of vessels—the brigs *Eliza* and *Ann*, the schooners *Columbia*, *Parkett*, *Enterprise*, *Rosanna* and another from Havre de Grace—to block the British ships away from entering Baltimore's harbor.[33] Additionally, eleven more floating barges—each with two guns—were stationed on the narrow inlet of the Patapsco River, with a boom (a large chain) laid across the inlet to keep the British from sailing past the well-armed walls of Fort McHenry and supporting their attacking land force with superior naval gun fire.

Fort McHenry was critical to Baltimore's survival. Years earlier, Smith had lobbied for funds to build the fort, and one year in advance of this moment he had been instrumental in raising local funds to augment the fort's defenses, even going so far as to put up his Montebello country estate as collateral for loans to help fund the defense of the city. It was Smith who lobbied for the appointment of Major Armistead to the position of Commander of the fort to replace the uncooperative Major Lloyd Beall. The wisdom of Smith's many preparations was now becoming apparent to all.[34]

Because the defense force of citizen soldiers was too inexperienced, and the time too short to thoroughly train for a mobile defense of the city, Smith needed to best determine where the British planned to land and what approach they would take on their march to Baltimore. The south side of the city was too wet and swampy, it would therefore be North Point —with a march up the peninsula to Baltimore—approaching the city from the northeast.

Smith then arrayed his main land defense force at a high point just outside the city, constructing an imposing earthen barrier of redoubts anchored by Hampstead Hill (modern day Patterson Park), which would offer his largely inexperienced defense force a tactical advantage. This main earthen work ran about a mile-and-a-half, a series of trenches that linked 62 cannon covering strategically chosen fields of fire. This was the center part of a larger almost three-mile-long "ring of iron" (a total of more than 100 cannon made up mainly of ships' guns) designed by Smith and his naval officers to specifically thwart the British land approach to the city of Baltimore.

Smith also created a mobile reconnaissance element with his militia under the command of his subordinate and fellow Revolutionary War comrade-in-arms, Brigadier General John Stricker.[35] At a series of choke points up the peninsula from North Point, Stricker quickly prepared ramparts and fighting positions that would allow his force of about 3,000 men to slow the march of the British and give those in the city much needed time for the final main defensive positions to be completed. In the event that British General Ross overcame all obstacles set in place, Smith had a final fall-back location where he could make a last stand: the thick foundation walls of the Catholic Cathedral of Baltimore—at that time just being constructed and not yet under roof—high atop the last remaining hill just before the entrance of Baltimore from the northeast.[36] If Hampstead Hill had not held, this would have been Baltimore's "Alamo."

At 3:00 a.m. on the morning of Monday, September 12, the British began to stir in the moonless night. By 6:00 a.m., they began landing troops at North Point (five to six miles by water from Fort McHenry) at the confluence of the Patapsco River and the Chesapeake Bay. A few miles inland from the landing zone, a warning was signaled from the Todd plantation house, being relayed up the line to Federal Hill in Baltimore. There, about ten miles away from the British landing sight, a signal cannon was fired alerting the town of Baltimore that the dreaded enemy was now polluting American soil. [37]

From a British perspective, this was the perfect place to disembark troops: sandy, gradually shallow, and far out of range of the guns at Fort McHenry. Witnessing these events firsthand was attorney, Francis Scott Key, who had helped to negotiate the release of physician William Beanes. Key was under British guard on board the American truce ship anchored with Cockburn's ships in Old Roads Bay, just below Sparrow's Point when the British commenced their dawn landing. By 10:00 a.m., General Ross had landed the entirety of his force: 2,500 soldiers, 1,300 Marines and sailors accompanied by a few small field artillery and light cavalry. High temperatures and intense humidity were already taking a toll on the British after only a march of four miles. Ross had stopped for a late breakfast at Gorsuch Farm. He had the farm owner taste the food he had prepared for the officers in case it was poisoned. Near the end of the meal, three captured American Light Cavalrymen were brought in and interrogated by Ross (one was the son of Sam Smith's business partner, James A. Buchanan). The Americans told Ross that Baltimore was defended by 20,000 soldiers and over 200 cannon, to which Ross quipped in response: "But they are mainly militia I presume, and I don't care if it rains militia!"[38] As the officers were laughing, the sound of musket fire rang out in the distance. Ross mounted his horse to ride forward to observe from a forward position. As he was leaving the farm, his reluctant American host asked sarcastically if the General expected to return for supper that evening. Ross replied, "I'll sup tonight in Baltimore, or Hell!" [39]

Upon Stricker's knowledge that the British Officers had stopped for breakfast, American Major Richard Heath and several officers, along with two companies of the 5th Maryland Regiment and Captain Edward Aisquith's rifle company, took 230 men and one cannon and volunteered to move forward. As Ross then rode forward on horseback, two of the Maryland militia sharpshooters from the 1st Rifle Battalion, Private Daniel Wells and Private Henry McComas, considered the fine British officer with many large feathers in his hat to be a good target; they are believed to have been the ones who took aim and fired what were possibly the most important shots of the War of 1812.[40] At just before 2:00 p.m., a shot struck 48-year-old Ross in the arm and came to rest in his chest. Wounded, he slumped over on his horse and slowly fell to the ground. One British account [41] describes the General as laying wounded alone for awhile. When his troops came up from the rear and found him, he complained that his right arm was broken. Eventually he was transported to the rear toward the British Flag Ship, but slowly bled to death about a mile and half from where he was shot. The young sharpshooters were among several American sharpshooters who were quickly killed by returning British fire.

Chaos broke out. The British force, confused and demoralized by the death of their beloved leader, tried to press the attack against Stricker and the Americans. Colonel Arthur Brooke, commander of the 1st Light Brigade, upon hearing of Ross's wounding, rode forward to the front and took command of the British landing force.[42]

The British resumed the attack in an orderly and disciplined manner as they closed in on the American lines. The Battle of North Point had begun.[43] General Stricker gave orders to engage the British in order to delay and attrite them until the American position became untenable and then disengage and make a disciplined tactical retreat to the earthen works just outside of Baltimore behind the defensive ring around the approach to the city.

Smith did not want to risk the loss of Stricker and the entirety of his only formal military force in the first round of combat. Stricker ordered his scant field artillery loaded with canister and fired on the advancing British troops. The effect was devastating, but barely slowed the British as they closed ranks and continued forward into the teeth of the American line. After two failed attempts to flank the Americans, and multiple futile charges into withering fire from the American muskets, the British were convinced that this time the "Yanks" would not drop their weapons and run in the face of the British infantry, Congreve rockets, and artillery assault.

These realizations forced the British to slow their attack, take cover, and reconfigure their formations for another fresh assault. After two hours of heavy fighting, the Americans calculated they had accomplished all they could at this position and retreated back through the dense woods to their supplementary positions at Bread-and-Cheese Creek. Unaware that Ross was dead, Stricker expected the British to press the attack. When it became apparent that the British would not attack again that afternoon, Stricker continued his planned withdrawal back to the main defensive line at Hampstead Hill. The first day of fighting was over. The Americans had sent a clear message that this fight would not be anything like Bladensburg.

Colonel Brooke, against the protestations of Admiral Cockburn, elected to camp on the battlefield for the night and postpone the further land invasion of Baltimore for the following morning. The body of General Ross had been evacuated earlier to North Point on a local farm cart and returned to Cochrane's flagship, the HMS *Tonnant,* where it was temporarily interred in a barrel of rum as a preservative for an ocean voyage. Ross was later buried at a cemetery near the North American British naval base at Halifax, Nova Scotia. American losses from the short battle of North Point numbered 24, with 139 wounded; miraculous considering the intensity of the brief battle.

British losses numbered 46 killed, including General Ross, with more than 300 wounded.

By late Monday afternoon, the rumble of an approaching thunderstorm could be heard in the distance and a cold early autumn rain arrived just as the sun set. The men in the British landing force, who had expected to be victorious by evening and spending the night in Baltimore, had left their tents and camping equipment at the North Point landing location. Instead, they suffered through a miserable, rainy and stormy night, exposed to the elements. Meanwhile, the British Navy had made its final preparations with its bomb and Congreve rocket platforms for the pending attack on Fort McHenry, which was scheduled by Admiral Cochrane to begin at first light, Tuesday the 13th. The bomb ships *Erebus, Meteor, Aetna, Terror, Heron,* and *Devastation* were now in position just two miles from the all-important American fort.[44]

Tuesday morning at sunrise, September 13, brought an oppressive humidity as Colonel Brooke rallied his land forces for the march down the eastern approach by way of the Philadelphia Road into Baltimore. Brooke and Cockburn thought they had faced and defeated the entire Baltimore defense force when they battled Stricker's skirmishers at North Point the previous day.

The British "Invincibles" now anticipated little resistance on the remainder of their march into Baltimore. In a spirit of retribution over the loss of their beloved Ross, and emboldened by the distant booms of the big British naval mortars now firing on Fort McHenry, the veteran British moved rapidly down the Philadelphia Road anticipating a quick victory. Instead, what awaited them as they approached the city was a reinforced line, several miles long, manned by thousands upon thousands of American defenders. In addition to the approximately 10,000 regular soldiers were several thousand local militia and irregulars who had come from throughout the region to aid in the Defense of Baltimore.[45] Brooke attempted to circle around the American left flank, but Smith had also anticipated this tactic. He sent General Stricker and General William Winder with about 400 American cavalry to attack the British flanking move. The British were stopped cold and suffered heavy casualties. Their dead were later buried near the site.

Admiral Cochrane's attempt to silence the American cannon at Fort McHenry was not faring much better than the British land assault. He must have felt particularly frustrated since he had a special score to settle with the Americans. His older brother, Charles, had been killed 33 years earlier at the culminating battle of the American Revolution at Yorktown, Virginia. Cochrane had been hesitant to approach the fort and come within range of its cannon, and therefore, could not range it with his direct fire naval guns. He was limited to the use of his mortars and the newly fitted rocket barges to reduce and silence the fort. These he kept just out of range of the fort's well-manned 60-plus cannon.

A fierce and imposing attack by a foreign power began that Tuesday morning. Many local citizens felt the physical shock waves of the booming naval attack as they watched the spectacle from atop Federal Hill and from the roof tops of their houses. Inside Fort McHenry, Major Armistead's force, a combined group of regular army soldiers from multiple units numbering approximately 1,000 men, held fast under 25 hours of deadly and nearly continuous fire by the British mortars and rockets. Miraculously, there were few casualties. Tragedy was averted when the main powder store of the fort was struck with a direct hit by one of the British 200 pound mortars, but the bomb failed to go off, whether by rain that snuffed out the fuse, or by chance that the mortar was simply a dud. Four Americans were killed in the barrage, one of whom was an African-American woman delivering supplies to the defenders.

All day, the British bombarded the American fort. The British were just beyond range of the American cannon while the British mortars and rockets were operating at their maximum, albeit inaccurate, distance of two miles. As the afternoon and the bombardment wore on, Admiral Cochrane realized that the fort would not be reduced by indirect fire alone; a special night amphibious landing force would, therefore, have to be called upon in an effort to sneak up on, and overrun, the strategically located fort in order to silence its powerful and threatening cannon.

That afternoon, back ashore on the other side of the Patapsco River from the fort, Colonel Brooke sent several patrols to probe and test Smith's land defenses. The Americans remained solid. The rain continued to turn the open area between the opposing forces into a wet, swampy mess and the afternoon afforded no opportunity for Brooke to attack without taking significant losses. He sent word back to Admiral Cochrane asking for advice. What returned was a cryptic response that led Brooke to believe he should not attack, but wait for the British naval guns to reduce Fort McHenry. Cochrane then believed he could move his ships closer to the harbor to engage his big naval guns in support of Brooke's intended land assault on the fortified American line centered on Hampstead Hill.

The cold, heavy rain continued and the British troops began their second night, September 13th into the 14th, camped and once again exposed to the elements on the outskirts of Baltimore (the grounds of what today is the Johns Hopkins Bay View Hospital Center). That night, around 11:00 p.m., Brooke called a last council of war to consider a night bayonet charge up Rodger's Bastion on Hampstead Hill. The decision was made not to attack as the defenses were too well prepared ,the rainy conditions too unfavorable, and the night was pitch black due to a new moon and cloud cover.[46] Not only did the rain render the British small arms

157

difficult to fire, but the muddy ground was too slippery for soldiers to keep their footing while attempting a bayonet charge uphill. By 3:00 a.m., the British land forces began their retreat, while leaving some men to maintain campfires to deceive the Americans, leading them to think the British were still encamped.

In a last-ditch effort, Admiral Cochrane, unaware that Colonel Brooke had decided to call off the land attack, assembled his special amphibious landing force of about 1,200 men. Shortly before midnight he launched them in an attempt to land on the southern peninsula just west of Fort McHenry. Unfortunately for Cochrane's landing force, General Smith had again successfully anticipated this move as well, and had positioned some of Rodgers' excellent junior naval officers and marines at Fort Babcock. As the amphibious raiding force approached around 1:00 a.m., believing they had bypassed the Fort McHenry cannon, they fired off a rocket barrage. The American supplementary Forts Babcock and Covington were waiting for the right time to open fire on the raiding force and the rocket launch served as a perfect aim point. The Americans even lit bales of hay in order to see the enemy through the pitch black night. They held their fire until the last possible moment, ensuring no escape for the enemy. When the Americans finally opened fire, they delivered a two-hour devastating blow to the British landing force. Nearly 200 British sailors and solders died from the cannon fire of the forts, most of them likely drowned; many who survived were taken prisoner. [47]

The cold and rainy night yielded to the brisk and windy morning of Wednesday, September 14th. Aboard his flagship, Admiral Cochrane took stock of his tactical situation. The first approximately 1,800 rounds of heavy mortars appeared to have had no significant impact on Fort McHenry. Risking the approach of his capital ships into direct fire range of the fort's cannon could potentially lose a Ship of the Line to an American fort. General Ross was dead, and it seemed that Colonel Brooke did not have the expertise, fortitude, or favorable weather conditions to attack Baltimore without support from the sea. At first light, therefore, Cochrane signaled a full naval withdrawal. At 9:00 a.m., the Americans lowered the drenched and battered small battle flag, then raised the massive Star-Spangled Banner high over Fort McHenry. As the military fife and drum corps loudly played "Yankee Doodle" inside the fort, the battle weary Americans stood cheering upon the ramparts, visible to the frustrated British, while shouting "Huzzah, Huzzah!"

The attack on Baltimore was over, legends and heroes were born, and Francis Scott Key, inspired by the sight of the unfurled flag in the distance, penned some poetic words from aboard his American sloop that would one day become our national anthem.

On Friday, September 16th, Sam Smith wrote a letter of appreciation to the troops who served under his command:

> Gentlemen, I avail myself of the first moments of respite from very arduous and active duty to tender you my own and my country's warmest acknowledgements and thanks for the all important aid which you have afforded to me as commanding officer of the very interesting service in which we have been, and still are engaged.
>
> To Gentlemen of your zeal and excelling judgments, I need offering no arguments to prove the propriety of a continuance of our joint and best exertions to sustain and improve one means of resistance. A suspension of our enemy's attack under the circumstances attending its suspension, would make it criminal in the military authority to abate their Vigilance; and therefore, reposing with confidence on your patriotism I shall draw liberally thereon for such aid as I may require.
>
> With the highest Esteem
>
> I am your fellow citizen
>
> Signed   S. Smith
>
> Major General Commanding [48]

On October 18th, Sam Smith tendered the resignation of his military commission. This ended his brilliant 44-year military career. His letter to the Baltimore Committee of Vigilance and Safety reads:

> Gentlemen: From the intimate connection which has existed between us and from the very important assistance you have rendered me in the defense of the city, I deem it proper to inform you of the resignation of my commission in the militia of the state. I take this opportunity of tendering to you my sincere thanks for the continued marks of attention you have shown me and for the confidence which you have on all occasions reposed in me. Accept Gentlemen the assurances of my very great esteem and respect.
>
> S. Smith [49]

The first public singing of "The Star-Spangled Banner" took place at the Holliday Street Theater on October 19, 1814. Today there is a plaque at the original site which is located across the street from the modern Baltimore City Hall.

The next day, on October 20, 1814, there was a special public church service conducted at the New Jerusalem Temple in Baltimore, located at Exeter and Baltimore Streets, and held for the special giving of thanks to God for the deliverance of the city. Reverend John Hargrove

161

offered public thanksgiving for God's protection of the city and its inhabitants from the united and formidable attack of the British fleet and army. He quoted Psalm 14, exhorting the people to humbly acknowledge God's Divine Providence in granting his mercy to "this land of civil and religious freedom". He went on to say "Except the Lord keep the city, the watchman watches in vain. This deliverance was of the Lord's doing and was marvelous in our eyes. So let all enemies of American freedom perish!"

He concluded with Psalm 124.

> If the LORD had not been on our side—let Israel say—[2] if the LORD had not been on our side when people attacked us,[3] they would have swallowed us alive when their anger flared against us;[4] the flood would have engulfed us, the torrent would have swept over us,[5] the raging waters would have swept us away.
> [6] Praise be to the LORD, who has not let us be torn by their teeth.[7] We have escaped like a bird from the fowler's snare;the snare has been broken, and we have escaped.[8] Our help is in the name of the LORD, the Maker of heaven and earth.[50]

Rev. Hargrove declared that people should renew their vows to the Lord so that when they call upon him in future times of trouble "he will deliver us and we shall glorify his Holy name".[51]

The following year, the city organized an effort to build a war memorial. The Baltimore City Archives still has the original leather-bound ledger listing all those who contributed. Sam Smith signed the ledger "Major General Sam Smith Commander in Chief" and made a donation. Today, the Battle Monument stands on North Calvert Street, located in front of two City Circuit Courthouses, and is the symbol of the City of Baltimore. Defenders' Day is celebrated every September 12 in Maryland. [52] Today, there are other War of 1812 monuments around the city of Baltimore worth noting as well.

The prescient leadership of Samuel Smith proved to make all the difference in the Defense of Baltimore.[53] His military planning for the protection of the city and his ability to anticipate the British moves at every turn allowed the Americans under his command to waste no effort, time, or resources. His experience with the British ways of warfare, and their hubris, made them predictable to Smith, and therefore able to be defeated.[54] Additionally, it was more than Smith's planning and leadership; it was his innate ability to leverage business interests, politics, and resources to meet the city's needs that saved the day. These authors believe it was this combination of heroic leadership on the part of Sam Smith that ultimately saved the sovereignty of the entire United States [55] at that critical moment in history.[56] For this epic battle, Smith truly

163

utilized all his experience, personal capital, and grit.[57] He was indeed the architect of victory.

That same week, the Americans also won the Battle of Lake Champlain on September 11, 1814. This ended British attempts to attack America from Canada. Some five weeks later the news reached London of the American victories at Baltimore and on Lake Champlain. These reversals triggered the British willingness to quickly negotiate an end to the war. Even the Duke of Wellington agreed that it was best to settle with the Americans quickly. The terms of the treaty were negotiated by Dec. 24, 1814. It was signed in London by the Prince Regent four days later, then sent by sea to America.

As the three official copies of the peace treaty with Britain were on their way aboard three ships to America, Admiral Cochrane sailed around Florida and into the Gulf of Mexico. He was joined by added reinforcements, bringing his total landing forces to some 12,000 troops with which to attack New Orleans. Since the time for news to travel from London was so slow (over a month depending on weather at sea), the British fleet had no idea that a peace treaty was in route for the offering at that very moment. In January of 1815, General Jackson paralleled General Smith's plan of defensive works used to channel the British into a single point of tactical advantage at the Battle of New Orleans. The American victory there was impressively decisive and ended all British hopes for inroads into the American South.

Today, the Battle of Baltimore should be recognized as one of the most famous moments in American history. Sadly, it has been almost wiped from our collective memory. The Defense of Baltimore was critical in the preservation of American Independence[58], and Sam Smith played the leading role as Commander of the brave American forces during that momentous battle. [59] Every American heart owes this great patriot a debt of gratitude for the freedoms we continue to enjoy to this very day. This is the story of how a country is preserved "when freemen shall stand!"

The Star-Spangled Banner

by

Francis Scott Key

Oh, say can you see, by the dawn's early light,
What so proudly we hailed at the twilight's last gleaming?
Whose broad stripes and bright stars, through the perilous
fight,
O'er the ramparts we watched, were so gallantly streaming?
And the rockets' red glare, the bombs bursting in air,
Gave proof through the night that our flag was still there.
O say, does that star-spangled banner yet wave
O'er the land of the free and the home of the brave?

On the shore, dimly seen through the mists of the deep,
Where the foe's haughty host in dread silence reposes,
What is that which the breeze, o'er the towering steep,
As it fitfully blows, half conceals, half discloses?
Now it catches the gleam of the morning's first beam,
In full glory reflected now shines on the stream:
'Tis the star-spangled banner! O long may it wave
O'er the land of the free and the home of the brave.

And where is that band who so vauntingly swore
That the havoc of war and the battle's confusion
A home and a country should leave us no more?
Their blood has wiped out their foul footstep's pollution.

166

No refuge could save the hireling and slave
From the terror of flight, or the gloom of the grave:
And the star-spangled banner in triumph doth wave
O'er the land of the free and the home of the brave.

Oh! thus be it ever, when freemen shall stand
Between their loved homes and the war's desolation!
Blest with victory and peace, may the heaven-rescued land
Praise the Power that hath made and preserved us a nation.
Then conquer we must, when our cause it is just,
And this be our motto: "In God is our trust."
And the star-spangled banner in triumph shall wave
O'er the land of the free and the home of the brave!

Leadership Lesson 9

"Where there is no vision, the people perish . . ."
(Proverbs 29:18)

Sam Smith was a devout Presbyterian. His family was part
of the founding parishioners that organized the First
Presbyterian Church of Baltimore, of which Sam Smith
was a life-long member. His brother, Robert, was president
of the nascent American Bible Society in 1813. Sam Smith
knew his Bible. He had read the Book of Proverbs many
times. He knew that: *"Where there is no vision, the people
perish."* As a man of Faith in a Higher Power, Sam Smith

167

oriented his life of service by the Scriptures of his Christian Religion (and its principles) as his *Moral Compass*. He knew that, in his role as a leader, it was his sacred duty to provide clear vision for his followers in their moment of need during the Battle of Baltimore. *When the time came for him to lead, Sam Smith did what it was his habit to do; he shared his clear vision with his followers* (the people of Baltimore and available military support) and by showing them his detailed, thoughtful, compelling, and desirable vision of the future, he was able to inspire all to do their duty in defense of their beloved city and country so that they would not perish at the onslaught of the British juggernaut.

No leader, past or present – not even Sam Smith, has ever had a magical crystal ball to accurately predict the future with absolute certainty, but that does not abrogate the leader's responsibility to provide clear vision – especially in times of great need. The question then becomes, *"How can a leader provide clear vision of the future without special powers to accurately predict the future with certainty?"* The answer is simply (yet profoundly) this: **"Predicting the future without uncertainty has nothing to do with leadership vision!"**

It is not the leader's role to predict the future. It is the leader's role – and duty – to provide a compelling vision that enables the followers to survive and not perish. It is the leader's role to size up the situation, discern the intervening variables, vectors and forces at work, assess strengths, weaknesses, opportunities, threats, and provide a "S.M.A.R.T." (Specific, Measureable, Attainable, Realistic, and Time-Focused) *vision of things that might be* - *if the followers do their part in making this possible vision come to fruition. This is the essence of the vision of leaders such as Sam Smith!*

Many Baltimoreans' "vision" of the future when the wolves were at the door was to just give up without a fight and give in to the demands of their would-be conquers. These men were not all cowards; brave patriotic men such as Charles Carroll of Carrolton (as has been noted, a Signer of the Declaration of Independence from Maryland, the only Catholic Signer, and the last Signer to die) *had hoped that a delegation from the city would meet the British in order to sue for peace without a Battle – even though there were indications that the British were bent on the destruction of the city.* Charles Carroll of Carrolton was a leader in his day - a Founding Father – yet the people did not feel compelled to follow his vision of what needed to be done. *In the end, it was Sam Smith's positive and compelling vision of the future which won the day!*

Sam Smith's vision came from his great wisdom, as practical knowledge, which in turn came from years of experience in getting things done through the efforts of others. His wisdom came also from his wounds received in battles long before, from his keen critical thinking skills

169

honed over the years, and from being true to the great wisdom found in the Book of Proverbs which set his Moral Compass aright. This properly aligned Moral Compass then served him in good stead, in his moment of great need. He was oriented toward what needed to be done in order to *craft the reality that needed to be, out of the morass of the "current situation" he faced.* The lesson in leadership, vis-à-vis "vision," here is this: There are two kinds of leaders in this world – *those who actively* **craft the future and make it happen** *through the compelling positive power of vision (such as Sam Smith)*, and those, unfortunately, to whom the future merely "happens." *Carpe Diem.*

[1] Hickey, D. (Editor) (2013). *The War of 1812: Writings from the Second War of Independence.* NY, NY: Literary Classics.

[2] Lord, W. (1994). *The Dawn's Early Light.* Baltimore, MD: Johns Hopkins University Press.

[3] Vogel, S. (2013). *Through the Perilous Fight: Six Weeks That Saved the Nation, pg. 269-270.* NY, NY: Random House.

[4] He even sent Captain Nicholson and his 80 Baltimore Fencibles home thinking the immediate danger of a British attack on Baltimore had passed.

[5] She gave birth to a girl, Margaret, on Thursday, the 15th.

[6] War of 1812 Collection, MS 1846, Letter to Louisa Armistead, September 10, 1814, Maryland Historical Society, Baltimore.

[7] Barber, B. (2004). *No Excuse Leadership: Lessons from the US Army's Elite Rangers*. Hoboken, NJ: Wiley & Sons.

[8] Blanchard, K. (2013). *The Servant Leader*. Nashville, TN: Thomas Nelson Publishing.

[9] Kemp papers, Maryland Episcopal Diocese archives, Baltimore

[10] Battle of Baltimore Records (British) MS 2322, Maryland Historical Society.

[11] Eshelman, R. (2011). *A Travel Guide to the War of 1812 in the Chesapeake*. Baltimore, MD: The Johns Hopkins University Press.

[12] Useem & Bennis (1999). *The Leadership Moment*. NY, NY: Random House.

[13] Maxwell & Covey (2007). *The 21 Irrefutable Laws of Leadership: Follow Them and People will Follow You.* Nashville, TN: Thomas Nelson Publishing.

[14] Elting, J. (1995). *Amateurs to Arms!: A Military History of the War of 1812.* Chapel Hill, NC: Da Capo Press.

[15] Paullin, C. (1910). *Commodore John Rodgers.* Cleveland, OH: The Arthur H. Clark Company.

[16] Robinson, R. (1944). "Controversy over the Command at Baltimore, in the War of 1812." *Maryland Historical Magazine* 39: pg. 177-198.

[17] Muller, C. (2003). *The Darkest Day: The Washington-Baltimore Campaign.* Philadelphia, PA: University of Pennsylvania Press.

[18] Pitch, A. (1998). *The Burning of Washington: The British Invasion of 1812.* Annapolis, MD: Naval Institute Press.

[19] Norton, L. (2000). *Joshua Barney: Hero of the Revolution and 1812.* Annapolis, MD: Naval Institute Press.

[20] Schroeder, J. (2006). *Commodore John Rodgers: Paragon of the Early American Navy.* University Press of Florida.

[21] Maxwell, J. (2007). *Be a People Person: Effective Leadership Through Effective Relationships.* Colorado Springs, CO: David C. Cook Publishers.

[22] "Nest of Pirates" appears to be a term associated with Baltimore only after the fact and normally cast by fellow Americans and attributed to the British. It is true, however, that Admiral Alexander Cochrane did receive orders from the British Admiralty in 1806 to set sail for Tortuga with intent *"To destroy the shipping and burn the town, in order to root out that nest of pirates, and privateersmen."* New York Spectator, July 30, 1806.

[23] Charles Jared Ingersoll, *Historical Sketch of the Second War between the United States and Great Britain (4 vols., Philadelphia, 1845-'52).* Ingersoll's account is likely based on personal knowledge rather than research due to his proximity and personal affiliation with the event.

[24] Arthur, B. (2011). *How Britain Won the War of 1812: The Royal Navy's Blockades of the United States, 1812-1815.* London, UK: Boydell Press.

[25] Brown, R. (1964). *The Republic In Peril; 1812.* NY, NY: Columbia University Press.

[26] Hybels, B. (2012) *Courageous Leadership.* Grand Rapids, MI: Zondervan Press.

[27] Goman, C. (2011). *The Silent Language of Leaders: How Body Language Can Help or Hurt How You Lead.* San Francisco, CA: Jossey-Bass.

[28] Crawford, Michael J. (Ed) (2002*). The Naval War of 1812: A Documentary History, Vol. 3.* Washington: United States Department of Defense, p. 273, Memo from Rear Admiral Codrington to Respective Captains dated 11 Sept 1814.

[29] Whitehorne, J. & Jones, C. (1997). *The Battle of Baltimore 1814.* Baltimore, MD: Nautical & Aviation Publishing Company of America.

[30] Von Schell, A. et. al., (2013). *Battle Leadership.* Echo Point Books.

[31] George, C. (2000). *Terror on the Chesapeake: The War of 1812 on the Bay.* Shippensburg, PA: White Maine Books.

[32] Miller, M. & Lencioni, P. (2013). *The Heart of Leadership: Becoming a Leader People Want to Follow.* San Francisco, CA: Berrett-Koehler Publishers.

[33] Port of Baltimore Papers, MS 2304, Maryland Historical Society

[34] Irwin, T. (2014). *Impact: Great Leadership Changes Everything.* Dallas, TX: BenBella Books.

[35] General John Stricker Papers: MS 1435, Maryland Historical Society

[36] Smith had ordered his engineer, Capt. Babcock, to scout out the thick foundation walls for this purpose.

[37] Vogel, S. (2013). *Through the Perilous Fight: Six Weeks That Saved the Nation, pg. 291-293.* NY, NY: Random House.

[38] This was later reported in the Niles Weekly Register. It is cited in the book *The British Invasion of Maryland 1812-1815 by William Marine, 1913, pg. 150.*

[39] A surgeon with the City Brigade, William George Hawkins, reported hearing Mr. Gorsuch recount the story a few days later. Vogel, ibid pg 293.

[40] Some claim that these two were as young as 14. It is certain that they were teenagers, inexperienced, and had no real idea at whom they were shooting, and certainly could not have understood that their single shots would change the course of the Battle of Baltimore and likely the entire war. See Jenkins, W. (1982). "The Shots that Saved Baltimore." *Maryland Historical Magazine 77: pg. 362-364.*

[41] The Naval History of Great Britain by William James, published in London, 1837, Vol. VI, page 318

[42] George, C. (1993). "The Family Papers of Maj. General Robert Ross, the Diary of Colonel Arthur Brooke, and the

British Attacks on Washington and Baltimore of 1814."
Maryland Historical Magazine 88: pg. 300-316.

[43] Marine, W. (1901). *The Battle of North Point.* Baltimore,
MD: Hanzsche and Co. Printers.

[44] Sheads, S. (2008). "H.M. Bombship Terror and the
Bombardment of Fort McHenry." *Maryland Historical
Magazine 103: pg. 257-267.*

[45] This inspired Key to write in his fourth stanza:
"Oh! thus be it ever, when freemen shall stand
Between their loved homes and the war's desolation!
Blest with victory and peace, may the heaven-rescued land
Praise the Power that hath made and preserved us a nation.
Then conquer we must, when our cause it is just,
And this be our motto: "In God is our trust."
And the star-spangled banner in triumph shall wave
O'er the land of the free and the home of the brave! "

[46] NASA moon phase chart:
http://eclipse.gsfc.nasa.gov/phase/phases1801.html

[47] *United States Naval Institute Proceedings*, Volume 35,
page 505-508, U.S. Naval Institute, Annapolis, 1909.

[48] Baltimore City Archives, BRG 22, 0838, document 538

[49] See the actual document at the Baltimore City Archives
website

[50] New International Version 2011

[51] John Hargrove Sermon, October 20, 1814. PAM 394, Maryland Historical Society, Baltimore.

[52] Sheads, S. and Von Lunz, A. (1998). "Defenders' Day, 1815-1998: A Brief History." *Maryland Historical Magazine 93: pg. 301-315.*

[53] Cohen, W. (2001). *The Stuff of Heroes: The Eight Universal Laws of Leadership*. Longstreet Press.

[54] Kaipa & Radjou (2013). *From Smart to Wise: Acting and Leading With Wisdom*. San Francisco, CA: Jossey-Bass.

[55] Google Battles that Saved America

[56] Wills, G. (1994). *Certain Trumpets: The Nature of Leadership*. NY, NY: Touchstone.

[57] Nye, R. (2001). *The Challenge of Command*. NY, NY: Berkley Publishing group.

[58] Borneman, W. (2004). *1812: The War that Forged a Nation*. NY, NY: Harper Collins.

[59] McCoy, B. (2006). *Passion of Command: The Moral Imperative of Leadership*. Marine Corps Association Bookstore.

Section III.

A Full Life

"It is harder to preserve

than obtain liberty."

John C. Calhoun

Chapter 10

Political Service

1814 to 1838

"The Union, next to our liberties,

is most dear. May we all remember

that it can only be preserved by

respecting the rights of the States,

and distributing equally the

benefits and burdens of the Union."

John C. Calhoun

The Peace Treaty between England and America was negotiated in Ghent, (today in Belgium) and was completed with its 11 Articles on December 24, 1814. One of three copies of the official documents arrived in New York City on a British ship of truce, the *Favorite,* in early February of 1815, carried by a young Mr. Carroll. A second copy arrived in Annapolis on February 13, aboard the U.S. schooner *Transit,* carried by Christopher Hughes of Baltimore.[1] The third copy arrived by the hand of a British diplomatic courier. Three ships were chosen as insurance against potential calamities at sea. These documents were then carefully delivered overland by carriage to Washington, DC. They were first received by Secretary of State, James Monroe, who delivered them to President Madison at his temporary residence, the Octagon House, at 18th and New York Avenue, NW. Madison quickly signed the Treaty and sent it to the Senate for ratification. Just days before he left office, on February 16, 1815, Senator Sam Smith joined with his colleagues in the U.S. Senate to unanimously ratify the "Treaty of Peace and Amity". The next day, President Madison exchanged ratification papers with a British diplomat in Washington, officially ending "Madison's War". The original American copy of the treaty is preserved at the National Archives. On Saturday, February 18th, President Madison sent a message to Congress which was read to the members presenting his concluding remarks about the war. Sam Smith, the hero of Baltimore, was there, reflecting on events and the country he loved.

The large flag at Fort McHenry was preserved by the Armistead family for several generations. It was only displayed publicly a few times until it came into the possession of the Smithsonian Institution in Washington

181

DC in July, 1907.[2] After the Battle of Baltimore, Major Armistead was quickly promoted by President Madison to Lt. Colonel. He was overcome by fatigue and shell shock for awhile, so General Smith placed the fort temporarily under the command of Commodore Rodgers. Armistead submitted his after action report to acting Secretary of State, James Monroe, on September 24, 1814. [3]

After the War of 1812, Smith's political career flourished for another 22 years. The United States of America had been miraculously preserved as an independent nation, and for the second time in his life, Smith had been honored and revered in Baltimore as a military hero.

The second half of his political career had now begun. In spite of being voted out of the U.S. Senate by the Maryland Federalist legislature in August of 1814, Smith continued to be respected as a seasoned elder statesman in national politics and local affairs[4]. In 1815, Smith was once again elected to the House of Representatives by the people of Baltimore and its surrounds. President Madison recovered from the disgraceful burning of Washington, and was celebrated for the final "victory" against the British[5]. The White House and Capitol were slowly rebuilt. The country began to recover economically as restored "amity" with Britain resulted in growing American trade with Europe and beyond.[6] The policies of Sam Smith played a key role.

The War of 1812 resulted in the preservation of American independence. Thanks to men like Sam Smith, the U.S. military was strengthened and expanded[7]. The Navy and Marine Corps continued to grow. The Military Academy at West Point continued to train a professional officer corps.

On the political and economic fronts, the Federalist Party was humiliated and ultimately disbanded. With Smith's ongoing advice, U.S. trade policies were improved. During the War of 1812, the "Indian Uprisings" in the Great Lakes region, as well as those in the American Southeast, led eventually to a decisive defeat for the British-supported Native Americans. The British were finally removed from forts on American territory. American control of the Mississippi River was assured with Jackson's decisive victory over the British at New Orleans in January of 1815. American Westward expansion was now wide open. The "War Hawks" finally got what they wanted[8].

In October of 1814, the controversial General Winder was replaced by 28-year-old Brevet Major General Winfield Scott as commander of the 10th Military District, which included Baltimore. Since the war was not yet officially over at that time, Smith's military leadership in Baltimore appeared once again to being undermined by the political appointment of a younger and less experienced officer of a lower rank. This was more political chess, and Smith had had enough. After 35 years as the head of the Maryland

Militia, he resigned his commission as a Major General. It was the end of an era.

Before he departed the U.S. Senate to reenter the House of Representatives, Smith witnessed the successful passage of his Reciprocity Act of 1815, which lowered import duties for foreign ships and thus, improved trade relations. This was one of Smith's most important legislative accomplishments, as it established better free trade relations and opened the way for American ships to compete more fairly in world trade. It became a model in international trade relations which still resonates today.

In 1816, Congress voted to re-charter the national central bank. Smith voted in favor of this, believing it was necessary to have a strong national financial system across state borders. Once again, the charter was set for 20 years, and would run from 1816 to 1836.

Returning to the U.S. House of Representatives, Smith sat on the influential Committee of Ways and Means. There he lobbied for moderate trade tariff legislation in an effort to pay off the national debt while protecting growing American industry from foreign competition. It was a balancing act of moderation. In addition, Smith promoted federal help to build roads and canals to aid the nation's expansion. Baltimore had become the nation's fastest growing city, and this would continue with the development of a National Road which would run from Baltimore to Ohio[9].

James Monroe was elected president in 1816, and the so called "Era of Good Feelings" began in earnest[10]. He would serve two terms. President Monroe and Smith were veterans of the American Revolution and were both members of the Society of the Cincinnati. Monroe respected the leading role Smith had played in the Defense of Baltimore in 1814, as well as his commercial expertise and advice[11]. In 1818, Smith became Chairman of the House Committee of Ways and Means and would serve in that capacity for the next four years. During this period Smith advocated for maintaining a strong military by promoting continued funds for the West Point Military Academy, ongoing coastal fortifications, and veterans' pensions.

In 1820, Smith supported the controversial Missouri Compromise. By 1822, he had moved back to the U.S. Senate. In 1823, Senator Smith supported the Monroe Doctrine[12] (written mostly by Secretary of State John Quincy Adams) which declared that European powers (monarchies at the time) should no longer colonize or otherwise intervene in the affairs of the Americas. This was in support of the independence movements in Latin America and formed the foundation for the present day Organization of American States (OAS), a defining moment in American foreign policy. Ironically, it was mostly enforced at the time by the British Navy, since the American Navy was so small. It was also in Britain's best interests to keep trade open across the Americas.

In 1824, Smith welcomed to Baltimore the visiting Marquis de Lafayette. This was the returning Frenchman's first American tour since his famed role in the American Revolution. Smith was president of the Baltimore Chapter of the Society of the Cincinnati, and as such led the welcoming committee for this esteemed guest and fellow Cincinnatian. There were parades through the city. The Marquis was also welcomed at Fort McHenry where the famous flag that had flown over the fort in 1814 was put on special display. There were private dinners at Smith's home as well as a grand banquet sponsored by the local Society of the Cincinnati, presided over by Smith.

In the fall presidential election of 1824, Smith backed William Crawford of Georgia, whom he had known since 1807 when Crawford entered the Senate. They had been friends over the years and worked well together when Crawford became Secretary of the Treasury and Smith was Chairman of the Committee of Ways and Means. During the campaign, however, Crawford suffered two strokes which ended his bid for the presidency. While Baltimoreans largely voted for Andrew Jackson (he won the most popular votes nationally), the election went to John Quincy Adams, whom Smith had not gotten along with for the past 15 years. Adams, like his father before him, would also be a one-term president[13]. Smith quickly switched his support to Andrew Jackson, who was widely expected to run again.

Smith became Chairman of the Senate Finance Committee. One of the major issues of the new Adams Administration was the trade policy with Great Britain. Once again, Smith would offer moderate and practical advice, preferring as much free and open trade as possible, but the President took a hard line, resulting in an increasingly adversarial trade relationship. Adams continued to push for high tariffs and protectionism, causing a backlash from Britain. Smith viewed Adams' hard line trade policies as disproportionately injurious and alienating to the Southern states, and warned that such measures could lead to regional hostilities in America. As a nationalist and elder statesman, Smith's policies moved more toward those of a nonpartisan independent than a party loyalist, even as the nation began to slide down the slippery slope of sectional differences[14].

From 1828 to 1832, Smith served as President Pro Tempore of the Senate for the second time. In that role he could further influence legislation, particularly on matters of commerce and finance. In 1828 he supported the presidential election of his friend and fellow war veteran, Andrew Jackson. He helped plan the Jackson inauguration as chairman of a joint congressional committee. He also conducted the swearing into office of the new Vice President, John C. Calhoun of South Carolina .

Smith was a respected voice during the Jackson Administration[15]. He worked on reducing tariffs to improve trade, explaining on the Senate floor how the current tariff system favored Northern industrialists over Southern planters. Such an imbalance was fueling talk of tariff nullification in South Carolina. Smith believed that the notion of allowing states to nullify federal laws as they chose was dangerous and could ultimately lead to the weakening or breaking apart of the Union[16]. He argued that Congress had the constitutional right to impose tariffs but that they should be modest and be applied fairly to all states. Smith was seeking to calm regional differences and head off what would later grow into the Secessionist Movement among Southern states. His instincts would eventually, again, be proved correct, but many of the younger politicians were not listening.

The second big issue of the Jackson presidency was the question of the re-charter of the National Bank. The 20-year expiration was coming up in 1836. President Jackson was opposed to the bank in its present form, which had only twenty percent government ownership and was weakened by corrupt management. He favored a bank with stock that was wholly owned by the American public and with directors that were from the government. There were fears over foreign ownership of bank stock. Smith sided with those in favor of a central bank that could provide a stable currency and national credit, but without foreign influences[17].

In September of 1831, the Anti-Masonic Party rose up in opposition to Andrew Jackson. Members held their national political convention at the Baltimore Athenaeum, located at St. Paul and Lexington Streets. They supported Baltimore lawyer William Wirt to oppose Jackson over the issue of Jackson's Masonic membership and the Masonic code of secrecy[18]. A second new political party from the John Quincy Adams era, the National Republicans, also met in Baltimore that same year, in the same building, to choose Henry Clay of Kentucky to run against Jackson. In May of 1832, Democrats met at the old First Universalist Church at North Calvert and East Pleasant Streets to support Martin Van Buren as Vice President to run on the Andrew Jackson ticket, replacing John C. Calhoun, who would return to the Senate to once again represent South Carolina and continue to promote nullification policies. This was the first Democrat National Convention in America. The presidential election year of 1832 proved to be a busy one in Baltimore.

As the election season revved up, Smith remained entangled in the ongoing bank re-charter controversy. Smith and the Senate Finance Committee held hearings and heard from Nicholas Biddle, the President of the national bank based in Philadelphia. The fate of the vote in the

Senate was uncertain, and Smith strategically counseled his fellow senators to postpone the vote on the bank until after Jackson's reelection to a second term in 1832 which would avoid making the bank controversy a test of party loyalty in a presidential election year. Nevertheless, in June of 1832, the Senate passed the bank re-charter bill by a close vote of 28 to 20. President Jackson quickly applied his veto, but there was not enough political support for Congress to override it . Jackson had been pushed into a corner on this issue and now the bank would die. As it turned out, this gave Jackson strong support over his rival Henry Clay in the 1832 election. However, it also led to an all-out bank war, which Smith was hoping to avoid for fear of the negative ramifications on the American economy[19].

By 1833, the re-elected President Jackson pulled government deposits out of the national bank in Philadelphia and distributed the funds to private banks across the country. He moved Roger Taney (brother-in-law of Francis Scott Key), of Frederick, Maryland, from Attorney General to Secretary of Treasury[20], to carry out his wishes. Bank President Biddle countered by constricting credit, which set off a prolonged national economic downturn and bank panic. The public was outraged by such manipulations from the national bank. As a result, politicians could no longer support any re-charter efforts. By 1836, the Bank of the United States failed to gain a re-charter. Jackson had won his war against what he felt was a Northern-manipulated elitist bank (and possibly the foreign Bank of England) that was not equally favorable to all Americans. Jacksonian Democracy was in full force. This, however, sparked the beginning of the Whig Party, which would oppose Jackson's bank policies well into the future.

Andrew Jackson took office for his second term in the spring of 1833, with Martin Van Buren as his Vice President. At that same time Sam Smith resigned from Congress. He was 80 years old.

For 40 consecutive years Smith held a national office, serving18 years in the House, and 22 years in the Senate. He had served under the first seven presidents of the United States and sponsored major bills that influenced commerce, defense, banking, and national infrastructure improvements. Smith's reputation for clear judgment and forward thinking resulted in an honorable career in public service with many accomplishments[21]. But it was not over yet. Upon his return to Baltimore, the octogenarian Smith, like the famed Cincinnatus, would once more heed the call to leadership.

Smith's intentions of resuming life with friends and family at Montebello outside of Baltimore likely did not include being called on to settle the challenges that were once again tearing the city of Baltimore apart. Local banks were being hard hit by the banking constrictions of Nicholas Biddle.

Credit was diminished and a financial panic resulted. Banks and insurance companies were collapsing, including the Bank of Maryland, of which Smith had been a founding director.

By the summer of 1835, those who had lost their money in the bank were so angry that there were riots in the streets of "Mob Town." Fierce battles with thousands of rioters broke out in and around Monument Square–where the War of 1812 War Memorial still stands. The mobs were out to destroy the mansions of the bank directors. The city government became overwhelmed. The Mayor of Baltimore resigned in the panic, and all public authority vanished into chaos and violence.

In stark contrast, a crowd gathered one day around the elderly Smith, speaking at age 83 to a crowd of like-minded decent citizens. Carrying an American flag, he proceeded to lead a march right through the riot-torn city toward Howard Park. Smith's son, John, who was the head of the local militia at that time, joined him there. The Smiths then ordered to arms the law-abiding citizens still left in the city, and organized them into patrols to quell the riots. The rebellion quickly ceased. On September 7, 1835, the citizens of Baltimore elected Sam Smith, age 83, as their new Mayor.

The population of Baltimore at that time was over 100,000. It was thriving as the fastest growing American city, beautiful as well, with lovely fountains and monuments along with many mansions. President John Quincy Adams called it the "Monumental City" after his visit in 1827. Smith improved the streets and the public marketplaces, as well as the harbor and its facilities. He helped with the extension of canals and the new railroads that improved Baltimore as a center for shipping. Smith maintained law and order and broke up the teenage gangs that roamed the streets. He led in the reorganization of city government. His portrait still hangs in the chambers of City Hall today.

In 1835, the Democrat National Convention was held at the First Presbyterian Church on the northwest corner of East Fayette and North Streets (now Guilford Avenue). There, Vice President Martin Van Buren was nominated to run for President. In 1836 he won the national election. In 1837, an economic panic once again struck the entire nation which lasted through the mid-1840s.

In the fall of 1838, after three years in office, the 86-year-old Smith resigned as Mayor. Six months later, on April 22, 1839 he departed this life. His nearly five decades of public service was now over. His obituary appeared as follows in the Baltimore newspaper, *The Sun*, on April 23:

> Death of General Smith. General Samuel Smith, died at his country residence, Montebello, yesterday afternoon, at 5

o'clock, in the 87th year of his age. He was a man of whom Baltimore was justly proud. A brave soldier, a sound statesman, and an honorable high-minded patriot; he ever obeyed the call of his country, and in two wars fought her battles, and in peace aided her in the legislature councils. Elected as mayor of the city, for his services in having restored the city from a state of anarchy in good order and respect for the laws, he labored by every means that a debilitated frame would permit, to perform the duties of his office. It was the last public honor conferred upon him, and it was one springing from the reverence of his fellow citizens for his virtue and integrity. He has lived to see the country for whose freedom he battled, a great and powerful nation, and the city he defended from the pollution of a foreign foe (during the War of 1812), rising to the height of opulence and prosperity. His long life has been well spent, and his name will be inscribed among the greatest of the American patriots – his memory revered, and his services remembered with gratitude. As a mark of respect, it is suggested that the flags of the public buildings and shipping be displayed at half-mast today, and until his corpse is consigned to the tomb in Westminster Cemetery in downtown Baltimore.

Leadership Lesson 10

Formative Leadership

and the Cardinal Virtues

In his elder years, Sam Smith was a paragon of the virtue of Prudence. Prudence, or Wisdom as practical knowledge, knowing what to do, when to do, and how to do the best thing according to the circumstances at hand. This is the essence of leadership. Below, is a diagram from the book, *Empowering the Leader Within: Four Essential Virtues*, which illustrates the concept of Formative Leadership:

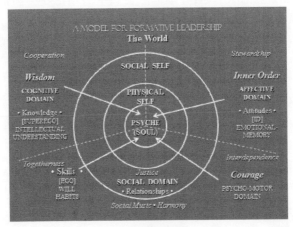

Sam Smith had the wisdom sufficient to operationalize all of the other cardinal virtues necessary to lead well:

1. Prudence – or Wisdom as Practical Knowledge,

2. Temperance – or Inner-Order as Moderation,

3. Fortitude – or Courage as Perseverance, and

4. Justice – both Distributive and Retributive.

As shown in the illustration above, Sam Smith was able to empower the leader within him and within others. His leadership abilities were formed (Formative Leadership) in the frequent repetition of desired good habits of behavior (virtues) so that when the occasion called for leadership, this "inside-out" development of leadership capabilities provided the ability needed for the specific situation at hand. The point is this, if one wants to be able to lead in times of crisis, one must first develop these "good habits" of leadership conducive behaviors in the day-to-day exercise of one's life experiences. *That way, like Sam Smith, one will be ready (in the head), willing (in the heart), and able (with the hands) to do one's duty. There are no short cuts to becoming an effective leader.*

---

[1] Christopher Hughes was married to Sam Smith's oldest daughter.

[2] Sheads, S. (1999). *Guardian of the Star Spangled Banner: Lt. Colonel George Armistead and the Fort McHenry Flag, pg. 39-41,* Baltimore, MD: Toomey Press.

[3] Printed in the Niles Weekly Register on October 1, 1814. Sheads, Ibid. pgs 13-17.

[4] Cashman, K. (2008). *Leadership from the Inside Out: Becoming a Leader for Life.* San Francisco, CA: Berrett-Koehler Publishing.

[5] Peterson, M. (Editor) (1974). *The Founding Fathers: James Madison, A Biography in His Own Words, Vol. 1 and 2.* NY, NY: Newsweek.

[6] Pancake, J. (1972). *Samuel Smith and the Politics of Business.* University of Alabama Press.

[7] Schwartz, P. (1996). *The Art of the Long View: Planning for the Future in an Uncertain World.* NY, NY: Doubleday Press.

[8] Nugent, W. (2008). *Habits of Empire: A History of American Expansion.* NY, NY: Vintage Books.

[9] Howe, D. (2007). *What Hath God Wrought: The Transformation of America, 1815-1848.* NY, NY: Oxford University Press.

[10] Ammon, H. (1990). *James Monroe: The Quest for National Identity.* Charlottesville, VA: The University Press of Virginia.

[11] Blanchard, K. et. al., (2013). *Trust Works: Four Keys to Building Lasting Relationships.* NY, NY: Harper Collins.

[12] This major non-interference policy was later applied to Mexico, Cuba, Puerto Rico, the Republic of Texas, the American Northwest, and even Hawaii. There have been later additions such as the Roosevelt Corollary, to "Speak softly and carry a big stick, and you will go far." Teddy Roosevelt learned the lessons of Sam Smith in his research for his book, <u>*The Naval War of 1812*</u>, which is still held in high esteem for its readability and scholarship. The book still has an impact on modern scholarship in the field and is still being reprinted since 1882.

[13] John Quincy Adams left the Presidency after only one term but he holds a special distinction of being one of only two American Presidents who served in Congress after being President (Andrew Johnson went on to the U.S. Senate). In fact, Adams went on to serve in the House of Representatives for 17 years, from 1831 to 1848. J.Q. Adams was the only President to both know the Founding Fathers and meet Abraham Lincoln. In 1847, he was the first U.S. President to have his photo taken. The next year he suffered a massive cerebral hemorrhage at his desk in

the halls of Congress on February 21, at age 80. He died two days later, in the Speaker's Room, inside the Capitol.

[14] Kaipa and Radjou (2013). *From Smart to Wise: Acting and Leading with Wisdom.* San Francisco, CA: Jossey-Bass.

[15] Meacham, J. (2008). *American Lion: Andrew Jackson in the White House.* NY, NY: Random House.

[16] Galford and Maruca (2006). *Your Leadership Legacy: Why Looking Toward the Future Will Make You a Better Leader Today.* Boston, MA: Harvard Business School Press.

[17] Cassell, F. (1971). *Merchant Congressman in the Young Republic: Sam Smith of Maryland, 1752-1839.* Madison, WI: University of Wisconsin Press.

[18] Bullock, S. (1996). *Revolutionary Brotherhood: Freemasonry and the Transformation of the American Social Order, 1730 to 1840.* Chapel Hill, NC: University of North Carolina.

Hagger, N. (2007). *The Secret Founding of America: The Real Story of Freemasons, Puritans and the Battle for the New World.* NY, NY: Sterling Publishing.

Hall, M. (2008). *The Secret Destiny of America.* NY, NY: Penguin Group.

Morse, S. (1924). *Freemasonry In The American Revolution.* NY, NY: Kessinger Publishing.

Sora, S. (2003). *Secret Societies of America's Elite: From the Knights Templar to Skull and Bones.* Rochester, VT: Destiny Books.

Tabbert, M. (2005). *American Freemasons: Three Centuries of Building Communities.* NY, NY: New York University Press.

[19] Zinn, H. (2006). *A People's History of the United States: 1492 to Present.* NY, NY: Harper Press.

[20] Jackson would later appoint Taney to Chief Justice of the US Supreme Court. Smith was supportive of Jackson's reelection and wrote positive election articles for various Maryland newspapers. Smith's hope was to smooth Jackson's reelection by avoiding an immediate showdown over the bank.

[21] Blanchard and Miller (2012). *Great Leaders Grow: Becoming a Leader for Life.* San Francisco, CA: Berrett-Koehler Publishing.

Chapter 11

A Living Legacy

"Carve your name on hearts, not tombstones. A legacy is etched into the minds of others and the stories they share about you."
Shannon L. Alder

"Live today the way you want to be remembered tomorrow."
Dillon Burroughs

"Everyone leaves a legacy, whether they want to or not. The question is, "What kind of legacy will you leave?"

Dillon Burroughs

Sam Smith died in the afternoon on Monday, April 22, 1839 at the age of 86[1]. Word travelled quickly, rippling through day-to-day life in the city of Baltimore. The funeral attendance plans of dignitaries and citizens alike took shape as people received the news. The next day, Sheppard C. Leakin, Mayor of Baltimore, who had also served as an officer in the Battle of Baltimore, summoned members of the First and Second Branches of the City Council with the following memo:

Gentlemen: —The death of our venerated and highly esteemed fellow citizen, General Samuel Smith, which occurred on Monday afternoon, has induced me to invite you, on a brief notice, to assemble to-day, that I might submit to your consideration, to decide in what manner the constituted authorities will unite with the other citizens of Baltimore in manifesting their estimation of the eminent qualities and services, and their respect for the memory of a man so highly distinguished both in peace and war, from an early period in the revolutionary struggle of our country to the close of his long and useful life.

I understand that the funeral will take place on Thursday—the hour will depend upon the decision of the Councils. Yours respectfully,

S.C. LEAKIN, Mayor.

On April 25th, Mayor Leakin's memo was published in *The Sun* newspaper, along with the following elegant response from the Councils, attesting to the wide sphere of influence and respect General Smith had garnered[2]:

> *Whereas*, Gen'l. SAMUEL SMITH, a hero of the Revolution, and late Mayor of the city of Baltimore, has been "gathered unto his fathers," at an advanced age, after having filled the measure of his glory in the "tented field" of two wars, and attained a distinguished rank in the councils of his country. A man who in all the relations of a merchant, a public spirited citizen, and in social life was an ornament to society. Therefore,

> *Be it resolved unanimously* by both branches of the City Council, That the Mayor and members of both branches of the City Council, and the other officers of the corporation, as a mark of respect, attend his funeral on Thursday next, at 3 o'clock, from his late residence, Exchange Place.

Resolved, That the Mayor and the City Council wear the usual badge of mourning for 30 days, and that the Chambers of both Branches be shrouded in black for the remainder of the session, and that they assemble in the Chamber of the First Branch, on Thursday next, at half past two o'clock, P.M., for the purpose of joining in the funeral procession of the deceased.

Resolved, That Rev. Clergy, the President of the United States, the heads of the Departments, Senators and Members of the House of Representatives, the members of the Society of Cincinnati, the Judges and officers of the several courts and members of the bar, the collector and officers of the customs, officers of the Army and Navy, the military of the city, the President and members of the Baltimore Fire Department, the Trustees and Regents of the Medical University, gentlemen of the Medical Faculty, Foreign Consuls, masters of vessels and seamen, citizens and strangers, be invited to attend the funeral, and take place in the procession in order assigned agreeably to this resolution.

Resolved, That persons having charge of churches to which bells are attached, be requested to have them tolled during the procession.

Resolved, That the owners or captains of vessels in the harbor, and the keepers of public buildings, be requested to have their colors hoisted half-mast from sunrise to sunset–and that the citizens generally are requested to close their stores and refrain from all business during the procession.

Resolved, That the Commanding Officer at Fort McHenry be respectfully requested to have minute guns fired during the ceremonies.

Resolved, That the Committee of Arrangements be directed to provide suitable carriages for the President of the United States, Heads of Department, and the Governor of Maryland.

Resolved, That a person be appointed by the Joint Committee of Arrangements, to act as Marshall-in-Chief, with full power and authority to carry into effect the object of these resolutions, and that he be authorized to appoint as many Assistant Marshals as he may think necessary.

Resolved, That the Judges of the City Court be respectfully requested to issue their orders to the officers under their control, to report themselves to the Mayor, for the purpose of preserving order for the procession.

Resolved, That a Joint Committee be appointed by the City Council to consist of three members from the First Branch and two from the Second, to be constituted a Committee of Arrangements to conduct the procession of the deceased, and to give such aid to the Marshall-in-Chief, as he may require.

Resolved, That a copy of these proceedings be signed by the Mayor and Presidents of both Branches of the City Council, and the same be communicated to the family of the deceased, and be published in all daily papers of the city.

PHILIP WALLACE,

JOHN L. YEATES,

JOSEPH BROWN,

Committee of the First Branch

SAMUEL JONES, Jr.,

JOSEPH HOOK, Jr.,

WILLIAM REANEY,

Committee of the Second Branch[3]

Sam Smith's funeral was the largest ever held in the city of Baltimore[4]. On Thursday, April 25, 1839, the streets were lined with crowds of mourners as Smith's funeral procession appeared in the afternoon. With cavalry in front, followed by infantry and artillery, the black hearse proceeded through the city pulled by four white horses and flanked on both sides by mounted dragoons. A long line of carriages then followed in procession, including a coach carrying the Smith family, followed by coaches carrying the Mayor of Baltimore, the Governor of Maryland, and the President of the United States, Martin Van Buren. Next, came members of the President's cabinet, U.S. senators and representatives, foreign diplomats, Maryland state legislators, local businessmen, the Society of the Cincinnati members, followed by more militia and local fire brigades. Crowds of local citizens then joined in the procession. As requested by the Mayor and City Councilors, church bells rang out. Businesses were closed, and ship flags in Baltimore Harbor were lowered to half-mast. Cannon were fired each minute from Fort McHenry, booming salutes across the harbor.[5]

The funeral procession began from Smith's downtown residence at Exchange Place, then moved past Federal Hill and Fort McHenry, over Hampstead Hill, and back toward town to the First Presbyterian Church, where Smith had been a lifetime member. He was eulogized with honors and laid to rest in the church cemetery in the Smith family vault at the Westminster Burial Grounds at 519 West Fayette Street (others interred there today include Robert Smith, James McHenry, John Stricker, and John Skinner) . Years later there was a church built over much of the burial grounds, but the Smith vault is still seen in the rear courtyard.

Samuel Smith's Last Will & Testament was filed May 1, 1839. He had named his son, John Spear Smith, as his Executor. The original will is now in the Maryland State Archives in Annapolis. [6]

Sam Smith was a true American hero, a man honored for his decisive leadership[7] that saved Baltimore, and ultimately the young American nation at a time when her patriotic defenders of freedom muscled on land and sea. Veterans from the Battle of Baltimore would remember General Smith for the rest of their lives[8]. Together, their efforts resulted in establishing a nation that would one day become a leader among reigning world powers[9].

Smith's legacy inspires us still today[10]. He saw and experienced a lot in his nearly nine decades. He had traveled to Europe, lived through two wars with the British, and witnessed American expansion into the west. He was a beloved family man. While he made and lost fortunes, he was always respected in his community as a decent and honest man[11]. He had served in national government under seven Presidents over 40 years. As a leader in national affairs, business, international trade, and his local community, his example still has the power to impact both present and future leaders to follow in his footsteps[12].

Today, visitors to Baltimore will find a striking statue of Sam Smith, dressed in full military regalia, located on Federal Hill overlooking the Baltimore Harbor. They will discover a Star Spangled history up close, and gain a fresh appreciation for those like Smith who were dedicated to preserving the "land of the free, and the home of the brave."

Leadership Lesson 11

How does One Develop into a Leader?

Today, there are four basic types of leadership training and development:

Type One – The "Personal Growth" Movement

This first type of leadership development and training maintains that, by becoming a "reflective practitioner" through the journey of "self-knowledge," one can grow as an individual, on the personal level, to become the leader that one wants or needs to be. Such things as psychometric tests (i.e. Myers-Briggs Type Indicator, etc., the Kersey Temperament Sorter, The Thomas-Kilmann Conflict Mode Indicator, the FIRO-B, and various "Leadership Inventories"), give one a "window to the soul" and allow someone to assess where one "is" (in terms of leadership ability of potential) and where one "needs to be" in terms of their personal growth toward becoming a more effective leader. These psychometric instruments, and some of the less scholarly rigorous leadership "Style" assessment instruments on the market today, are seen as the first step toward helping the budding leader to learn "How to Win Friends and Influence People," as Dale Carnegie would have said, but there is no conclusive body of empirical research which indicates that those who solely rely on this type of leadership development and training will attain the growth they desire. That having been stated, it probably wouldn't hurt to learn about oneself. Socrates himself did enjoin: "Know Thyself."

Type Two – "Skill Building"

The thinking here is as direct as it simple: find out what desirable skills effective leaders possess, then find out where the gaps are between those who are acknowledged as examples of effective leaders and ones' own current skill level in these areas, and finally attend some specifically targeted seminars to acquire the necessary skills to bridge the identified gaps. So, if one is a procrastinator – not a desirable trait in a leader – then one attends a good "Time Management" seminar and learns to manage multiple priorities. If stress is your downfall, a "Stress Management" program will do as a ticket to successful leadership. "Effective Communication Skills" are seen as essential to effective leadership, so sign up for that course, or any one of over a hundred different offerings. "Effective Delegating Skills," etc., the list of leadership training offerings goes on and on. Certain leadership training companies have sprouted up in recent times; their four-color glossy brochures sounding like the modern-day leadership training equivalent of the "Earl Scheib" Discount Auto Painting Shop commercials of the 1960's. You can almost hear the barkers crying: "Get your leadership training right here – only $99.95!" In spite of all the hype and the hawkers selling dreams fulfilled, learning new skills to correct deficits in key behaviors may not necessarily be a totally bad idea if one wishes to become a better leader. The military, and many businesses, favor a form of this basic approach (without the hype) to this day.

Type Three – The "Feedback" School of Thought

This type of leadership development and training works, usually, by sequestering potential leaders in a retreat like setting and putting them in (sometimes contrived) situations in which they are required to engage in typical leadership related activities and behaviors through simulations and role-plays, and then afterwards the

211

"situation" is "processed." The would-be leaders are then either given "feedback," or asked to give feedback to others. This feedback comes in several varieties of "pitching" and "catching." The learner is shown such valuable leadership behaviors as "How to Request Feedback on a Message Sent to Ensure Another's Understanding of Your Message or Intentions," "How to Give Feedback to Others to Confirm Your Understanding of Another's Message or Intentions," and then receives details on what are considered to be the most ultimate insights of all through "Behavioral Feedback" on their own performance in the simulations, etc., rendered by qualified expert observers, as to "How Your Behavior as a Leader Affects Others," etc. The desired outcome is that one will be sufficiently, humbled, mortified, cajoled, or enlightened by learning the impact of one's behavior on others, so as to make better "behavioral choices" in real life situations as one functions as a leader in the future in the "real world." This is the most psychologically intrusive and emotionally intensive form of leadership development and training, and has had a dramatic effect on some – to the point of being hailed as a life-changing experience; others find it tedious and manipulative and of little professional value. Several prestigious universities offer variations of this form of leadership development to corporate executives and government officials for tens of thousands of dollars per participant.

Type Four - Conceptual Awareness

The last main avenue of leadership training and development activities involves raising one's intellectual or conceptual awareness pertaining to all things related to effective leadership, so as to educate a potential leader to be able to assume the responsibilities of leadership. Various leadership theories, models, and practical applications through review of case studies, etc., all from the scholarly literature in the field and based on empirical research and scientific studies using rigorous methodologies, are presented for the would-be leader for their edification and enlightenment. The leader-in-training learns about the different styles, models, theories, and practices of effective leadership. "Best Practices" in leadership are investigated through "Case Studies" and "Benchmarking" against "proven" highly effective leadership practices, etc. These are used to develop "leadership potential" through training and educational offerings. There are even those who have written books on the subject – some after completing years of acclaimed research – who have doctorates in the field, and are respected experts and distinguished professors, who have never been a leader nor engaged in any of the theoretical "best practices" they espouse to others.

The question still remains: "Can leadership really be taught?" Or, as we discussed earlier, is it "one's Nature not Nurture" which makes one excel as a leader and another falter. Or, perhaps leadership may actually be something that is "caught, not taught" by being "nurtured" by good "role models" who work with the natural gifts of the learner and shows them the way to become an effective leader. "How can one become a leader like Sam Smith?"

Today, many believe that it is a false dichotomy, and that, paradoxically, leaders are developed through *both* nature *and* nurture - and by *neither* nature *nor* nurture exclusively. They assert that all types of leadership development and training can help everyone – in varying degrees and to a varying extent – depending on what nature has given an individual, and by utilizing the type (from the four types above), or multiple types, of leadership training and developmental activities that resonate best with that particular individual.

Of all the above types of leadership development and training types, most people have a dominant "preference," that they tend to resonate with most, a sub-dominant type that is their second choice, a tertiary choice that they can either take or leave based on the lack of the two above, and a forth type of training which they tend to avoid like the plague. All types, regardless of personal preference, add something to the leader's tool chest. None work all the time for every person. Still, any of them is better than none at all. In fact, sometimes just engaging in the type which one loathes the most can actually produce the best results. But is there a better way to become the leader that one wants or needs to be?

In the previous chapter, Chapter 10, we looked at Sam Smith through the lens of Formative Leadership, or developing one's leadership potential by acquiring the good habits (or virtues) of an effective leader and thereby "empowering the leader within" through practicing the four cardinal virtues as they pertain to leadership. According to this theoretical format, the cardinal virtues may be seen as main headings, or categories of germane subsidiary virtues (or could also be called related effective leadership habits) that one should practice in order to develop leadership potential (see illustration at the end of the previous chapter).

Below, is taxonomy of cardinal and subsidiary leadership-related virtues arrayed to show the process (from left to right, top to bottom) of Formative Leadership:

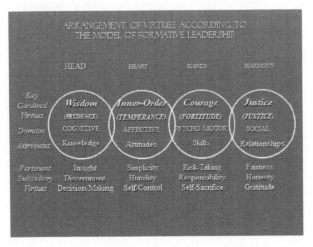

A positive change in behavior starts with the head, convinces the heart, and directs the hands in the new desirable behavior. The "totus personalis" or whole person is involved. One cannot prepare for every obstacle one may encounter in the risky business of leadership. *Even Sam Smith could not have predicted which skills, etc. he would need to lead others over his long career – especially in the crises he encountered. In the end, all one can do is identify what good leadership habits one possesses (from the lists above) and which ones that are lacking, and set a course in life to acquire the virtues one lacks through training and development of various types, so that, as Sam Smith did, one can empower the leader within oneself and others to do their duty in life in all hazards.* This is the leadership lesson of Sam Smith – become the leader one needs to be, from the inside out, so that others can learn from that example how to lead others when fate puts one to the test.

In addition to leadership virtues, or good habits, we would be remiss if we neglected to spend a moment considering core leadership competencies. Sam Smith was acknowledge – even by his enemies and detractors – as being the most competent man to lead the Defense of Baltimore during the War of 1812. Below is an array of four main leadership competencies. Review the diagram (below) starting with:

1. Power, then (going counter-clockwise to)

2. Influence,

3. Authority, and finally to

4. Control.

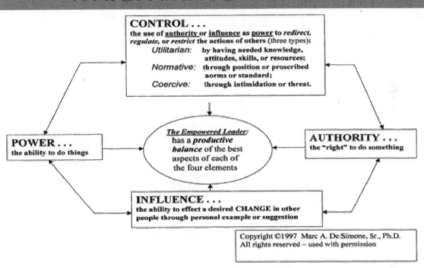

Sam Smith was a powerful leader. He had the ability to do things – to make good things happen for those who followed him. He had a positive influence on others – even in times of crisis and dire necessity. Sam Smith assumed authority that he possessed and used that right to do what was necessary to make important things happen for the common good. And finally, Sam Smith exercised utilitarian control (because he was of use to those who followed him in their hour of need), normative control (by taking charge by virtue of his rank when the situation called for decisive action), and coercive control (through ordering those who would have rather capitulated to the British in 1814) to stand firm and do their duty. He used all three types of licit control as a leader to redirect, regulate, and restrict the actions of others through the use of his licit authority and positive influence, to empower himself and others to do what needed to be done. *This is the leadership lesson, and legacy, of Samuel Smith, the Man who Saved America.*

---

[1] His was an unusually long life span for that period. A few other long lived founders included Benjamin Franklin who lived to the age of 84. Washington lived to 66. Jefferson lived to 83. John Adams lived to 90. Charles Carroll of Carrollton lived to the amazing age of 95 and died in 1832, becoming the longest surviving original signer of the Declaration of Independence. James Madison died at age 85 in 1836, just 3 years before Smith's death.

[2] Maryland State Archives, Baltimore Sun 25 April, 1839; "Honors to General Smith, City Council"; "The Late General Smith."

[3]

http://msa.maryland.gov/megafile/msa/speccol/sc3500/sc3520/002800/002827/pdf/mdgazette.pdf

[4] Niles Register   56, pg. 129-130

[5] *The Biographical Cyclopedia of Representative Men of Maryland and District of Columbia.* Baltimore: National Biographical Publishing Co., 1879. Biographical sketch on pp. 237-238.

[6] See the Sam Smith Collection at the Maryland State Archives. This Will was written the year (1838) before his death (1839) and was witnessed by Sam's younger brother Robert as well as Dabney S. Carr, John Smith Hollins and William Spears. Most of Smith's assets had been passed on during his lifetime. Upon his death he bequeathed to his son, John, the following: his Congressional Sword; his pistols; his Society of the Cincinnati Diploma; his Congressional Gold Medal; his father's portrait; the portrait of himself (used for the cover of this book) and of his wife; two marble busts from Montebello (of Washington & Franklin); four marble busts from his downtown Baltimore home; his books; and a gold watch. To his oldest daughter he gave Baltimore land and chattels. To his grand-nephew "Carr" he gave some books and his Congressional letter opener.

[7] Irwin, T. (2014). *Impact: Great Leadership Changes Everything.* Dallas, TX: BenBella Books.

[8]

http://freepages.history.rootsweb.ancestry.com/~wcarr1/Lossing2/Chap40.html1850's History of the War of 1812

[9] Schwartz, P. (1996). *The Art of the Long View: Planning for the Future in An Uncertain World.* NY, NY: Doubleday Press.

[10] Snyder, S. and George, B. (2013). *Leadership and the Art of Struggle: How Great Leaders Grow Through Challenge and Adversity.* San Francisco, CA: Berrett-Koehler Publishers.

[11] Price, T. (2008). *Leadership Ethics: An Introduction.* NY, NY: Cambridge University Press.

[12] Galford and Maruca (2006). *Your Leadership Legacy: Why Looking Toward the Future Will Make You a Better Leader Today.* Boston, MA: Harvard Business School Press.

Cassell, F. (1971). *Merchant Congressman in the Young Republic: Sam Smith of Maryland, 1752-1839.* Madison, WI: University of Wisconsin Press.

George et. al. (2007). *True North: Discover Your Authentic Leadership.* San Francisco, CA: Jossey-Bass.

Kaipa and Radjou (2013). *From Smart to Wise: Acting and Leading With Wisdom.* San Francisco, CA: Jossey-Bass.

Kaplan, R. (2013). *What You're Really Meant to Do: A Road Map for Reaching Your Unique Potential.* Boston, MA: Harvard Business School Publishing.

Linsky and Heifetz (2002). *Leadership on the Line: Staying Alive through the Dangers of Leading.* Boston, MA: Harvard Business School Publishing.

Mahler, M. (2011). *Live Life Aggressively.*

McIntosh and Rima (2007). *Overcoming the Dark Side of Leadership.* Grand Rapids, MI: Baker Books.

Pancake, J.(1972). *Samuel Smith and the Politics of Business.* University of Alabama Press.

Parks, S. (2005). *Leadership Can Be Taught: A Bold Approach for a Complex World.* Boston, MA: Harvard Business School Publishing.

Wills, G. (1994). *Certain Trumpets: The Nature of Leadership.* NY, NY: Touchstone.

Conclusion

Sam Smith was instrumental in saving Baltimore in the War of 1812. As a result, he helped save the United States of America! This patriot turned a near loss into a win during America's Second War for Independence.

The successful Defense of Baltimore not only saved the city from brutal retribution and ultimate destruction at the hands of the British, but also saved the country from otherwise certain defeat. Had Baltimore fallen, the rest of the country would most certainly have succumbed in short order. The Federalists who controlled New England were prepared to capitulate. The US economy was quickly collapsing. The massive British naval blockade was highly effective. The British fully intended to take America back, and came very close to succeeding. As the British sailed away from Baltimore and out of the Chesapeake Bay, news of the survival of Baltimore, and the death of the British General Ross, reached London within five weeks. Only then did the British Government finally make the clear decision to quickly end the war. The British were war weary. Their lack of military success in Baltimore, as well as the economic costs of the war ultimately convinced the British to expedite a negotiated peace settlement with the

Americans. In just over three months after the battle of Baltimore, the British negotiators had concluded the Treaty of Ghent on Christmas Eve of 1814; it was signed in London just four days later. The Battle of Baltimore had proven to be the pivotal turning point in the war, and Sam Smith's leadership had won the day.

As a final tribute to this brave man, let it not be forgotten that no foreign military has ever dared invade the homeland of the United States since the peace treaty with Britain was finalized in February of 1815.

Let's Review 21 Ways Sam Smith Impacted American History

(1) Smith had a vision for a strong US Navy. He voted in favor of building the first six frigates of the US Navy in 1794. Let it be noted that as a Congressman, James Madison voted against this bill. Sam Smith's leadership and efforts in Congress helped establish the principle of maritime defense of American merchant trade and freedom of the seas that has held strong ever since.

(2) Smith urged and voted in favor of the creation of the US Marine Corps in 1798. This elite corps has been the "First to Fight" ever since. In the War of 1812 Sam Smith strategically utilized the Marines who played a key role in the defense of Baltimore.

(3) Smith also helped create the Department of the Navy in 1798. To the great surprise of the British Navy, the young US Navy truly established itself in the War of 1812 and has since grown to become the finest Navy in the world today.

(4) Smith led Congress in the decision and the overseeing of the building of Ft. McHenry from 1798 to 1800. This fort served as the centerpiece for the plans to defend the port and city of Baltimore. This same legislation provided for additional American coastal and port defenses.

(5) For over a decade leading up to the War of 1812 Smith advised Jefferson, Madison , Monroe and Gallatin on the possibility of war with Britain and how best to prepare. He supported diplomacy to avoid war but ultimately realized that the British were seeking to retake America and that in order to maintain American independence, war was inevitable. Smith was always a realist in the defense of freedom.

(6) Due to his background and experience in the American Revolution, Smith recommended and supported the 1802 creation of the US Military Academy at WestPoint for the training of a professional US Army Officer Corps.

(7) Both Sam Smith and his brother Robert served as Secretary of the Navy under President Jefferson. Robert went on to serve as Secretary of State under President

Madison. Together, the Smith brothers were very influential on American foreign policy during the decade leading up to the War of 1812.

(8) While in the US Senate, Smith voted in favor of declaring war on Britain in June, 1812. This was a close vote and Smith recognized the unavoidable need to defend American Independence against all odds.

(9) As Major General, Sam Smith served as Commander of the Maryland State Militia. He oversaw their equipping and training in preparation for their brave and essential service in the War of 1812.

(10) In 1813 and 1814 Smith led the effort in raising private local funds for the needed preparations of the defense of Baltimore. He helped organize the Baltimore Committee of Safety & Vigilance which oversaw and synchronized local efforts to prepare the city's defenses. These funds were used to train, feed, equip and pay men; purchase weapons and ammunition; bolster defenses; plus repair needed infrastructure such as strategic roads and bridges in advance of the battle. Both the state and federal governments were slow to act in this regard so Sam Smith decisively and energetically led his local community in doing what needed to be done in time to make all the difference.

(11) Smith played a behind-the-scenes role in the recruitment and appointment of Major George Armistead

as the new commander of Ft. McHenry in 1813. Armistead was young and cooperative compared to his predecessor, Major Lloyd Beall who was 61, slow and often uncooperative. This change in commanders made a big difference in the preparations and battle operations at Ft. McHenry.

(12) In spite of political attacks by the Federalists and being voted out of the US Senate by the Federalist-controlled Maryland State Legislature in August of 1814, Sam Smith nevertheless rose to stand for American freedom and the defense of his home no matter what. He allowed nothing to get in the way of defending America, not even the hardball politics of the Federalists who were pro-British.

(13) Smith was the architect of the battle strategy for the defense of Ft. McHenry. He led in the preparations for the proper mounting of over 50 new large cannon at the fort plus the he insured the specialized training needed to effectively operate them. He also substantially increased the number of men at the fort from under 100 to 1,000.

(14) Smith correctly anticipated the location of the British amphibious landing at North Point. He ordered the advance preparations of earthen works along the North Point Road and planned for the ambush of the over 4,000 veteran British land forces when they arrived. These actions fortuitously resulted in the death of the British

Commander, Major General Robert Ross which very negatively impacted British morale.

(15) Smith adamantly rejected any local thoughts of capitulation to the British. While some were vacillating, he was activated to Regular Army status by authority of Governor Levin Winder and accepted Command as the senior officer over all American forces in Maryland in late August of 1814, shortly after the American leadership failures at Bladensburg and the resulting burning of the US Capital. The Federal Government was in total disarray but Sam Smith was gearing up for the fight of his life. His long preparations and fierce resolve inspired the men under his command.

(16) Smith rallied quality military leaders around himself. He then directed their individual and collective talents most effectively. His unified command included forces of the US Navy, US Marines, US Army, and a wide range of volunteer militia. Gallant subordinate officers included Captain Oliver Hazard Perry, Commodore John Rodgers, General John Stricker, and Major George Armistead.

(17) Smith directed the preparations of additional defenses to protect strategic American positions around Baltimore. These included Roger's Bastion on Hampstead Hill with its powerful cannon; the connected three miles of earthen works employing even more cannon; North Point

earthen works preparations; organizing a substantial cavalry; the building, equipping and manning of Ft. Babcock, Ft. Covington, Ft. Lookout and the Lazaretto; a blockade of sunken ships protecting the entrance of the harbor; utilizing an effective system of reconnaissance, intelligence and signaling throughout the area; plus preparations for a potential final stand from within the foundations of the strategically located under construction Catholic Basilica.

(18) Smith helped rally thousands of additional volunteers from across Maryland, Virginia, and Pennsylvania. He placed them strategically for maximum effectiveness.

(19) When the critical British assault came, Smith oversaw all combat operations and personally directed the brave defense of the city from multiple field headquarters. He was 62 years old at the time.

(20) Sam Smith set the country on the path to a stronger military as well as better international fair trade policies. As he predicted, government revenues from the rapid growth in the merchant shipping trade quickly paid off the war debt. Smith supported American industrialization and infrastructure developments. He also backed the Monroe Doctrine as well as supported American westward expansion.

(21) From an American perspective, the positive results of the outcome of the War of 1812 included the following: first and foremost, American Independence was preserved; the American military was built up with a long-term strategy of peace through strength; the British Government recognized the legitimate naturalized American citizenship of Irish, Scottish, and British immigrants to the United States; there was much improved American free trade and economic growth; there was an end to the British incitement of and military supplies to American Indian tribes; the American continent was opened up for expansion across North America; the pro-British Federalist Party was ultimately dissolved; and finally, America became much more unified with a newfound sense of national pride and identity.

Sam Smith's insights, preparations, and resolve combined to save America, win a war, and propel the country forward at one of the most dramatic moments in its early history. His 40 years in Congress, three years as Mayor of Baltimore, combined with his 40 year military career are rare in American history. He was a real hero in two wars for Independence. His legacy is one of great integrity, bravery, statesmanship, and patriotic service.

In conclusion, one must ask the question "What would have happened to America without Sam Smith?" He turned around what appeared to be a hopeless loss and led his country back to freedom. It is hoped this book will inspire other future valiant leaders to do same!

Addendum

Here are a few "follow-up" vignettes about some of the people and places in this book.

Adams, John

On July 4th, 1826, 50 years after the Declaration of Independence was signed, both John Adams and Thomas Jefferson died. At age 83 Jefferson was buried on the grounds of his Monticello estate near Charlottesville, Virginia. Adams was 90 and is buried at the United First Parish Church in Quincy, Massachusetts. His wife Abigail is also buried there, having died of typhoid in 1818. Their son, John Quincy Adams, was President at the time of John Adams death.

Adams, John Quincy

The son of President John Adams, John Quincy, like Sam Smith, had left the Federalist Party and became a Democrat-Republican. He was appointed Minister to Russia by President Madison from 1809 to 1814. He then became the leading American negotiator for the Treaty of Ghent, the document which officially ended the War of 1812. After the War, he became American Minister to the Court of St. James in London for three years. Next, he served for eight years as US Secretary of State under President Monroe and authored the Monroe Doctrine. He was elected President for one term in 1824 (the first father-son presidency in American history). He went on to serve for 17 years in Congress after being President and died in the Capitol on February 23, 1848 at age 80. He is buried next to his parents in the family crypt in the United First Parish Church in Quincy, Massachusetts. John Quincy kept a lifetime diary which is about 50 volumes. He was an accomplished linguist.

Armistead, George

Major George Armistead was born in Virginia and was one of five brothers who served in the War of 1812. He had been second in command of Fort McHenry in 1810 and married in Baltimore that same year. He became the brother-in-law to Sam Smith's son-in-law, Christopher Hughes. Early in the War of 1812 he was sent to fight on the Canadian front. When the Americans captured Fort George from the British in May of 1813, it was Armistead who carried the captured flags and presented them to President Madison in Washington, DC. After the bombardment of Fort McHenry, his wife gave birth to a girl. He was quickly promoted to Lt. Colonel by President Madison. Armistead never fully recovered from the shock of the bombardment of Fort McHenry. He suffered from what today is known as post traumatic stress syndrome. About ten days after the battle, he wrote his after action report on the events for Secretary of War Monroe. He died only three and one half years after the battle on April 25, 1818 at the young age of 38. He is buried at the Old St. Paul's Cemetery in Baltimore. Today, his statue stands in front of Fort McHenry. His nephew, Lewis Addison Armistead, later became a General in the Confederacy during the Civil War and died in a charge at Gettysburg. He is buried near his uncle in Baltimore at the Old St. Paul's Cemetery.

Barney, Joshua

Commodore Joshua Barney had served in the American Revolution in the Continental Navy and became a member of the Society of the Cincinnati. Afterwards, he joined the French navy as the commander of a squadron. He was 55 years old at the time of the Battle of Bladensburg in the War of 1812. His valiant stand at Bladensburg employed 360 of his sailors and 120 of his Marines. He was seriously wounded by a bullet in the thigh which festered for the next four years. He died at age 59 in Pittsburgh, Pennsylvania and is buried there in Allegheny Cemetery. He is remembered as the Father of the Chesapeake Flotilla.

Bonaparte, Elizabeth "Betsy" Patterson

Elizabeth Patterson, known as "Betsy", was Sam Smith's niece and was married to Jerome Bonaparte, younger brother of Napoleon, in Baltimore on December 24, 1803. Her father, William Patterson, like Smith, was an affluent Baltimore merchant of Irish descent, and was a fellow Presbyterian. Betsy was said to be the most beautiful woman in America when she married at age 18. Some have speculated that Sam Smith may have encouraged the marriage in order to gain diplomatic advantages with Napoleon, who was First Consul of France at the time. On May 8, 1804 war broke out between France and Britain. Napoleon crowned himself Emperor December 2, 1804. Napoleon did not approve of his brother's marriage and ordered Jerome back to Europe. In the summer of 1804, a pregnant Betsy traveled with her husband, Jerome, to Europe in order to attend Napoleon's coronation. Betsy was refused entry to the Continent and instead traveled on to London where she gave birth to a son, Jerome Napoleon Bonaparte. She was abandoned by her husband Jerome and returned to Baltimore. Jerome went on to marry a German princess. In 1815, by special act of the Maryland Legislature, Betsy secured a divorce. She never remarried.

She outlived her son (a graduate of Mt. St. Mary's College) who died in Baltimore in 1870 at the age of 65. Betsy died in Baltimore on April 4, 1879 at the age of 94. She is buried in the Green Mount Cemetery, Baltimore.

Bonaparte, Napoleon

Napoleon's abdication in April of 1814 changed the momentum of the War of 1812 in America, causing the British to shift their focus from Europe to America. Napoleon was taken to the Italian island of Elba while European heads of state sought to recreate a new European order at the Congress of Vienna.

In 1815, after the Treaty of Ghent ended the war between America and Britain, Napoleon escaped Elba, returned to France, and fielded another army. A combined European force finished the French at the famous Battle of Waterloo and Napoleon was permanently exiled to the remote island of St. Helena in the South Atlantic, escorted by Admiral Cockburn of Chesapeake infamy. He died there May 5, 1821 at the age of 51. There are theories that he may have been poisoned. He is buried in Paris beneath a golden dome in a crypt at Les Invalides, part of Europe's greatest military museum.

Burr, Aaron

Aaron Burr's father was a Presbyterian minister and second president of the College of New Jersey, as Princeton University was known prior to 1896. His grandfather was the formidable Calvinist preacher Jonathan Edwards. Burr had served well in the Continental Army during the American Revolution reaching the rank of Lt. Colonel. He went on to complete his legal studies and practiced law in

New York City. He helped Jefferson's election in 1800 by rallying the Tammany Hall political machine. When it turned out that he tied Jefferson, the election went to the House of Representatives to be decided. Jefferson ultimately won by one vote (Delaware cast a blank vote). Burr then became Vice President for one term.

Burr and James Madison had been fellow students at the College of New Jersey. In 1790 they also served in the U.S. Congress together in Philadelphia. In 1794, Burr was living in a rooming house in Philadelphia where the recently widowed Dolley Payne Todd also lived. Burr introduced the 26 year old widow Dolley to the 43 year old bachelor, James Madison. Madison married Dolley in September, 1794 at Harewood House, the home of her sister Lucy, near present day Charles Town, West Virginia. A few years later, the capital was moved to Washington, DC. While Madison served as Secretary of State under President Jefferson, Dolley assumed the role of hostess (surrogate first lady) since Jefferson was a widower.

On July 11, 1804 Alexander Hamilton was killed by Burr in a duel. Murder charges were filed against Burr in both New York and New Jersey (dueling was outlawed in both states), but the charges were eventually dropped.

After leaving the Vice Presidency in 1805, Burr went west. In 1807, he was arrested for treason based on an order issued by President Jefferson. This was based on an alleged conspiracy to aid in a Mexican revolution to overthrow Spanish control of the Southwest. Burr was brought to Richmond, Virginia for trial in U.S. District Court. The trial was presided over by the Federalist Chief Justice John Marshall. Burr was acquitted.

Burr then traveled to Europe for several years leading up to the war of 1812. During the War of 1812 he lost a daughter on the schooner *Patriot* off the coast of the Carolinas. He continued to practice law in New York. A notorious womanizer, he is one of the most controversial of America's founding fathers. He died on Staten Island at a boarding house in 1836, and is buried in Princeton, New Jersey.

Carroll, Charles

Charles Carroll of Carrollton, a staunch Federalist, was one of the richest men in Maryland. He was not in favor of defending Baltimore against the British in the War of 1812. After the war, he went on to help create the Baltimore and Ohio Railroad in 1827. He also served as President of the State Colonization Society of Maryland. He died on November 14, 1832 in Baltimore at age 95, being the last living signer of the Declaration of Independence. He is buried in the chapel at his Manor on what was originally a 13,500 acre estate near Ellicott City in Howard County, Maryland. Carroll County, Maryland was created in 1837 and named after him.

Carroll, John

John Carroll is of Irish descent and was born in Upper Marlborough, Maryland and died in Baltimore on December 3, 1815 at age 80. He was the cousin of Charles Carroll of Carrollton. He became a Jesuit at age 18 and studied for the Catholic priesthood in France. He returned to Maryland from France at age 40 soon after the Pope suppressed the Jesuits in 1773. He helped to organize the Catholic Church in America beginning in Baltimore. John Carroll became the first Catholic Bishop in America in 1789. He helped found the Jesuit Georgetown University in 1791. In 1803 he conducted the wedding of Betsy Patterson to Jerome Bonaparte in Baltimore. In 1806 he helped oversee the beginning of construction of the first Catholic Cathedral in the United States, what today is called the Basilica of the National Shrine of the Assumption of the Blessed Virgin Mary, in Baltimore. The cathedral was designed by Benjamin Latrobe, the architect of the U.S. Capitol and was constructed from 1806 to 1821. In 1808 John Carroll became the first Catholic Archbishop in America. The cathedral was not complete in 1814 when Baltimore was attacked by the British. Sam Smith used it as the final defensive position for protection of the city. John Carroll is buried in a crypt at the Basilica. Today, tours are available to this National Historic Site.

Cochrane, Alexander

British Vice Admiral Sir Alexander Cochrane was knighted for his service in the War of 1812. After his failure to take Baltimore, Cochrane sailed to New Orleans where the British were decisively defeated by General Andrew Jackson in January, 1815. The British failure was later blamed on Cochrane by the Duke of Wellington. Nevertheless, Cochrane was promoted to full Admiral in 1819. He died in Paris in 1832 at the age of 73. Sam Smith outlived him by 7 years.

Cockburn, George

British Rear Admiral Sir George Cockburn was one of the most hated British naval officers in America. He had been promoted to Rear Admiral August 12, 1812. His "Terror on the Chesapeake" in the summer of 1813 earned him his reputation for cruelty and brutality. It was Cockburn who strongly urged General Ross to attack and burn Washington, D.C. in August of 1814. When General Ross was shot and killed several weeks later in Baltimore, Cockburn's intentions to burn Baltimore were thwarted. In August of 1815, it was Cockburn who transported Napoleon Bonaparte to the South Atlantic island of St. Helena. He later became a Tory member of the British Parliament from Portsmouth. In 1828 he was elevated to the position of First Naval Lord. He was promoted to full

Admiral in 1837 and Admiral of the Fleet in 1851. Cockburn died in England in 1853 at the age of 81.

Decatur, Stephen

Stephen Decatur was of French and Irish descent, born on Eastern Shore of Maryland and raised in Philadelphia. He was the youngest man to become a Captain in the U.S. Navy at the age of 25. He played a key role in the development of the young navy and was personal friends with James Monroe. As a Midshipman, he served under Commodore John Barry on the launching of the frigate USS *United States* out of Philadelphia and later commanded that same ship. He fought in the Quasi-War against France, the Barbary Wars, and the War of 1812. He was considered the hero of the first Barbary War of 1805 where he lost his brother James. Returning to America, he became the most popular navy man of his era.

Decatur married Susan Wheeler, daughter of the mayor of Norfolk, Virginia. (She had previously declined marriage offers from Aaron Burr and Jerome Bonaparte). At the end of the War of 1812 Decatur was captured by the British and briefly imprisoned in Bermuda. After the war he was awarded the Congressional Gold Medal for his distinguished service. He went on to receive the rank of Commodore and fought in the Second Barbary War in 1815, capturing the Algerian flag ship. Because he received all his demands from Tripoli and Tunis, Decatur was known as the Conqueror of the Barbary Pirates. He later became a member of the Board of Navy Commissioners. The Decatur House on Lafayette Square, opposite the White House in Washington, DC is today a museum. In 1820 Decatur was shot in a duel at Bladensburg with Commodore James Barron. After being wounded, he was escorted back to his Washington home by Commodore John Rodgers, and died that night at the age of 41. His funeral was attended by Washington's elite, including President Monroe. Decatur is buried in Philadelphia.

Defenders Day

Since 1815, September 12th of each year has been commemorated as "Defenders Day" in Baltimore. On April 1, 1908 it was made a state holiday for Maryland. 2014 marked the 200 year Commemoration of the Defense of Baltimore. The celebration included several days of events such as fireworks, the Navy Blue Angels Air Show, sailing ships filling the harbor, and more.

French & Indian War

The French and Indian War, also known as the Seven Years War (1756 to 1763), was a major international conflict between England and France; some would say the first "world war." The conflict between these two "super powers" of the day was a contest for dominance over global colonial empires that would impact many countries for the next half century. America was caught in the middle of this struggle as well. This competition between France and Britain resulted in the next 60 years of warfare: 7 Years War, the American Revolution, the French Revolution, the Napoleonic Wars, and the War of 1812.

George Washington served as a Colonel under the British during the French & Indian War. Sam Smith was born in 1752 and saw soldiers from this war as a young boy in Carlisle, Pennsylvania. In fact his boyhood home became the headquarters for a British General. That contest in North America resulted in the loss of most French territory to the British except for Quebec and New Orleans. The British economic costs of the war in North America were soon passed on to the American Colonists. The resulting heavy taxation eventually led to the American Revolution. The French helped the Americans win their Revolution against the British. Then the French Revolution toppled the French monarchy. This resulted in two more decades of war across Europe. The Napoleonic Wars threatened the status quo of many European powers and the monarchial system. America helped Napoleon by purchasing the Louisiana Territory. This seriously upset the British for two reasons. It provided much needed money for Napoleon to fight his European wars and it also gave America a great deal of western lands which further inspired their future westward movement, something the British wanted desperately to prevent. Upon the abdication of Napoleon in April 1814, the British shifted their entire focus on their hopes to regain control of North America once and for all. 1814 was an all out effort by the British to break up America, destroy its government, decimate its economy, destroy its small navy, control its port cities, and finally gain control of the future of the entire North American Continent, something Britain had envisioned since the days of the French and Indian War. America's future as an independent nation was truly on the line.

Gallatin, Albert

Albert Gallatin served the longest tenure as Secretary of the Treasury in American history (1801 to 1814). Sam Smith and his brother Robert were often at odds with Gallatin's tight purse strings when it came to defense spending. Sam and Robert Smith were ostracized from President Madison in order to keep Gallatin in the cabinet. Gallatin eventually resigned the Treasury to participate in the American peace negotiations in Europe to end the war. He was a signatory as an American negotiator to the Treaty of Ghent. From 1816 to 1823 he served as U.S. Minister to France, and later moved to New York City where he helped found New York University. Gallatin died in Astoria, New York, August 12, 1849 at age 88. He is buried at the Trinity Churchyard in Lower Manhattan. A statue of him stands today in front of the U.S. Treasury Building next to the White House in Washington, DC.

Howard, John Eager

Howard was born near Baltimore in 1752 and was a veteran of the Revolutionary War and hero of the 1781 Battle of Cowpens in South Carolina. He inherited a large amount of land in and around Baltimore and grew his real estate holdings over his lifetime. He served as Governor of Maryland in 1789. Colonel Howard later declined an offer by President Washington to be Secretary of War. He became a U.S. Senator from Maryland at a time when Sam Smith was a Congressman. Howard was a fellow member of the Society of the Cincinnati and a Freemason. His 1814 speech before the Baltimore Committee of Vigilance and Safety was profound and helped sway the city to fight in its defense of American liberty. In 1816, he ran as a candidate for Vice President against the Monroe ticket, but lost.

Howard's son Charles married Francis Scott Key's oldest daughter, Elizabeth Phoebe Key in 1825. They lived in Baltimore, where a Methodist church is currently located on Mt. Vernon Place. The Washington Monument there is the first public monument to George Washington in America and was built on land donated by John Eager Howard. It was there, at Charles Howard's home, where Francis Scott Key died while visiting his daughter in January 1843. Key was originally buried in the Howard family vault at the Old St. Paul's Cemetery in Baltimore. The Howards were members of St. Paul's Episcopal Church in Baltimore, where Francis Scott Key had been offered the position of Assistant Rector in the spring of 1814, but turned it down.

John Eager Howard died at his Belvedere estate at age 75, in October of 1827. He is buried at the Old St. Paul's Cemetery in Baltimore, and is memorialized by an equestrian statue that stands today at Mt. Vernon Place. Howard County, Maryland is named for him.

Jackson, Andrew

Like Sam Smith, Andrew Jackson descended from Scots-Irish Presbyterians who emigrated from Ireland. He hated the British ever since he was a prisoner during the American Revolution and lost two brothers and his mother during the war. He was an orphan at age 14. In January 1815 he became famous for his victory at the Battle of New Orleans. For this he received a Congressional Gold Medal. Prior to that, he led the fight against the Creek Indians during the War of 1812. After the war, Jackson led the fight against the Seminoles who were being supported by the Spanish and the British. This led to the eventual acquisition of Florida from Spain in 1821.

Jackson ran for President in 1824 and won the popular vote but did not have a majority of the electoral votes. He lost to John Quincy Adams in a runoff in the House of Representatives. Sam Smith supported him for President in 1828 and oversaw his inauguration (one of the wildest in American history). Jackson lost his wife just before taking office. As President, he generally promoted State's Rights, but not nullification of federal laws. He strengthened the office of the President and served two terms. He is often remembered for his breaking of the National Bank and for Indian removal. On January 30, 1835 there was an assassination attempt on Jackson on the east steps of the Capitol. Two guns misfired. Francis Scott Key defended the shooter in court who was eventually declared insane (first use of the insanity defense in American jurisprudence).

Francis Scott Key recommended his brother-in-law, Roger Taney, to Jackson as Attorney General. Jackson also appointed Taney Secretary of the Treasury. After an initial rejection to the Supreme Court, Taney was successfully appointed by Jackson as Chief Justice in 1836 (Taney later swore in Lincoln and died in 1864 at age 87).

After eight years of retirement from the presidency, Andrew Jackson died on June 8, 1845 at age 78. He is buried next to his wife, Rachel, at his home, The Hermitage (1,000 acres at its peak), 10 miles outside of Nashville, Tennessee. Jackson was a longtime Mason and was Grandmaster of the Tennessee State Lodge.

Jefferson, Thomas

Jefferson had struggled for years with the issues that led up to the War of 1812. He followed the war with great concern from Monticello. After the burning of the U.S. Capitol in

1814, which destroyed the Library of Congress, Jefferson sold the bulk of his personal library (6,487 volumes) to Congress in 1815 to begin the modern Library of Congress (his collection is still there). On July 4th, 1826, 50 years after the Declaration of Independence was signed, both Thomas Jefferson and John Adams died. Jefferson was 83 and is buried on the grounds of Monticello near Charlottesville, Virginia. Adams was 90 and is buried at the United First Parish Church in Quincy, Massachusetts.

Key, Francis Scott

In later August of 1814, Francis Scott Key had been sitting at his Georgetown home very depressed on the heels of the Bladensburg disaster where he "raced" with the rest of the militia. His brother-in-law, Roger Taney (who with Key's help later became Secretary of the Treasury, Attorney General and then Chief Justice of the Supreme Court) had come down from Frederick, Maryland with a wagon to convince "Frankie" to travel back with him for safety. Shortly thereafter, another brother-in-law and fellow Episcopalian, Richard West, from Upper Marlborough, arrived with bad news about their mutual friend Doctor Beanes. Key knew Beanes from their Episcopal Church vestrymen duties as well as from earlier Annapolis days. Taney returned to Frederick while Key made arrangements to rescue Dr. Beanes with authorization from President Madison.

Key sailed out of Baltimore with John Skinner in search of the British fleet. Several days later, on September 7, 1814 they located the flagship HMS *Tonnant* at the southern end of the Chesapeake Bay. Key dined with General Ross and Admirals Cochrane and Cockburn, while Skinner negotiated Beanes' release. Together, they sailed north to Baltimore for the largest battle of the War. After observing the landing of General Ross at North Point and the formidable bombardment of Fort McHenry, Key was inspired to write a poem to express his overwhelming patriotic feelings.

Following their release, the three Americans and crew disembarked Friday evening on Hugh's wharf at Fell's Point. Key went to the Indian Queen Hotel (at the southeast corner of Hanover and Baltimore streets) to recover from his nearly two week ordeal. It was there that he took out the scribbled notes that he had made on the back of a letter. He then wrote on a new single sheet of paper the four stanzas of his poem. He did not title or sign it. The actual document is today in the possession of the Maryland Historical Society.

Key then reconnected with another of his brother-in-laws, Judge Joseph Hopper Nicholson. The judge was a prominent lawyer in Baltimore, a fellow Episcopalian and Federalist, and had just served as the second in command of Fort McHenry during the bombardment. Key gave his poem to the judge who, in turn, had a local printer produce posters of the poem called "broadsides". It was soon posted all over town with the added title "The Defense of Baltimore". Baltimore newspapers began printing the poem and it quickly spread across the country. The poem was put to music and first formally sung in Baltimore at the Holiday Street Theater in late October. Sheet music was first printed in Baltimore, and then sold widely. Key had no idea this one-page poem would make him famous. Nicholson kept the original and passed it on to his son.

Key traveled to Frederick for a family reunion. His parents, wife and children welcomed him back to Terra Rubra, the family farm (which he would inherit). They all shared his firsthand account of the recent series of amazing events, including seeing a printed copy of the poem he had written.

He went on to a long legal career in Washington, DC, representing cases before the U.S. Supreme Court. He eventually became District Attorney for Washington, DC. From 1817 until his death in 1843, Key also served as Vice President of the American Bible Society. He helped start a Theological Seminary in Alexandria which today is the largest Episcopal Seminary in America, and was an active member of the American Colonization Society.

Key had a total of 12 children but suffered several family tragedies in his lifetime. One of his children drowned in the Potomac at about age nine. Another son, Daniel Key, was a naval cadet who was killed at age 22 in a senseless duel at Bladensburg in 1836.

Francis Scott Key died unexpectedly on January 11, 1843, while visiting his daughter, Elizabeth Howard, in Baltimore. He was sick for several days at her home and this author suspects for various reasons that he may have died from a burst appendix. He was buried in the Howard Vault at the Old St. Paul's Cemetery in Baltimore. Decades later, he was reinterred at the Mount Olivet Seminary in Frederick, Maryland, where today there is a majestic monument and Chapel in memory of the author of the poem that became the American National Anthem.

Key's wife, **Mary "Polly" Tayloe Lloyd Key**, outlived him by 16 years, and died in Baltimore, about a week before her 75th birthday, May 18, 1859. She is buried at her husband's side at the Key Monument, Mount Olivet Cemetery, in Frederick, Maryland.

Key, John Ross (father of Francis Scott Key)

John Ross Key was about 60 years old at the time of the Battle of Baltimore in 1814. He knew Sam Smith since they served together – both from Maryland - in the American Revolution. They both fought at the major Battle of Long Island and played strategic roles in the "Maryland Line". In 1792, then President, George Washington visited the Keys at their home in Frederick while on his way to Philadelphia for the Fourth of July celebration there.

Francis Scott Key was almost 12 years old at the time. It was a moment the young boy would never forget.

John Ross Key served as Justice of the Peace, Judge, and Associate Justice of the Western Maryland Judicial District covering Allegheny, Washington, and Frederick Counties. He was proud of his oldest son, Francis, and would have been quite interested in hearing the firsthand accounts of the Battle of Bladensburg, as well as the Battle of Baltimore. He lived another seven years after those events and enjoyed the annual Summer visits of Francis and the many grandchildren. John Ross Key died at his country home in Frederick, Maryland, on October 11, 1821, at the age of 67. Francis Scott Key inherited the several thousand acre estate of Terra Rubra.

John's wife, **Anne Arnold Phoebe Charlton Key** bore John Ross six children, only three of whom survived to adulthood. She died at her home in Frederick on July 8, 1830, at the age of 74. Both of Francis Scott Key's parents are buried next to each other at the Mt. Olivet Cemetery in Frederick, Maryland.

Madison, Dolley

Dolley Madison was born in North Carolina, and raised as a Quaker. She had four brothers and three sisters. She eventually moved with her parents to Philadelphia. In 1790, at age 22, young Dolley married a Quaker lawyer named John Todd. In August of 1793, a yellow fever epidemic broke out in Philadelphia killing more than 5,000 people, including Dolley's husband and one of her two young sons. The following year, 1794, 26 year old Dolley was introduced by Aaron Burr to 43 year old James Madison, whom she married in September. Since James was not a Quaker, Dolley was expelled from the Society of Friends for marrying outside her faith.

Dolley Madison became known as the most dynamic "First Lady" in early American history. She hosted weekly parties at the White House as well as special balls, teas, private dinners, and other events in the new capital. On March 29, 1812, just weeks before war was declared, she hosted the first wedding in the White House—that of her younger sister Lucy to U.S. Supreme Court Justice Thomas Todd.

When the British invaded Washington, DC in the summer of 1814, Dolley fled the White House at the last possible moment. She was escorted by Daniel Carroll (Madison had sent him specifically to care for her at that moment) and taken to his home in Georgetown. She spent the next several days on the move in Virginia and Maryland amid the confusion. By her request, the famous Gilbert Stuart painting of George Washington was indeed saved from the British, but not by Dolley personally. The historic portrait hangs today in the White House. Importantly, documents such as the Declaration of Independence and the Constitution were also saved that same day by a civil servant named Steven Pleasonton.

After President Madison's second term, James and Dolley retired to their country estate in Virginia. While they enjoyed many visitors at Montpelier, Dolley missed the excitement of the Washington social scene. She also hoped James would take her on a trip to Paris, but that never happened.

After James Madison died in 1836, Dolley was welcomed back to Washington as the social grand dame of the city. She lived about a block from the White House, at what today is called the Dolley Madison House, which occasionally offers private tours. Congress purchased the valuable James Madison notes from the Constitutional Convention of 1787, and Dolley was able to live off those proceeds. She lived to the age of 81, and died July 24, 1849 in her D.C. home. Her funeral was one of the largest in Washington's history at that time. Steven Pleasonton was one of her pall bearers. Dolley is buried next to her husband in the family cemetery at the Montpelier estate in Virginia.

Madison, James

Upon returning to Washington, DC in late August of 1814, President James Madison and Dolley eventually moved into the Octagon House at 18th and New York Avenue, NW. It was there, in the second story parlor, that he signed the Treaty of Ghent in February of 1815, officially ending the War of 1812. It took several years for the White House to be restored after being burned to the ground by the British.

After the War of 1812, President Madison completed his second term of office, leaving Washington in 1817 as he retired at age 65 to his Virginia plantation home of Montpelier. Although Madison was a member of the American Colonization Society, he never freed any of his slaves, which numbered more than a hundred. He sold one-fourth of his slaves to help his finances near the end of his life. Madison's personal servant, Paul Jennings, later wrote a book (the first White House memoir), *"A Colored Man's Reminiscences of James Madison."* Jennings was 15 years old in 1814 and personally helped save the Gilbert Stuart portrait of George Washington that hung in the formal dining room of the White House. That day Jennings had set the table for a 3:00 p.m. dinner, which included preparing the ale, cider, and wine in coolers. That night, Admiral Cockburn, General Ross and other British officers dinned at the White House and toasted to "Jemmy's hospitality" before burning the Presidential Mansion. When Madison signed the Treaty of Ghent at the Octagon House in February of 1815, it was Paul Jennings who played *"The President's March"* on his violin to start the celebration. Jennings was with Madison at Montpelier when he died in 1836. Dolley sold Paul Jennings to Daniel Webster for $120 in 1847. He worked off the debt at $8 a day, finally earning his freedom. His three sons later fought for the

Union during the Civil War. Paul Jennings bought a home, at 1804 "L" Street, NW in Washington, DC and died there surrounded by his family in 1874 at the age of 75.

Madison's personal finances declined as the years went by. Madison had no children of his own, but adopted Dolley's son, John Payne Todd, who took a major financial toll on the Madisons over the years. He spent several years preparing his notes on the Constitutional Convention which were sold after his death in order to support Dolley in her old age. He has long been considered the Father of the American Constitution and was a co-author of the Federalist Papers. After Jefferson's death in 1826, Madison became Rector of the University of Virginia until his death in 1836.

For six months before his death, Madison could not walk but his mind was alert, as he conversed with numerous visitors. He died suddenly, on the morning of June 28, 1836, at Montpelier, at the age of 85. He is buried at Montpelier, in the family cemetery. By 1844, Dolley had sold both the mansion and the plantation. She moved back to Washington, DC, and lived there until her death 13 years later, in 1849. Today you can visit the historic Madison home, Montpelier, and the James Madison Museum, in Orange, Virginia.

Maryland Historical Society and Museum

The Maryland Historical Society is a private non-profit entity founded in 1844. Today it is located at 201 West Monument Street in Baltimore. It includes historical archives, a library, a quarterly journal, special speaking events, and a museum. Its first President was John Spear Smith, son of Sam Smith.

McHenry, James

In 1813, McHenry had been elected President of the Baltimore Bible Society. He was in Baltimore at the time of the British attack in 1814, but was not healthy. That year, he suffered paralysis resulting in the complete loss of the use of his legs. He was very concerned about the War of 1812 and received letters from friends keeping him informed of what was happening. On September 13, 1814, in the middle of the Battle of Baltimore, a letter was written to McHenry from Philadelphia. It was penned by a French engineer named Jean Foncin who years earlier had designed Fort McHenry. In the postscript, Foncin wrote the following: "It is a painful idea to me that the beautiful city of Baltimore be exposed to the disasters of war, but my mind will be a little solaced, if Fort McHenry does answer the purpose for which it was established, and affords me the satisfaction of having contributed to your defense." (Maryland Historical Society, MS 1846)

McHenry lived to see the successful defense of his beloved city and the effectiveness of the now famous Fort. He died in his hometown of Baltimore, two years later, at age 62. He was a member of the same Presbyterian Church as Sam Smith and is buried at the same Westminster Burial Grounds, in Baltimore. As a young man he had studied medicine under Benjamin Rush in Philadelphia. During the American Revolution he served as a surgeon and then aid to General Washington. He was a signer of the U.S. Constitution, a member of the Society of the Cincinnati, and served as U.S. Secretary of War. He will always be remembered by the fort which bears his name.

Monroe, James

James Monroe, a Virginian, went on to complete serving as Secretary of State to the end of Madison's second presidential term. He then served two terms as President and worked collaboratively with Sam Smith, whom he always respected for his military service.

Monroe is regarded as the last U.S. President to be a Revolutionary War Veteran – the last of the "Three-Cornered Hat" presidents. He had been wounded in the left shoulder at the Battle of Trenton. He then studied law under Thomas Jefferson in Philadelphia, followed by serving in the Continental Congress. Next, he was elected from Virginia to the U.S. Senate.

257

Monroe had served as Minister to France under President Washington. He also served several terms as Governor of Virginia. He eventually returned to France to help negotiate the Louisiana Purchase for President Jefferson. He was appointed Minister to the Court of St. James where he corresponded with Sam Smith about possible war plans against Britain.

Monroe's Presidency is most remembered as the "Era of Good Feelings." He signed the Monroe Doctrine (which was drafted by John Quincy Adams) and saw the passing of the Missouri Compromise of 1820. Under Monroe, Florida was ceded from Spain to the U.S. in 1821. Five new states were admitted to the Union under his Presidency.

Monroe departed the Presidency in March of 1825. In August, the Marquis de Lafayette and President John Quincy Adams visited the Monroes at their home of Oak Hill Mansion, Virginia.

Monroe owned several slave plantations. He supported the American Colonization Society in an effort to repatriate freed slaves back to Africa. The African capital of Liberia, Monrovia, was named after him.

Monroe died at his daughter's home in New York City, at age 73, on July 4, 1831. He is entombed in Richmond, Virginia.

Montebello

This was the name of the Smith country estate. It was completed by Sam Smith around 1800. He built it on 600 acres which overlooked a southern view of Baltimore and its harbor. The estate was purchased by the Garrett family after the death of John Spear Smith. The mansion was eventually torn down in 1907, and today this is the site of a high school known as the Baltimore City College, in the area south of 33rd Street and west of Alameda.

National Bank of the United States

Located in Philadelphia, the First National Bank was chartered for 20 years from 1791 to 1811 and was the first central bank in America. Madison and Jefferson led in the opposition of such a federal institution, considering it unconstitutional because it was not exclusively government owned. Twenty years later its charter was not renewed during the administration of President Madison, but was allowed to expire just prior to the War of 1812. At the heart of the national bank controversy was the fact that the First National Bank was privately owned; hence even foreigners were allowed to be stockholders. Many people at the time felt that powerful interests in England held a great deal of the bank stock and through additional financial entanglements, the British exerted strong influence over the Federalist Party in America. This is one reason why New

England and the Federalists were not supportive of the war to defend America from British abuses.

After the war, in 1816, a second bank charter was approved by Congress to run for 20 years from 1816 to 1836. The bank controversy did not go away. Only twenty percent of its capital was owned by the Federal Government and only one fifth of the directors were from the government. Sam Smith was caught in the middle; he sat on Congressional Banking Committees, and was a Director of a Bank in Baltimore.

When Andrew Jackson became President in 1828, one of his goals was to destroy the "foreign controlled" central bank and replace it with a new central bank that was fully owned and controlled by the U.S. Government, eliminating private (and especially foreign) control. The election of 1832 was a showdown moment. Nicholas Biddle, the bank president was called into Sam Smith's Committee and grilled. When Congress quickly passed a recharter bill, President Jackson immediately vetoed it. Jackson was reelected but the Bank War that followed in retaliation caused havoc in the economy, including in Baltimore. Riots there led to Sam Smith coming out of retirement and becoming Mayor. In 1836 the bank charter expired. The privately owned bank was now officially dead. The controversy over Central Banking ownership continued through the Civil War period and culminated in the creation of the modern Federal Reserve System in 1913.

This contemporary American Central Bank is also a privately held corporation which controls American finance. The question still remains, who are the shareholders? To control a nation's finances is to control that nation.

Nicholson, Joseph Hopper

Judge Joseph Hopper Nicholson was a prominent Baltimore lawyer and judge. He served in the U.S. House of Representatives as a staunch Federalist and although he was in favor of the War of 1812, he was adamantly opposed to the leadership of Sam Smith in the defense of Baltimore. Nicholson contributed personal funds to help establish the Baltimore Fencibles and was present, serving as a Captain and second in command inside Fort McHenry during the bombardment in 1814.

Nicholson was married to Rebecca Lloyd, the sister of Francis Scott Key's wife Mary Lloyd. Like Key, Nicholson was a Federalist, a lawyer, and Episcopalian. He met with Key in Baltimore upon Key's return from British detainment. It was Nicholson who was responsible for Key's poem being published. The Nicholsons held the original handwritten poem for 93 years. It was eventually sold in 1953 to the Maryland Historical Society. Nicholson died in Baltimore on March 4, 1817 at age 47, and is buried at the Lloyd Estate of "Wye House" in Easton, Maryland.

Octagon House

The Octagon house was built in 1799, by John Tayloe III, as a winter residence. He was the richest man in Virginia in the early 1800s, and had been educated at Eton and Oxford, in England. He was friends with James Madison, and together they co-owned several race horses. John Tayloe was the uncle of Francis Scott Key's wife, Mary Tayloe Lloyd, who lived nearby in Georgetown. After the British attack on Washington, the Madison's moved into the Octagon house for about two years while the White House was being rebuilt. This is where the Treaty of Ghent was signed which ended the War of 1812. Today, the Octagon House still stands and is the home of the American Institute of Architects.

Original Six Frigates of the U.S. Navy and the Modern Navy

In 1794 Congress authorized the building of the original six frigates of the U.S. Navy. This was in response to the Barbary Wars of North Africa. The votes were very close and Congressman Madison voted against the bill while Sam Smith voted in favor. Secretary of War Henry Knox oversaw the first half of the project. In 1797 the first three ships were launched in this order: USS *United States* from Philadelphia; USS *Constellation* from Baltimore; USS *Constitution* from Boston. With leadership from Sam Smith, the Department of the Navy was created in 1798 and oversaw the construction of the next three frigates as follows: in 1799, the USS *Congress* from Portsmouth, NH; USS *Chesapeake* from Norfolk, VA; and in 1800, the USS *President* from New York City. Each of these ships displayed American valor during the War of 1812.

The USS *United States* was seized in Norfolk, VA in 1861 by the Confederacy. She was eventually broken up by the Union in 1865.

The original USS *Constellation* was broken up in 1853. Some of the original timbers were re-used in the construction of a reproduction vessel. A third version is docked in Baltimore today.

The USS *Chesapeake* was captured by the British in 1813. She was later broken up in Portsmouth, England in 1820.

The USS *Congress* was the first American Warship to sail to China. She was eventually broken up in 1834.

USS *President* was captured by the British in mid-January of 1815. She was broken up in 1818.

The USS *Constitution* is the best known of the original six frigates. She defeated four British warships during the War of 1812 and gained the nickname "Old Ironsides". She circumnavigated the world and during the American Civil War she served as a training ship for the U.S. Naval Academy. Today, she is berthed in Boston Harbor and is the oldest commissioned vessel in the world.

263

Sam Smith would be proud to know that the modern U.S. Navy is the largest navy in the world. The National Museum of the U.S. Navy is located at the Navy Yard in Washington, DC. Other navy museums include the Naval Museum at Hampton Roads, Virginia; the Great Lakes Naval Museum near Chicago; the National Naval Aviation Museum in Pensacola, Florida (home of the Blue Angels); the Naval Undersea Museum, Keyport, Washington; the Puget Sound Naval Museum near Seattle, Washington; the Submarine Force Museum in Groton, Connecticut. The U.S. Naval War College is in Newport, Rhode Island. The U.S. Naval Academy is located in Annapolis, Maryland. The Navy Seals have become legendary as special operators.

Perry, Oliver Hazard

Captain Oliver Hazard Perry was a direct descendant of William Wallace, of "Braveheart" fame. In January of 1814, he received the Congressional Gold Medal, in Washington, DC, for his brave actions in the Battle of Lake Erie. He was made an honorary member of the New York Society of the Cincinnati. He was in Baltimore overseeing the building of the USS *Java* when the British arrived in September of 1814. Following the Defense of Baltimore, Perry commanded the USS *Java* which sailed out of Baltimore. He sailed to the Mediterranean for the Second Barbary War in 1815. Perry was given the rank of Commodore by President Monroe. In Venezuela, Perry contracted yellow fever and died at the age of 34 on his return trip to America. He was ultimately buried in his hometown of Newport, Rhode Island, where there is a memorial statue in his honor.

His younger brother, Matthew, had served under him in his early naval career. In later years, Matthew famously played a key role in the opening of Japan to the West, in 1854. He helped develop curricula for the U.S. Naval Academy and became known as the "Father of the Steam Navy." He also became Commodore, in 1840. He died in 1858, in New York City at the age of 63, and is buried next to his brother, in Newport, Rhode Island. Today, the Navy War College is located in the Perry's hometown of Newport, Rhode Island.

Rodgers, John

After the Defense of Baltimore, Rodgers temporarily commanded Ft. McHenry while Major Armistead recovered from what we would refer to now days as "shell shock." The Commodore was asked to head up a new Board of Navy Commission, which he did for most of the rest of his life. He also served as Secretary of the Navy for a brief time. In his lifetime he tested Robert Fulton's experimental torpedoes in 1810, was present at the Bladensburg duel that killed Stephen Decatur in 1820, and he introduced steam power to the U.S. Navy. At age 66 Rodgers died in Philadelphia one year before the death of his mentor and friend, Sam Smith. He is buried in the

Congressional Cemetery in Washington DC. Rodgers' son, several grandsons, and great-grandsons, became Commodores and Admirals in the U.S. Navy. Today, there is a marker in Patterson Park, Baltimore where "Rodger's Bastion" stood that September of 1814. Commodore Rodgers, when under the command of Sam Smith in Baltimore, played a major role in saving America.

Ross, Robert

After dying at North Point from a sharpshooter's ball, Major General Robert Ross was preserved in a barrel of Jamaican Rum on board the British flagship, HMS *Tonnant*. He was later transferred to the HMS *Royal Oak* which transported his body for burial in Halifax, Nova Scotia. Admiral Cockburn wrote a letter of regret to Ross' wife who was staying with Ross' brother who was a clergyman in southwest England. Ross was a graduate of Trinity College Dublin and played the violin. He had seen significant action in Spain, Egypt, Italy, and the Netherlands. He was wounded three times, and had a horse shot out from under him both at Bladensburg and later the same day upon his entry into Washington. There is a memorial in his memory at his hometown (Rostrevor, County Down) in Northern Ireland as well as a memorial in St. Paul's Cathedral, London. Ross was loved by his men and was a highly decorated officer who is regarded as a hero in Great Britain today, being remembered as General Ross of Bladensburg, the man who captured Washington.

Scott, Winfield

Winfield Scott fought in the early northern campaigns of the War of 1812. He became a prisoner of war and was paroled by the British. He was promoted to Colonel and in March, 1814 he was made Brigadier General at age 27. In July he was promoted to Brevet Major General. That Fall he replaced William Winder as Commander of the 10th Military District which led to Sam Smith's resignation from the Maryland Militia. In 1815 he became an honorary member of the Pennsylvania Society of the Cincinnati.

Scott went on to serve the longest on active duty of any General in American military history. He fought in three wars. He played a key role in the Mexican War in 1847. He consequently became the Military Commander of Mexico City.

In 1852 Scott ran for US President but lost to Franklin Pierce. He became a Lieutenant General in 1855. When the Civil War broke out in 1861, Scott was 74 and too old to participate in the field. He offered the top command position to Col. Robert E. Lee. Lee resigned and joined the Confederacy. Scott, who was also a Virginian, remained loyal to the Union and retained his commission. Scott devised the "Anaconda Plan" for a naval blockade to slowly strangle and defeat the Confederacy. He resigned the army in November of 1861. Scott died May 29, 1866 at West Point at the age of 79 and is buried at the West Point

Cemetery. He served 53 years active service, 47 as a General.

Skinner, John Stuart

John Skinner was a young Maryland lawyer and had served for a time with Joshua Barney. At the beginning of the War of 1812 he served in the neutral port of Annapolis overseeing all incoming European mail. He had been commissioned as a Colonel in 1813 as a U.S. Government negotiating officer and agent for prisoner-of-war exchange and parole, opening an office in Baltimore. He was paid $1800 per annum. When the British fleet arrived off of Point Lookout in August of 1814, Skinner rode 90 miles to warn Madison and became known as "Maryland's Paul Revere." As a consequence, the British burned buildings on Skinner's St. Leonard's Creek estate. In early September of 1814 Skinner sailed out of Baltimore accompanying Francis Scott Key on a sloop of truce to seek the release of Dr. Beanes from the British. He was 26 years old at the time. Together, these men witnessed the bombardment of Fort McHenry while anchored among the British fleet.

In later years, Skinner published *The American Farmer,* the first widely recognized agricultural periodical. He later published *The Plough, the Loom, and the Anvil.* He also served as Postmaster of Baltimore from 1816 to 1849. In 1824 Skinner was chosen by Lafayette to mange 20,000 acres that were granted to the General by Congress.

Skinner died in Baltimore March 21, 1851 at the age of 63 from "a contusion of the brain caused by falling through a trap door at the post office" (*Lewisburg Chronicle*, March 26, 1851). He is buried at the Westminster Burial Ground in Baltimore.

Smith, Robert (brother of Sam Smith)

Sam Smith's younger brother, Robert, left the Madison administration under a cloud in 1811. He sought to defend himself in a published letter, "*Robert Smith's Address to the People of the United States.*" He later turned down an offer to serve as Minister to Russia and never served in public office again. In 1813 he was elected Provost of the University of Maryland. He died in Baltimore at the age of 85, on November 26, 1842, and is buried at Westminster Burial grounds in Baltimore near his brother.

Smith, Margaret Spear (wife of Sam Smith)

Sam Smith's wife outlived him by three years and died December 22, 1842 at the age of 83. She is buried at Westminster Burial Grounds in Baltimore. Sam and Margaret were married about 60 years at the time of Sam's death in 1839. Together, they raised three children: John, Sidney, and Mary.

Smith, John Spear (son of Sam Smith)

John was the oldest son of General Sam Smith. He was born in Baltimore, in 1786, and died in Baltimore, in 1866, at the age of 80. He was married with several children. He moved into Sam Smith's Montebello estate and purchased it, working the plantation to save it from Sam Smith's bankruptcy. In 1844, on the formation of the Maryland Historical Society, he was elected its first president, a position he held for the next 22 years. He also served as General of the Maryland State Militia.

Society of the Cincinnati

This society was formed by John Knox in 1783 in Newburg, New York. George Washington was its first President. It was established for officers of the American Revolution who had served at least three years of active duty. Future membership was hereditary to firstborn sons. It was controversial in its earlier days. This society still exists with its national headquarters located in Washington, DC at the Anderson House, 2118 Massachusetts Avenue NW. They have a research library, historical archives, and host special events. Tours are available. Sam Smith's presentation sword from the Continental Congress is housed in their archives, donated by an heir of Sam Smith.

Star-Spangled Banner (flag)

The original flag that flew over Fort McHenry in 1814 was kept for years by the family and descendants of Major Armistead, the fort's Commander. In 1907 it came into the possession of the Smithsonian Institution and has been there ever since. Today, it is on display at the American History Museum in Washington, DC.

Star-Spangled Banner (lyrics and song)

The original tune came from a British song, "To Anacreon in Heaven". Within days of Francis Scott Key writing his four stanza lyrics in Baltimore, it was printed and posted around town on September 17 under the title of "The Defense of Baltimore". Two local newspapers, *The Baltimore Patriot* and *The American*, printed the words on September 20 with the note "Tune: Anacreon in Heaven." In October it was first performed at the Baltimore Holliday Street Theater, set to the British tune. Sheet music was printed by the Carr Music Store in Baltimore and the song became popular as it spread around the country. As the years went by, the U.S. military used it more and more. It was first performed at a baseball game in the 1918 World Series in Chicago during the seventh inning stretch. In 1931, Congress passed a bill designating the "Star Spangled Banner" as the official National Anthem of the United States. The bill was signed by President Herbert Hoover, and the original document is on display today at Fort McHenry.

The original document that Key penned was given to his brother-in-law, Judge Joseph Hopper Nicolson. It then passed to his son who lived in a house in Annapolis on the site of what today in the U.S. Naval Academy. For a

271

number of years, the famous poem sat in a desk drawer until it was rediscovered in 1847 when the house was purchased by the expanding Naval Academy. Today there is a historic marker near the location of that house, in front of the Chapel of the Naval Academy. There is also a bandstand nearby where the "Star Spangled Banner" is played with special recognition for the years the original manuscript spent at that site. The historic document was passed down through the Nicholson family until it was sold in 1907 to Henry Walters of Baltimore. In 1934 it was purchased at auction in New York by the Walters Art Gallery for $26,400. In 1953 it was purchased by the Maryland Historical Society in Baltimore for the same amount. Another manuscript was handwritten in Washington, DC, titled and signed by Key in 1840. It is in the Library of Congress today.

Stricker, John

Brigadier General John Stricker is one of the heroes of the Defense of Baltimore. He was very close to Sam Smith. He is especially remembered for his leadership at the Battle of North Point. Stricker died in Baltimore, June 23, 1825 at the age of 66. He was a member of the Society of the Cincinnati. He is buried at the Westminster Burial Grounds in Baltimore.

Treaty of Ghent (which ended the War of 1812)

The city of Ghent was actually a part of the Netherlands in 1814. This treaty was completed by negotiators on Dec. 24, 1814. It was signed 4 days later in London by the Prince Regent. It arrived in New York City on the ship *Favorite* in early February, 1815 and was then sent overland to Washington DC carried by young Carroll. It was signed by President Madison in the Octagon House on Feb. 16, then approved by the U.S. Senate the following day. A second copy of the Treaty was delivered by a secretary to the American Peace Delegation, Christopher Hughes Jr. of Baltimore. He was Sam Smith's son-in-law. Hughes had married Sam Smith's daughter, Laura Sophia Smith in 1811in Baltimore. He was also the brother-in-law of George Armistead, Commander of Ft. McHenry, who married Christopher's sister, Louisa Hughes, on October 26, 1810 in Baltimore. He arrived in Annapolis aboard the U.S. schooner *Transit* February 13, 1815 carrying the second of three copies of the treaty. He spent 30 years in the U.S. diplomatic corps. The retained American copy of the Treaty is preserved in the U.S. National Archives in Washington DC.

United States Army War College

Sam Smith was born in Carlisle, Pennsylvania. Today, his birthplace is the home of the U.S. Army War College. This institution was founded in 1901 in Washington, DC. Since

1951 it has resided at the now 500-acre campus on the site of the historic Carlisle Barracks, the nation's second oldest active military base. Upper level officers, some civilians, and some foreign guests attend this college to study strategic leadership at The Center for Strategic Leadership and Development, as well as military history at The Military History Institute. This graduate level school grants a Masters Degree in Strategic Studies. Notable alumni include John Pershing, John Lejeune, Dwight Eisenhower, George Patton, Omar Bradley, Alexander Haig, Norman Schwarzkopf, and Tommy Franks.

United States Marine Corps

Sam Smith helped produce the legislation that created the U.S. Marine Corps in 1798. The marines played a key role in the successful defense of Baltimore in the War of 1812. Today the Marine Corps has about 200,000 active duty members. The National Museum of the Marine Corps is located at Quantico, Virginia.

United States Military Academy at West Point

West Point is the oldest continuously operating army-post in the United States. It was established in 1802 as a military academy by President Thomas Jefferson and with major support from Sam Smith. Jefferson was not a great supporter of a standing army (and had never served in the military) but Sam Smith, who had served as an army officer in the Continental Army during the American

Revolution, helped convince him of the importance of a trained officer corps. The Corps of Cadets increased to 250 in anticipation of the War of 1812. Grey uniforms were introduced in 1814 giving the basis for the expression "The Long Grey Line." The Academy was the first engineering school in America, supplying leadership to the Army Corps of Engineers. Most American forts up to that time, including Fort McHenry, were designed by French engineers. After the War of 1812, the curriculum developed further and a trained officer corps with the idea of a standing army became fully accepted. Sam Smith led continuing congressional action to provide financial support of the academy in the 1820's when some in Congress were wavering. West Point houses the oldest military museum in the country. It is West Point that began the collegiate tradition of the class ring. A popular song at the academy today is "The Corps." Sam Smith retired as a Major General and would be most proud of today's U.S. Army and its well trained leaders.

United States Naval Academy

After the War of 1812, it became clear that America needed a strong navy with a trained officer corps. The U.S. Naval Academy was founded in 1845. It was located in Annapolis on the ten-acre site of the U.S. Army's Fort Severn. The first class consisted of 50 midshipmen students and seven instructors. Prior to the founding of the Academy, formal navy training took place on various ships and at various Naval Institutes.

Today the Naval Academy campus has expanded to about 340 acres and includes over 4,000 students. Its Bancroft Hall houses the largest college dormitory in the world. The Academy is rated at the top of Liberal Arts Colleges in the country. It is home to the Nimitz library and archives. On campus is the Naval Academy Museum which displays one of the world's finest collections of warship models in the world. John Paul Jones, considered by many to be the Father of the U.S. Navy, lies in the crypt beneath the Chapel. There is a band shell in front of the Chapel where the Star Spangled Banner is often played in memory of Key's original document being resident at that location for a number of years.

Veterans of the Battle of Baltimore

The veterans of the Battle of Baltimore never forgot Sam Smith and those historic days of defending freedom. Battle Monument was constructed from 1815 to 1825 to commemorate the saving of the city. Since 1827 the monument is depicted on the seal of the City of Baltimore. Defenders' Day became a holiday in Baltimore and is still celebrated each year on September 12. In 1876, a famous photo was taken of some elderly Baltimore veterans on Defenders Day.

Winder, William Henry

William Winder, Brigadier General, will always be most remembered as the Commanding Officer overseeing the debacle at the Battle of Bladensburg. He had no real military training or experience. His military appointment was a political move to please the Federalist Governor of Maryland, his uncle Levin Winder. To be fair, he was greatly hindered at Bladensburg by Secretary of War Armstrong as well as President Madison and Secretary of State James Monroe. Sam Smith Commanded all American forces in Baltimore, ultimately outranking Winder by the agreement of Governor Winder and Secretary of War James Monroe. General Winder did in fact serve well under Major General Sam Smith during the Defense of Baltimore. He was a Federalist and a Baltimore lawyer, having studied law under Judge Gabriel Duvall of Annapolis. He became a close lifelong friend of Roger Taney (Francis Scott Key's brother-in-law) from his Annapolis days, and Taney visited Winder on his death bed. After the War of 1812 he returned to the practice of law. He died in Baltimore May 24, 1824 at the age of 49. At the time of his death his law practice was the largest before the Baltimore Bar and one of the largest before the U.S. Supreme Court. The funeral cavalry escort was commanded by Brigadier General John S. Smith (Sam Smith's son). He is buried at Green Mount Cemetery in Baltimore.

Sam Smith

Timeline

1728 Smith's grandfather (Samuel Smith, 1698-1784), grandmother (Sidney Gamble Smith (abt. 1693-1759), along with their son (John Spear Smith, 1723-1794) emigrate from Ulster, Northern Ireland to Lancaster County, Pennsylvania along with three other Protestant families: the Spear, the Sterret, and the Buchanan families.

1750 The Smith, Spear, Sterret, and Buchanan families move to Carlisle, Pennsylvania; John Smith marries Mary "Molly" Buchanan

1752 Sam Smith is born in Carlisle, Pennsylvania, the first of five children, on July 27.

1759-1760 Due to the terrors of the French and Indian War in and around Carlisle, the Smith, Spear, Sterret, and Buchanan families move to Baltimore.

1766 Fourteen-year-old Sam Smith begins a six-year apprenticeship in his father's shipping business.

1771-1774 Smith tours Europe, building business contacts for his father.

1774 Smith returns to America, landing in Philadelphia at the time the First Continental Congress is convening

1775 Smith joins the Baltimore Cadets; the American Revolution begins in Boston.

1776 Smith, as a Captain in Colonel Smallwood's Maryland Regiment, is sent to Annapolis to arrest the Maryland Colonial Governor Robert Eden (which was unsuccessful). In August, he experiences his first combat at the Battle of Brooklyn Heights in New York. In December, Smith is promoted to Major.

1777 Smith is promoted to Lt. Colonel; he becomes engaged to Margaret Spear; that fall, Smith heroically commands the defense of Fort Mifflin near Philadelphia (for which he is later recognized by the Continental Congress).

1778 Sam Smith marries Margaret Spear at the First Presbyterian Church in Baltimore on December 31. Twelve children would be born to them; only six of them survived.

1779 Smith resigns from the Continental Army. He begins privateering and restores his family fortune while continuing to support the Revolutionary cause by recruiting for the Army, providing food and armaments to the American military, and running the British Naval Blockade.

1780-1781 Smith becomes the State of Maryland broker for food and armaments; builds a brewery in Baltimore; buys real estate. In September, the American victory at Battle of Yorktown ends the American Revolution.

1783 The Society of the Cincinnati is founded; General George Washington is the first President. Sam Smith becomes a founding member of the Maryland Society of the Cincinnati in Annapolis. The Treaty of Paris is ratified in Annapolis; General Washington resigns his Commission there on December 24.

1780s Smith builds his shipping business and other enterprises in Baltimore; he is appointed Brigadier General over the Maryland Militia by the Governor.

1786 Smith receives a special ceremonial sword awarded by the Continental Congress for his heroic leadership in the defense of Fort Mifflin.

1787 The Constitution of the United States is drafted in Philadelphia.

1789 President-Elect George Washington travels through Baltimore on his way to his inauguration in New York City. He is hosted by Sam Smith. In Paris, the French Revolution begins.

1790 The first U.S. Census is taken. Smith enters politics and becomes a Maryland state delegate to Annapolis.

1791 The first Bank of the United States (central bank) is given a 20 year charter and is located in Philadelphia.

1792-1800 Smith becomes a U.S. Congressman and serves in Philadelphia; Washington, DC is being built.

1793 France declares war on England; President Washington declares America neutral.

1794 With federal troops, President Washington squelches the Whiskey Rebellion in western Pennsylvania; Sam Smith leads the Maryland Militia to Frederick.

1795 In April Smith is promoted to the rank of Major General in the Maryland Militia by Governor Stone.

1796 Congress passes the controversial Jay Treaty with England; Sam Smith opposes it.

1797 The USS *Constellation* is launched in Baltimore.

1798 Smith votes to establish the Department of the Navy and the U.S. Marine Corps. The Irish Rebellion against Britain results in large numbers of Irish immigrants to America, with many arriving in Baltimore.

1798 -1800 The U.S. fights an undeclared "Quasi-War" at sea with France during the Adams Presidency. Smith promotes the building of Fort McHenry on the site of the old Fort Whetstone in Baltimore to improve the city's defenses.

1800 Washington, DC becomes the new capital of the United States of America.

1801 Thomas Jefferson is elected President, breaking a tie with Aaron Burr by a vote in the House of Representatives in which Sam Smith plays a key role. Smith becomes acting Secretary of the Navy; Smith's brother, Robert, an Admiralty lawyer from Baltimore, takes over as Secretary of the Navy for the next eight years.

1801–1805 The Barbary Wars occupy America's fledgling Navy and Marines in the Mediterranean.

1803 The Napoleonic Wars begin in Europe (which will last to 1815). President Jefferson buys the Louisiana Territory from France for $15 million. Sam Smith becomes U.S. Senator from Maryland

1804 The Lewis & Clark Expedition begins, departing in May from St. Louis.

1805 The naval Battle of Trafalgar results in a major British victory over the French and Spanish navies. Smith becomes President pro tem of the Senate, 1805 to 1808 (second in the line of succession to the presidency). He corresponds with Madison and Monroe on future potential war strategies against Britain.

1807 The *Leopard Affair* results in Jefferson's Embargo Act. Albert Gallatin, Secretary of the Treasury, writes Sam

Smith asking for advice on how to prepare for war with Britain.

1808 The legal importation of slaves to America ends.

1809 James Madison becomes President and signs the Non-Intercourse Act; Robert Smith is appointed Secretary of State.

1811 The 20 year National Bank Charter (central bank) ends and is not renewed; Sam Smith plays a key role in shutting that down. In April, Robert Smith is fired as Secretary of State creating a major fallout between the Smiths and President Madison.

1812 In spite of a very close vote in the U.S. Senate, America declares war on Britain on June 18 (Sam Smith votes for war). Napoleon loses his Grand Army to the Russian Winter.

1813 The British Navy under Vice Admiral Sir George Cockburn unleashes a year of terror with his "Red Squadron" on the Chesapeake. On September 10, Oliver Hazard Perry is victorious over the British Navy on Lake Erie. Napoleon suffers a major defeat at the Battle of Leipzig, which sets up his abdication the following spring. Smith works energetically to build up the defenses of Baltimore in anticipation of a potential British invasion. Major Armistead orders a large garrison flag to be sewn by Mary Pickersgill for Fort McHenry, which is delivered and flown over the fort by late August. Robert Smith becomes the President of the not-yet-fully-organized American Bible Society

1814

April 6: Napoleon is defeated by England and Prussia, abdicating his roles as Emperor of France and King of Italy. He is removed to the island of Elba.

June: The British General Robert Ross sails with several thousand men from Bordeaux, France to America by way of Bermuda. Sam Smith is voted out of the U.S. Senate by the Federalist-controlled Maryland Legislature.

July: General Ross arrives in Bermuda, joining forces with British Vice Admiral Sir Alexander Cochrane. The combined force sets sail for the Chesapeake Bay and arrive to rendezvous with Rear Admiral George Cockburn making a total of approximately 50 warships. That same month Sam Smith is voted out of the U.S. Senate.

August 21: British forces land nearly 5,000 troops under General Ross at Benedict, Maryland.

August 24: – British forces defeat the Americans at Battle of Bladensburg, Maryland. President Madison is present, but leaves in haste with his cohort and is unreachable for several days. The British march to Washington, D.C., where they burn the U.S. Capitol, the White House, and other government buildings.

August 25: The British continue to set fires in the city. Late in the afternoon a rare tornado tears through the city, killing and injuring British soldiers. Torrential rains follow, dousing many of the fires. The British decide to leave town that night, beginning the 50-mile return march to their ships. Concurrently in Baltimore, the City *Committee of Safety and Vigilance* meets to name Sam Smith as Commanding Officer over all forces there. Final efforts to prepare for an attack are begun in earnest. A call for volunteer militia goes out via newspapers across the region. Patriots are mobilized to meet the British for what could be a "last stand" in Baltimore.

September 11: Sunday, around noon, the British fleet of about 50 warships arrives just outside of Baltimore Harbor. Sam Smith orders all forces into action; volunteers pour into the Baltimore area.

September 12: Monday morning, General Ross lands nearly 5,000 troops at North Point and begins the march to Baltimore. He is shot dead by advance sharpshooters. The Battle of North Point takes place that afternoon. Brigadier General John Stricker of the Maryland Militia fights for several hours as a delaying action, then retreats. The British camp in the field that night in the rain.

September 13: Tuesday at dawn, the naval bombardment of Fort McHenry begins. It lasts for 25 hours. Meanwhile, the British army seeks to outflank the Americans in order to attack the City of Baltimore, but with no success. Sam Smith oversees all military developments.

September 14: Wednesday, at 1:00 a.m., the British Navy attempts to land some 1,000 troops in a flanking move on Fort McHenry but fails. The British Army issues orders to begin their land retreat at 3:00 a.m. By 9 a.m., the large garrison flag is raised over Fort McHenry. Francis Scott Key sees it and is inspired to write the lyrics of what becomes "The Star-Spangled Banner." The Defense of Baltimore is a success; the British Army departs for the West Indies.

October: the Star Spangled Banner is sung for the first time at the Holliday Street Theater in Baltimore. Sam Smith resigns his Commission as Major General. It is the end of an era.

November: the US Government defaults on its debts.

December 24: The Peace Treaty in Ghent, (today Belgium) is finalized. Once signed and ratified, it will officially end the War of 1812. It is signed by the British Prince Regent four days later in London, then three copies are sent by three separate ships to America for signature and ratification.

1815

January 8: News that the war was over has not yet reached America in time to stop The Battle of New Orleans. It is won decisively by the Americans under the command of General Andrew Jackson against the invading British army.

February 16 to 18: President James Madison signs the Treaty of Ghent in Washington, D.C. at the Octagon House. The Senate, including Sam Smith, ratifies the treaty on the 17th. Documents are exchanged with the British on the 18th officially ending the War of 1812. Madison submits a concluding message before Congress that day.

June 18: Napoleon is defeated at the Battle of Waterloo in Belgium. The Napoleonic Wars are finally over. Napoleon is permanently banished to the remote island of St. Helena in the south Atlantic. He is escorted by Admiral Cockburn.

1816 James Monroe is elected President. The 2nd Bank of the U.S. is chartered for 20 years. The American Bible Society is founded in New York City.

1817 The American Colonization Society is founded along with the Maryland Colonization Society. Smith participates in the colonization efforts. Francis Scott Key becomes Vice President of the American Bible Society and remains so until his death in 1843. He is also a member of the American Colonization Society.

1818 Smith becomes Chairman of the House Committee on Ways and Means, and for the next four years he works closely with President Monroe.

1819 Smith is dragged into bankruptcy by the unethical dealings of his brother-in-law. It takes him seven years to pay off all related debts.

1820 Smith votes for the Missouri Compromise.

1822 Smith is again elected to the U.S. Senate.

1823 Smith supports the Monroe Doctrine.

1824 John Quincy Adams is elected President. The Marquis de Lafayette returns to America and visits Baltimore and Fort McHenry. Smith hosts this visit.

1828 Smith supports the election of Andrew Jackson as President. Smith becomes Chairman of the Senate Finance Committee and President Pro Tempore of the Senate for the second time.

1829 Smith heads up the Inauguration Committee for President Jackson in March. Smith swears in John C. Calhoun as Vice President of the United States.

1831 The Anti -Masonic Party is formed and holds its Convention in Baltimore.

1832 The Second Bank of the U.S. is effectively killed by Jackson's veto (there will be no re-charter in 1836). Andrew Jackson is elected to a second term as President.

1833 Smith retires from national politics in March, at the age of 80.

1834 Smith begins to write his memoirs.

1835 With riots in Baltimore over the banking crisis, Smith calms the crowds and brings civil order back to the city. On September 7, Smith is elected Mayor of Baltimore at age 83.

1836 Martin Van Buren is nominated for President in Baltimore at the Whig National Convention (held at Sam Smith's 1st Presbyterian Church), and wins the national election in the fall.

1838 Smith retires as Mayor of Baltimore at age 86.

1839

April 22: Monday, Smith dies in Baltimore at age 86.

April 25: Thursday, Smith's funeral is attended by President Van Buren, his Cabinet, U.S. Senators and Congressmen, the Governor, the Mayor, and thousands of mourners. A funeral procession through the streets of Baltimore lasts for hours. The guns of Fort McHenry are fired in his honor. Smith is laid to rest at the Westminster Burial Grounds in Baltimore.

Glossary of Terms

Anti-Masonic Party **(AMP)** Formed in 1828 in New York as the first 3rd Party in American politics. This party invented the political convention. It was a single-issue party to oppose Freemasonry due to its secrecy. This was the year that Andrew Jackson, who was a leading Mason, won the Presidency. Jackson was supported by Sam Smith who was also a Mason. In the 1832 election the AMP nominated for President the Virginian, William Wirt (a former Mason), at their Baltimore convention. Some prominent names associated with the party included: Millard Fillmore, John Quincy Adams, Thaddeus Stevens, and Daniel Webster. The party later merged into the Whig Party.

Baltimore Clipper This is the common name for fast sailing schooners which were mostly two-masted ships. These ships were built from around the turn of the 19th century and into the current era and were popular in Baltimore for use by Privateers during the War of 1812. Today the Pride of Baltimore II, based out of the Baltimore Harbor, is an example of a period Clipper.

Baltimore Committee of Safety and Vigilance In August, 1814, the City of Baltimore organized this committee of 30 civic leaders to oversee the efforts to protect the city from British attack. Many of the members were friends of Sam Smith. It was this committee who responded affirmatively to a team of military leaders who asked that Sam Smith be made commanding officer over the Defense of Baltimore.

Baltimore Fencibles   The Baltimore Fencibles was a volunteer artillery company recruited from private citizens of the City of Baltimore, in 1813. The word "fencible" was used by many units in the era to represent local defenders, or the Home Guard. The Baltimore Fencibles, led by Captain Joseph Hopper Nicholson (brother-in-law of Francis Scott Key), were Federalized militia. They were the only non-regulars to serve within Fort McHenry.

Barbary Wars   America fought two wars against the North African Ottoman Corsairs (1801-1805 and 1815). These Muslim fighters, also known to history as the "Barbary Pirates" operated mostly in the Mediterranean Sea, and sought tribute payments from merchant ships in order to prevent their attacks on international trade. They also took prisoners and made them slaves. President Jefferson sent the US Navy and Marines to defeat them. In fact, the Barbary Pirates were the original reason for America building its first six frigates for the US Navy in the 1790's. America has never paid tribute to pirates since and seeks to protect open trade on the high seas. This war is immortalized in a stanza of the Marine Corps Hymn: ". . . to the shores of Tripoli."

Bastion   A defensive wall that consists of two faces allowing for two angles of fire. Ft. McHenry has five bastions which allowed for interlocking fields of fire to fend off land and sea attacks.

Bermuda Station Known as "His Majesty's Royal Naval Dockyard," in the War of 1812 this was the principle British Royal Navy center for operations in the Western Atlantic, where its North American fleet was based. The British blockade of American ports was orchestrated out of Bermuda, a chain of islands located about 600 miles east of the US mid-Atlantic coastline. It included shipbuilding dockyards as well as an army base. This was an ideal resting place in the Winter for the British Navy operating in North America. In June, 1814, a large British fleet arrived carrying Major General Ross and his nearly 5,000 veteran troops sailing from Bordeaux, France, fresh from their victory in the Napoleonic Wars. They were bound for Washington DC and Baltimore.

Bladensburg   This is a small town located about eight miles East of Washington DC. It sat at a strategic crossroads. The road north went to Baltimore, and Philadelphia. The road East went to Annapolis and Upper Marlborough (home of Dr. Beanes). The road West went to Washington DC. It is the location of the battle that preceded the British invasion of Washington DC in August of 1814. President Madison was there that day, along with Joshua Barney, James Monroe, and Francis Scott Key. When the main body of the American Army ran in retreat during the battle, the British dubbed it the "Bladensburg Races." One observer said it was "like sheep chased by dogs." It was also known for its dueling grounds. Many duels were conducted there since dueling was illegal in Washington DC. Stephen Decatur, a naval hero, was killed there in 1820. It was there also that one of Francis Scott Key's sons, 22 year old Daniel Key, died in a senseless duel with a fellow Naval Academy cadet in 1836.

British Naval Blockades   During the War of 1812 the British Navy set up a naval blockade along the American Atlantic and Gulf coasts. The goal was to hurt the American economy by blocking its sea trade and drying up government revenues from import duties. The blockade also served to stop American Navy ships and Privateers from setting out to sea. The blockade ran from New England, South around Florida, to New Orleans. It was highly effective. From New York to Boston, however, the British allowed specified ships to trade in an effort to reinforce New England's support for England and in hopes of breaking that region away from the United States of America. The blockade caused inflation, unemployment, shortages, a bankrupt U.S. treasury, and severe discontent with the war – especially in New England. Nevertheless, it was not highly successful in stopping American Privateers who posed a major adverse impact on British merchant shipping. The US gave over 500 commissions to ships as Privateers who in turn captured over 1300 British prizes, even in spite of the blockade.

British Royal Navy Admiralty Ranks (Highest to Lowest) Lord of the Admiralty; Admiral; Vice Admiral; Rear Admiral

(The) Chesapeake Bay The Chesapeake Bay is the largest estuary in North America. It contains freshwater, saltwater and brackish water. It is located along the mid-Atlantic coast region and borders six states, but mainly Virginia and Maryland. It is about 200 miles long from north to south and drains more than 150 rivers and streams. This is where the British sailed to attack Washington DC and Baltimore in the 1814.

Chesapeake Flotilla In July of 1813 Joshua Barney, age 54, presented his plan to build 18 small craft (gunboats and barges) that could be sailed or rowed to harass British ships in the Chesapeake Bay. The flotilla was built in Baltimore with the enthusiastic support of Sam Smith and put into action by the Spring of 1814 manned by nearly 900 men. There were several engagements until the flotilla was cornered by the British on the Patuxent River, August 22, 1814. The flotilla was abandoned, lit on fire and blown up by Barney. The men then marched to Bladensburg where

360 of his sailors and 120 of his marines fought bravely against the British. Barney himself was seriously wounded, captured and paroled by the British (due mainly to his bravery in battle against them). He died four years later due to complications from his wounds. Another 500 of his men escaped to Baltimore and fought in the defense of the city.

Cincinnatus He was a Roman aristocrat and statesman who lived 519 to 430 BC. He was called from his life as a farmer to defend Rome. Upon his success he resigned and returned to his farm. This made him a model of civic virtue, serving for the good of the state and not for his own ambition. This became the inspiration for the Society which George Washington founded after the American Revolution called the Society of the Cincinnati. The parallels between Cincinnatus and Sam Smith are striking and include being "re-commissioned" by public acclamation for other crises into their 80's.

Colonization Societies In this book, this term refers to American organizations in the early 1800's which sought to return "Manumitted Negroes" from America back to Africa. The largest such group began in 1817, and was called the *American Colonization Society* which founded the colony of Liberia in West Africa. Other such organizations included the Maryland Colonization Society, the African Colonization Society (Virginia), and the New York Colonization Society. Sam Smith was a leader in the Maryland Society.

Constitutional Convention   The U.S. Constitution was written the Summer of 1787, in Philadelphia. The convention that accomplished this consisted of 55 delegates representing the 13 states. George Washington presided over the convention. James Madison played a leading role, and kept the most complete notes. Ultimately, 39 delegates signed the Constitution. The Bill of Rights was added and ratification by the states followed. James McHenry (for whom Ft. McHenry was named) represented Maryland.

Continental Congress/ Congress of the Confederation/ Congress of the United States   The   **Continental Congress** was a organization of delegates from the original 13 Colonies which met at various times in various places during the early stages of the development of the United States. The first meeting was in Philadelphia, in the Fall of 1774. The second meeting led to the Declaration of Independence, announced in July of 1776. During the American Revolution, there were meetings in Baltimore, Lancaster, and York PA. In 1781, the Articles of Confederation were adopted and the new name became the **Congress of the Confederation**. At the end of the war, it met in 1783, at Princeton, New Jersey, then Annapolis, to accept the resignation of General George Washington. There were meetings in Trenton, New Jersey, and New York City. In 1787, a Constitutional Convention was convened in Philadelphia, which resulted in the creation of the U.S. Constitution. Upon ratification the Congress of the

Confederation became the **Congress of the United States** which first convened in New York City, in 1789.

Continentals   This was the name given to the American soldiers during the American Revolution. They were regulars who were led by the Commander-In-Chief, General George Washington. They were joined by state militia as well. There were varying enlistment periods and high turnover.

Democrat-Republican Party This party was organized by Thomas Jefferson and James Madison between 1791 and 1793 in opposition to the dominant Federalist Party and Alexander Hamilton. Its party power took hold in 1801 with the election of Jefferson, and ran until 1824, when it was split into the Democratic Party, the Whig Party, and the National Republican Party. The early party has also been called the Jeffersonian Republicans. This party denounced the national bank, favored states' rights, and was strongest in the South. It strongly opposed Britain, while it favored France. The party dominated the House and the Senate from 1800 to 1824. Sam Smith was originally a Federalist, but became a member of this party while still showing a great deal of independent thought and action over the years.

Federal Hill   This is a high point directly across the Patapsco River basin overlooking the Baltimore Inner-Harbor. It is located in South Baltimore. It was used as a lookout point to see ships coming into the harbor and to signal their arrival to the docks below. Today, a distinguished statue of Sam Smith sits atop Federal Hill gazing across the Harbor at the city.

Federalist Party   This was the first political party in America. It was started by Alexander Hamilton, of New York. It was dominated by merchants and businessmen of major cities and strongly supported a national bank. They favored national power over state's rights. This party controlled American politics through the 1790's. None of the Federalists voted in favor of the War of 1812. Congregationalists and Episcopalians supported the Federalists. It was a Federalist newspaper in Baltimore, which ignited a major riot there in 1812, due to editorial opposition to the war. New England was controlled by the Federalists, and they actually held a convention in Hartford, CT in December of 1814 to discuss New England possible secession from the United States of America over the war issue.

Fort Whetstone   Whetstone Point is the narrow peninsula overlooking Baltimore Inner-Harbor where Ft. McHenry stands today. During the American Revolution, an early earthen fort was built there called Fort Whetstone. In 1794, federal funds were granted to improve the fort. From 1789 to 1800 a more substantial masonry fort was erected and named Ft. McHenry.

"Free Trade and Sailor's Rights" This was an American rallying cry during the War of 1812. The British and the French had impeded American sailing ships on the open seas for decades. Thousands of American ships had been confiscated. Sailors on American ships were often taken by force to serve in the British Navy. The British believed that anyone born in England, Wales, Ireland, or Scotland, could never renounce their British sovereignty and become a citizen of the United States by immigration, and so they took thousands of immigrants off of American vessels by force, or so called impressments. This was not the only reason for the War of 1812, but it was touted as one of the main causes by those who favored the war. The city of Baltimore and Sam Smith were supporters of American free trade and sailors rights. The result of the War of 1812 was improvements in America's free trade as well as protected immigration to America and internationally recognized American citizenship through legal naturalization.

French and Indian War This is sometimes called the first real "World War." It was primarily a war between England and France, but fought in various locations around the world. It is mentioned in this book because it is the beginning of the same English-French rivalry that extended through the American Revolution and the War of 1812. It is helpful to see the grand sweep of these three related conflicts and how they are so interwoven. In America, the war was fought from 1754 to 1763. In Europe the conflict was called the Seven Years War (1756 to 1763). In this war, the Americans served under the British against the French and their Indian allies. George Washington was a Colonel in the Virginia militia and gained his early military experience in this war. The French lost the war and lost their territories in North America except for Quebec. New Orleans and the Louisiana Territory were ceded to Spain. Florida went to the British. The high economic cost to Britain for this war led to high taxes on the American colonies which led to the American Revolution. The Americans won the Revolution largely due to French help. Then the British and the French went at it again in the 1790's and again in the Napoleonic Wars from 1803 to 1815. America was caught in the crossfire of all these conflicts.

Frigate   This term comes from an Italian word *fregata,* referring to a lighter type of ship built for speed and maneuverability. It was the name for a class of naval war ships of the early American period which had from 36 to 50 mounted cannon. The only larger ships of that era were called ships of the line, of which America had none. In 1794, the U.S. passed the Naval Act to build the first six frigates to make up the US Navy. It took several years to build these ships. They were built with American live oak and were very strong. Their names became the USS Chesapeake, USS Constitution, USS President, USS United

States, USS Congress, and USS Constellation (which was built in Baltimore). Sam Smith was very supportive of this project and also played a role in the creation of the Department of the Navy as well as the Marine Corps in 1798. Today, a reproduction of the frigate USS Constellation (with some original wood and other fixtures) is on display in Baltimore's Inner-Harbor. The original USS Constitution is still commissioned and on display in Boston Harbor.

General Ranks, US - (Lowest to Highest) Brigadier General, Major General, Lieutenant General, General. Sam Smith was a Major General over the Maryland Militia. Active duty regular army outranked militia but when Smith was activated under the Federal Government (by the Governor of Maryland) his rank as Major General then outranked Brigadier General Winder of the regular army.

Gun Battery   This refers to a group of guns such as a group of cannon in a fixed fortification such as Ft. McHenry.

Hampstead Hill   This was the geographical highest point that was East of old Baltimore. Today the area is called Patterson Park, and is in the city limits. Sam Smith used this location to place some 34 naval cannon to provide the major defense against the British land attack in 1814. He utilized the naval expertise of Commodore Rodgers and his 350 U.S. Marines and sailors to oversee the cannon at this strategic location, which became known as Rodger's Bastion. It became the center point of a one-and-one-half mile entrenchment line of redoubts where there were over 3,000 men assigned defensive positions.

Jacksonian Democracy   Named after President Andrew Jackson, this political movement refers to an emphasis on the common man and the beginnings of the Democrat Party. Jackson expanded the power of the Executive Branch. All adult white males were given the vote. Judges became elected rather than appointed. Jackson ended the national bank since he believed it was corrupt and run by elites who took advantage of the common people. Westward expansion was a major theme of this period which lasted from 1828 to about 1850. Jackson's influence has lived on through the history of the modern Democrat Party.

Jeffersonian Democracy   This refers to the policies of the Democrat-Republican Party which was started by Thomas Jefferson and first developed in the 1790's. This political system dominated American politics from 1800 to 1824. Preference was for an agrarian society of farmers in opposition to elitist financiers, merchants, manufacturers and factory workers. Westward expansion was promoted to provide new lands for farmers. This movement was strongly opposed to the Federalist Party. Emphasis was on the Bill of Rights, particularly the separation of Church and State. The theme was the spread of the "Empire of

Liberty". There was a preference for economic coercion over military action. This led to weak responses to British abuses and resulted in a weak military when war came. There was also a general desire for states' rights while limiting the power of the Federal Government. The War of 1812 was fought during the period of Jeffersonian Democracy. Sam Smith moderately supported much of this movement but also believed in a stronger military and the protection of maritime trade.

Kent Island   This is the largest island in the Chesapeake Bay and was occupied by the British during the War of 1812. The first English establishment there dates back to 1631. In the summer of 1813 over 2,000 British soldiers with some 17 ships landed on Kent Island and used it as a launching point for raids in the Chesapeake Bay.

Loyalists/Tories   These were American colonists who remained loyal to Britain during the American Revolution. It is estimated to have been about 20 - 30% of the colonial population before the war. Loyalists were generally conservative, afraid of mob rule, non-violent, sentimental towards Britain, and committed to the system of English law. After the Revolution, some loyalists left America. A large number settled in Canada, however, most remained in America, primarily in New England. During the War of 1812, New England was very pro-British due largely to the legacy of the loyalists. British spies operated out of Canada and one of their major objectives was to manipulate public opinion and events to get New England to secede from America. Many loyalists in America continued to help the British during the War of 1812 by providing supplies and intelligence.

Magazine A storehouse for gunpowder or other ammunition

Manumission This term means to free one's slaves. There were manumission societies promoting the abolition of slavery. Freed blacks led to other legal questions regarding their status and rights in early America.

Marine Fencibles During the War of 1812, defense of American ports and harbors was delegated to a corps of Fencibles. These were seafaring men of maritime trades who were able to man large guns. This corps only lasted for two years. There were two companies raised for Baltimore. One was quartered at Ft. McHenry, and the other at Ft. Covington. Each company consisted of 107 men.

Maryland Line, The Old Line State This refers to the Maryland Regiments which became part of the Continental Army during the American Revolution. The Maryland Line was considered one of the best by General George Washington who referred to Maryland Units as his "Old Line". This is how the state gained its official nickname as "The Old Line State." There were seven main regiments plus the Maryland and Virginia Rifle Regiment.

It was the 1st Maryland Regiment that fought bravely at the Battle of Brooklyn Heights providing the "Maryland 400" who ultimately stood against the British, charging them six times and saving the American Army and General Washington. Sam Smith and John Ross Key were part of this historic event. John Ross Key (father of Francis Scott Key) served at this battle in the Maryland and Virginia Rifle Regiment under Otho Holland Williams and the direct command of General Washington as an Extra Continental Regiment. These riflemen were specialized sharpshooters known for their long range marksman capabilities. They were typically deployed as forward skirmishers, flanking elements, scouts and escorts.

Masons/Freemasonry Masonry is a fraternal organization first established in Scotland around 1450. Legend has it that the suppressed Templar Knights who settled there about that time integrated into the stonemason guilds (operative lodges) but then expanded to persons who were not stone masons (speculative lodges). Today, Scottish Rite Freemasonry has 33 degrees whereas the York Rite has three. What is historically known for certain is that in 1717, the first Grand Lodge was established in London. Today, this is the largest Grand Lodge in the world. The French Grand Orient Lodge is the largest in Continental Europe. Freemasons progress through various levels or degrees within the organization based on ceremonial rites, oaths, and studying Gnostic-type esoteric secret knowledge that has been passed down through the ages. They share secret oaths, code words, code sayings, signs and handshakes. The Blue Lodge has only three degrees. Masonry played a key role in the American Revolution. The Sons of Liberty were Masons. George Washington was a Mason as were many of his top Officers. Both the American and British Armies had mobile field lodges during the war. Benjamin Franklin was the Grand Master of the Philadelphia Lodge and used his Masonic connections in France to recruit the critical help that won the Revolution. Sam Smith was a Mason and many other officers in the War of 1812 were as well. The Catholic Church bans its members from becoming Masons as does the Orthodox Church of Greece. See Anti-Masonry Party for comments on opposition to Masonry in American politics. Conspiracy theorists discuss the possibilities of Masonry connected to the Illuminati and aspirations to create a New World Order. Of particular note in this regard is the book "The Secret Destiny of America".

Mercantilism   This is an economic system based on a positive balance of trade for the accumulation of reserved wealth which seeks to import mostly raw materials and sell mostly finished goods. This was the force behind building colonial empires and was used as a form of economic warfare between colonial powers. Aspects of this system included developing monopolies, high tariffs to bloc competing imports, banning the export of gold and silver, providing export subsidies, banning trade from being carried by foreign ships, restricting domestic consumption, and promoting research for manufacturing. This was the dominant economic philosophy in Europe from the Renaissance through the 18th century. The term was coined by Adam Smith who criticized the policy in his *Wealth of Nations* in 1776. Mercantilism was the basis of the Triangular Trade of the North Atlantic. Understanding this economic system helps us make better sense of the trade wars that drove foreign policy and contributed to the wars of early American history.

Merchant Ships   These are non-military ships used for transporting raw materials, other goods and merchandize. Merchant shipping was an integral part of the life of Sam Smith. His personal wealth came primarily from his ownership of merchant ships. Merchant fleets sailed the world at that time. There was a lively cod fishing industry in the North Atlantic, substantial merchant transport between American ports, large Caribbean merchant trade, large European merchant trade, large South American merchant trade as well as a large Asian merchant trade, which sailed around the tip of South America to destinations including China and India. Early America prospered heavily from merchant shipping since most taxes for the Federal Government came from duties on imported goods and coastal cities boomed with the frenzy of international trade.

Militia　　In early America this term referred to combatant forces made up of non-professional fighters. These were part-time citizen soldiers who were largely untrained and were only used at the time of a war. At the Battle of Baltimore, there were over 12,000 volunteer American militiamen compared to about 2,000 regular (full-time professional) American forces (naval, marine and army). The military quality of militia was often low compared to regular fighters. For this reason, the British had disdain for the American militia. In Baltimore, the British General Ross was quoted as saying that he didn't care if it rained militia. This was just moments before he was fatally shot by militia sharpshooters at North Point.

Missouri Compromise　　　　The debate over slavery in America grew decade by decade. In 1820, during the Presidency of James Monroe, Congress narrowly passed the Missouri Compromise. This allowed Missouri to be admitted as a slave state along with Alabama. Maine was admitted as a free state and slavery was to be banned from any territory north of the parallel line 36' 30" within the Louisiana Territory. The votes in both Houses of Congress were very close which showed how divided the country was on the expansion of slavery. In just over three decades, all this would unravel with the Kansas-Nebraska Act of 1854, followed by the explosion of the American Civil War in 1861 . Sam Smith voted for the 1820 compromise, since he hoped that the efforts at African Colonization would resolve the slave issue over time.

Monroe Doctrine   President James Monroe is most noted for this 1823 policy which barred European nations from further colonizing or otherwise interfering in the affairs of North or South America. It was a bold move which still stands today. This was intended to free newly independent Latin American countries from future European intervention. This was largely enforced by the British Royal Navy to ensure open trade. This policy was drafted primarily by John Quincy Adams. Sam Smith was in favor of this policy so as to ensure neutral trade.

Napoleonic Wars   Napoleon Bonaparte led the French all across Europe from 1803 to 1815 in one of the most notorious epic sagas of modern warfare. He defeated five of the seven international coalitions arrayed against him. This was the peak of a longer struggle between France and England that had lasted nearly 100 years. The costs were high in lives and treasure. America was caught in the crossfire of this struggle, particularly at sea with its merchant fleet impacted greatly. In 1812, Napoleon lost his army due to the brutal Russian Winter. By the Spring of 1814, Napoleon abdicated from power and the British immediately sent thousands of their veteran troops to America in an attempt to tilt the balance of the War of 1812. Some 5,000 of these crack British troops sailed into the Chesapeake Bay that summer to attack Washington DC and Baltimore. While the British failed to regain their former American Colonies, they did become the dominant world power for the next 100 years as a result of the defeat of Napoleon. It is important to understand the Napoleonic period as it provides the greater context for the American War of 1812.

National Bank   This refers to the establishment of an American central bank. The first such bank was founded by Alexander Hamilton in 1791, located in Philadelphia, and chartered for 20 years. The story of central banking in America has been controversial from the beginning because of the question of who owns and ultimately controls such an institution. Such banks have always had stock owned by private and often foreign interests. Sam Smith wanted a central bank but one that was purely government owned. This was in the spirit of the Constitution. But it has never happened. Even today, the Federal Reserve Bank is privately owned and stockholders are secret. This lack of transparency affords opportunity for corruption and manipulation by unseen forces. In 1811, the Bank Charter expired. The War of 1812 was fought without a central bank and it was chaotic financially for the country. The Second Bank was chartered in 1816 for another 20 years. Then Andrew Jackson killed that Bank in 1836. Sam Smith weighed in on each of these milestones. He was also a Director of the Bank of Maryland in Baltimore which collapsed in the 1830's leading to riots in Baltimore and propelling him to Mayor by acclimation in his 80's to reestablish order and instill confidence in the people toward the city government.

North Point, Maryland   This is the site of the British landing for the attack on Baltimore, in September, 1814. Sam Smith correctly anticipated that this would be the site of a British landing well in advance and he was well prepared for the British invasion. There were lookouts there so Smith had timely intelligence. North Point is a peninsula extending southeast 15 miles from old Baltimore and jutting into the Chesapeake Bay on the Lower Patapsco River. It has also been referred to as the Patapsco Neck. It is here that Major General Ross landed 3,700 army troops and 1,000 Royal Marines in the early morning of September 12. The British were engaged that very afternoon about 7.5 miles along the North Point Road by some 3,200 American forces led by Brigadier General John Stricker. This engagement was originally referred to as the Battle of Patapsco Neck. General Ross was killed that day prior to the main engagement by advance snipers.

Nullification   This term refers to states individually deciding which federal laws are constitutional. This is an assertion of state sovereignty to limit the power of the federal government. The Federal courts have rejected this by asserting the Supremacy Clause in Article 6 of the Constitution, stating that federal law supersedes state law. Nullification was debated by Jefferson. Later this is what

311

led to secession by southern states which resulted in the American Civil War.

President Pro Tem of the Senate   This is the second highest-ranking official of the U.S. Senate just under the Vice President of the United States. The President Pro Tem presides over the Senate in the absence of the Vice President. Sam Smith served as President Pro Tem from 1805 to 1807 and again from 1827 to 1831. In those days, the President Pro Tem was second in line to the succession of the President following the Vice President.

Privateers   These were merchant ship owners who were given legal status by a government (letters of marquee) to attack foreign merchant ships during wartime. Captured cargo and vessels became prizes to the Privateers. European powers had used Privateers for hundreds of years. During the American Revolution Sam Smith sailed out of Baltimore as a Privateer and was quite successful, thus rebuilding his family finances. This was the primary way America fought the British at sea during the War of 1812 since there was only a very small American Navy. In the War of 1812 over 200 American Privateer ships were captured by the British Royal Navy. American Privateers captured some 1200 British merchant ships during the war. The British blockade of American ports and the invasion of Maryland at Baltimore were both partly intended to stop Privateers.

Protectionism   This is a trade policy which seeks to protect domestic products from foreign competition. This is usually done by levying high protective tariffs to discourage imports of foreign goods. This was a popular policy of those who pursued mercantilism. Sam Smith was a leading voice for decades on trade policy in Congress. He pushed for fair trade and minimal tariffs as a means to increase overall trade.

Quasi War   From 1798 to 1800 America was engaged in an undeclared war with France fought mostly at sea. As a result of the French Revolution, the French monarchy was toppled. At that time, the US stopped paying on its American Revolutionary War debts to the French monarch in the 1790's plus the Jay Treaty with England upset France further. The result was that French privateers attacked American merchant ships. By war's end it is estimated some 2,000 American merchant ships were captured by the French. This spurred further development of the US Navy which Sam Smith strongly supported. The Navy Department was created in 1798 along with the US Marine Corps. This conflict cost President Adams his reelection.

Rampart   The broad brick and earthen walls of a fort

Redoubt   This is a type of defensive wall. It usually refers to city walls or walls around a fort. It also applies to the defensive earthen wall that ran 1 1/2 miles through Hampstead Hill as the major land defense for Baltimore.

Regular Army   These are troops made up of full-time professional soldiers. They are paid, supplied and trained. Their quality is generally higher than that of militia.

Royal Navy   This refers to the British Navy. In early American history the British Navy was the largest in the world with over 1,000 war ships. After the Battle of Trafalgar in 1805, it ruled the waves for the next 100 years protecting its merchant fleet which dominated international trade. The names of Royal Navy ships begins with HMS which stands for His/Her Majesty's Ship.

Schooner   A type of sailing vessel with two or more masts. Such vessels were designed to be fast. They were first designed by the Dutch, then further developed in Bermuda and adapted still further by the Americans. The most popular type of schooner in America was the two masted Baltimore Clipper. Schooners played a major role as privateers during the War of 1812. They were widely used for American shipping on the great lakes, along the Atlantic coast, and around the world. They were also popular fishing vessels for the Grand Banks. American schooners were built all along the Atlantic coast. Baltimore was particularly noted for its shipyards and in the War of 1812 was called by the British "that nest of pirates". This was the primary reason the British attacked Baltimore.

Secession   This is the act of withdrawing from an organization. In American history this refers to states seeking to withdraw from the National Union. During the War of 1812, the New England states, led by the Federalist Party, contemplated secession and openly discussed this at the Hartford Convention in December, 1814. Madison sought to preserve the Union. One of the outcomes to the War of 1812 was a greater unity and sense of national identity for Americans.

Second War of Independence   This phrase has been used to describe the War of 1812. America was fighting to preserve its independence from Britain for the second time in less than 40 years.

Secretary of War   This is the cabinet position whereby a civilian oversees the US military. Today this is called the Secretary of Defense.

Ships of the Line   This was a type of naval warship built from the 1600's to the mid 1800's. They were the largest fighting ships of their age and would face off in a line (hence the name) firing at their enemies with great broadsides. In the War of 1812 the British had large ships of the line that carried over 74 cannon on two firing decks. The Americans had no ships to match such firing power. Francis Scott Key boarded the Royal Navy Flag ship HMS Tonnant in the Chesapeake Bay to negotiate the release of Dr. Beanes. This ship was commanded by Vice Admiral

Sir Alexander Cochrane and carried 80 guns. The body of Major General Robert Ross was preserved on board the Tonnant in a barrel of 129 gallons of Jamaican rum. This was transferred to another ship and sent to Nova Scotia where he was buried. The HMS Tonnant sailed on to New Orleans.

Society of the Cincinnati   This is the nation's oldest patriotic organization. Founded by Major General Henry Knox in 1783, this organization was for officers of the Revolution, both American and French. George Washington served as the Society's first President from 1783 until his death in 1799. There was some public controversy for fear that this group could pose the threat of a military coup to the fledgling country, or establish hereditary nobility in America. It was designed to address and calm the frustrations of officers over monetary compensation after the war. It helped provide pensions, land grants, and financial help to widows and orphans of officers. Membership was originally passed to the oldest male heir of each member. There are 13 Societies, one for each original state. The society still exists today, with its national headquarters in Washington, DC at the Anderson House, 2118 Massachusetts Ave., NW. See: www.societyofthecincinnati.org

Tangier Island   Located in the Chesapeake Bay, this island was used by the British during the War of 1812 as a staging area with as many as 1,200 British troops recorded on the island at one time. Many African American slaves escaped to the British on Tangier and were given their freedom. Some joined the British Corps of Colonial Marines. Tangier was used as a launching point for the failed British assault on Baltimore.

Treaty of Ghent   This treaty that officially ended the War of 1812 between Britain and America. It was signed in Ghent, Belgium, December 24, 1814. The official copies arrived in Washington DC in February of 1815. In between these dates, the Battle of New Orleans was fought.

Treaty of Paris   This officially ended the American Revolution. It was negotiated in Paris and signed in Annapolis in December 1783.

Triangular Trade   The Atlantic sailing trade route was triangular. Ships from Europe would sail south to the trade winds then sail west to the Caribbean. They would then sail north along the Gulf Stream along the American coast and back to Europe. From Europe came textiles, guns and manufactured goods to Africa. From Africa would come slaves to the Caribbean and the Americas. From the Western Hemisphere would come rum, sugar, cotton, and tobacco to Europe. This trade system thrived for nearly 300 years.

US Marine Corps   There were Continental Marines organized in Philadelphia in 1775 to fight in the American Revolution. The United States Marine Corps was officially founded on July 11, 1798 by an act of Congress. Sam Smith played a key role in its creation. Marines played a key role in the Defense of Baltimore in September, 1814.

US Navy　　The US Navy began with the construction of six frigates during the 1790's. The Department of the Navy was established by an act of Congress in 1798. Sam Smith played a major role in all this and he was later offered the Cabinet position of Secretary of the Navy in 1801 by President Thomas Jefferson. He served briefly in that position followed by his brother, Robert, who oversaw the navy for eight years.

War Hawks　　Term used in the War of 1812 for those in Congress who voted in favor of the war because they wanted an opportunity to drive the British from North America and be free to expand westward. These politicians were mostly from southern states and were led by Speaker of the House Henry Clay of Kentucky. Sam Smith originally wanted to prevent war through diplomacy but ultimately he concluded that war was the only way to resolve the abuses of the British.

Whig Party　　This political party was formed in opposition to Andrew Jackson in the 1830's. This party lasted for 20 years and stood for the supremacy of Congress over the Presidency while favoring modernization of roads and manufacturing, economic protectionism and westward expansion. Famous Whigs included Henry Clay, Daniel Webster, William Henry Harrison, John Tyler, Zachary Taylor, Winfield Scott, Millard Fillmore, and, for a time, Abraham Lincoln. Five of these men became President, though Lincoln as a Republican.

Appendix I

Sam Smith: Selected Official Military Documents

Sam Smith's Commission as a Major in the Continental Army

In Congress.

The delegations of the United States of New Hampshire, Massachusetts-Bay, Rhode-Island, Connecticut, New-York, New-Jersey, the Counties of New Castle, Kent and Sussex on Delaware, Maryland, Virginia, North-Carolina, South-Carolina, and Georgia, TO Samuel Smith (son John) Esquire

WE, reposing especial Trust and Confidence in your Patriotism, Valor, Conduct and Fidelity, DO, by these Presents, constitute and appoint you to be Major of Colonel Gist's Battalion of the Maryland Forces in the Army of the United States, raised for the Defense of American Liberty, and for repelling every hostile Invasion thereof. You are therefore carefully and diligently to discharge the Duty of Major by doing and performing all manner of Things thereunto belonging. And we do strictly charge and require all Officers and Soldiers under your Command, to be obedient to your Orders as Major And you are to observe and follow such Orders and Directions from Time to Time, as you shall receive from this or a future Congress of the United States, or Committee of Congress, for that Purpose appointed, or Commander in Chief for the Time being of the Army of the United States, or any other your superior Officer, according to the Rules and Discipline of War, in Pursuance of the Trust reposed in you. This Commission to continue in Force until revoked by this or a future Congress.

Dated at Philadelphia the 10th December Seventeen Hundred and Seventy Six.

By Order of Congress,

John Hancock   President

Source: Maryland Historical Society, Baltimore
Sam Smith Collection
MS 1790

Sam Smith's Congressional Sword Commendation Letter

War Office of the United States

New York   May 31st 1786

Sir

The United States in Congress assembled having been pleased by their resolve of the 4th of November 1777 to express their high sense of your merit and of the officers and soldiers under your command for the gallant defense of Fort Mifflin on the Delaware and to direct that an elegant sword should be presented to you I have the honor agreeably thereto to transmit to you by colonel Senf this honorable memorial of your service on that occasion.

The enlightened historian in consigning to posterity a detail of the brilliant events of the late war will experience peculiar satisfaction in illustrating the noble defense of Fort Mifflin. The glory of that defense is inseperable from you and your brave companions.

That your happiness in society may be equal to your reputation in the field is the sincere wish.

Sir

of Your most obedient and very humble servant

J Knox

Source: Maryland Historical Society, Baltimore Sam Smith Collection MS 1790

Sam Smith's Commission as Major General

The State of Maryland to Samuel Smith Esquire Greeting.

BE IT KNOWN, That reposing especial Trust and Confidence in your Fidelity, Courage, Good Conduct, and Attachment to the State of Maryland and the United States, you are by these Presents constituted and appointed Major General of the

Upper Division of Militia on the Western Shore of the State aforesaid. You are therefore carefully to discipline the Officers and Soldiers under your Command, who are hereby strictly enjoined to obey you as their Major General and in this, and all other Respects, you are diligently to discharge the Trust committed to you by these Presents, according to the Laws and Constitution of this State, and of the United States, and such Rules and Regulations as under the Authority thereof are or may be established: This Commission to be in Force until lawfully revoked.

GIVEN at Annapolis, this Eighth Day of April Anno Domini One Thousand Seven Hundred and Ninety five.

J. H. Stone

Source:　Maryland Historical Society, Baltimore
　　　　　Sam Smith Collection MS 1790

Appendix II

Letter from Jonathan Dayton to Samuel Smith

Elizabethtown N. Jersey Jan. 26th 1813

Sir,

The disgrace which the American arms have sustained on our lake frontier has so much affected me, that I cannot forbear to write to you, whose feelings as a soldier, and as a patriot, must I am sure, be equally alive on the occasion. It is needless for me, especially in addressing myself to you, to point out the real sources of our disasters - sufficient it is to know that under such Officers as were most injudiciously named for the commands at the three various and distant points of attack, success was impossible.

Dearborn is utterly unqualified for the office of Commander in chief, or even for that of Commander of a Division of the Army, and you must be perfectly sensible of it. Neither he, nor Hull, nor Smyth (Alex) are the men capable of leading our troops to conquest, and to glory- A change, a great, a complete change must take place, and that speedily, or our next campaign will be even more disastrous than the last. You must yourself again come forward, and reassume your military character - take the command of our Armies, or if that be already promised to Mr. Munro, as report says it is - take the command of that important portion of them which will be destined in the spring to invade Canada. You will reinspire all with that all essential in a General, confidence, which under most unhappy auspices has nearly expired and cannot be revived without extraordinary efforts on the part of our Government. Why is it, my dear Sir, that Congress are so infatuated as to direct enlistments of their 20,000 men for one year only? No error can be more unpardonable - none more fatal. By the time they are sufficiently trained and disciplined to deserve the name of Regulars - by the time they are enured to the regimen of the camps and the duties of the field, they will be dismissed, and this too before they can have effected the objects for which they were raised. I need not tell you - but those who do not know ought to be told, that the whole of both the Canadas cannot be conquered in one campaign, by any force which you can raise. All of the Upper, and so much of the lower, as extends to Montreal be subdued, and here it is that Advance and main body of the army must pass the first winter, preparatory to a descent again on Quebec in the spring before the St. Lawrence is open for the admitting of ships with supplies and reinforcements. Place all this, I entreat, in the debate on the new Army bill, in that strong clear and striking point of view, of which you are so capable, and have the term of enlistment of consequence extended from one to at least two years. Having done this, and whatever else you can towards establishing the military system on a firm and proper basis with a view to the coming crisis and emergency within the few short weeks which remain of the present season, let us then hear of you, and see you on a character in which you are not only more wanted, but can be so much more useful.

With great respect and regard I am

Dear Sir Your very hum. servant

Jona: Dayton

General Samuel Smith

Source: Maryland Historical Society, Baltimore
                    Sam Smith Collection MS 1790

Bibliography

Special Archives

Baltimore City Archives, Baltimore MD

Ft. McHenry Archives, Baltimore MD

Library of Congress Archives, Washington DC

Maryland Historical Society Archives, Baltimore MD

Maryland State Archives, Annapolis MD

Society of the Cincinnati Archives, National Headquarters, Washington DC

U.S. National Archives, Washington DC

U.S. Naval Academy Archives, Nimitz Library, Annapolis MD

U.S. Navy Yard Library Archives, Washington DC

University of Virginia Archives, Charlottesville VA

Manuscripts

Maryland Historical Society, Baltimore

John Eager Howard Papers

James McHenry Papers

Samuel Smith Collection

General John Stricker Papers, MS 1435

Library of Congress, Washington, DC

James Monroe Papers

Samuel Smith Family Papers (Manuscript Division, Madison Building)

University of Virginia, Charlottesville

James Madison Papers

Smith-Carter Family Papers

Newspapers and Magazines

Annapolis

Maryland Gazette

Baltimore

American

Architectural Review

Fowler, L. (1909). "Montebello." November, pgs 146-149.

Federal Republican

Maryland Historical Magazine

Cassell, F. (1971). "Response to Crisis: Baltimore in 1814." *Maryland Historical Magazine 66: pg. 261-287.*

Chew, R. (2009). "The Origins of Mob Town: Social Division and Racial Conflict in the Baltimore Riots of 1812." *Maryland Historical Magazine 104: pgs 272-301.*

Colston, F. (1907). "The Battle of North Point." *Maryland Historical Magazine* Vol. 2, pgs 111-125.

George, C. (1993). "The Family Papers of Maj. General Robert Ross, the Diary of Colonel Arthur Brooke, and the British Attacks on Washington and Baltimore of 1814." *Maryland Historical Magazine 88: pg. 300-316.*

Robinson, R. (1944). "Controversy over the Command at Baltimore." *Maryland Historical Magazine* Vol. 39, pgs. 177-198.

Sheads, S. (2008). "H.M. Bombship Terror and the Bombardment of Fort McHenry."

Maryland Historical Magazine 103: pg. 257-267.

Sheads, S. and Von Lunz, A. (1998). "Defenders' Day, 1815-1998 A Brief History." *Maryland Historical Magazine 93: pg. 301-315.*

Smith, Samuel (1910). "The Defense of Fort Mifflin." *Maryland Historical Magazine* Vol. 5, pgs. 211-228. Letters from Smith & General Washington during the defense of Fort Mifflin, Sept. 27 to Nov. 11, 1777.

Stricker, J. Jr. (1914). "General John Stricker." *Maryland Historical Magazine* Vol. 9, pgs 209-218.

Weeks, B. (1989). "This Present Time of Alarm: Baltimoreans Prepare for Invasion." *Maryland Historical Magazine 84: pg. 259-266.*

Nile's Weekly Register

Patriot

Sun

Smith, R. (1811). *Address to the People of Baltimore*

Washington, DC

National Intelligencer

The American Secretaries of State and Their Diplomacy

Tansill, C. "Robert Smith", edited by Samuel Flagg Bemis, Vol. 3, pgs 151-200.

New York City

Historical Review

Smith, Samuel (1870). XVII pgs. 81-93. "The Papers of General Samuel Smith." Submitted to the editor, Henry B. Dawson, by John Spear Smith. This was a biographical sketch of Sam Smith up to his resignation from the regular army during the American Revolution. The original manuscript is in the Samuel Smith Family Papers of the Manuscript Division of the Library of Congress (Microfilm Reel 5).

Books by Subject Area

1. War of 1812

Arthur, B. (2011). *How Britain Won the War of 1812: The Royal Navy's Blockades of the United States, 1812-1815.* London, UK: Boydell Press.

Borneman, W. (2004). *1812: The War That Forged A Nation.* NY, NY: Harper Collins.

Brown, R. (1964). *The Republic In Peril; 1812.* NY, NY: Columbia University Press.

Cranwell, J. (1940). *Men of Marque: A History of Private Armed Vessels out of Baltimore during the War of 1812.* NY, NY: Norton & Co.

Crawford, Michael J. (Ed) (2002). *The Naval War of 1812: A Documentary History, Vol. 3.* Washington: United States Department of Defense

Cress, L. (1982). *Citizens in Arms: The Army and the Militia in American Society to 1812.* UNC Press.

Dudley, W. (Editor) (2011). *The Naval War of 1812: A Documentary History, Vols. 1-3.* Washington, DC: Naval Historical Center.

Eshelman, R. (2011). *A Travel Guide To The War of 1812 In The Chesapeake.* Baltimore, MD: The Johns Hopkins University Press.

Eshelman, R. and Sheads, S. (2013). *Chesapeake Legends and Lore from the War of 1812.* Charleston, SC: History Press.

George, C. (2000). *Terror on the Chesapeake: The War of 1812 on the Bay.* Shippensburg, PA: White Maine Books.

Gleig, g. (1821). *Narrative of the Campaigns of the British Army at Washington and New Orleans.* London

Hickey, D. (Editor) (2013). *The War of 1812: Writings from the Second War of Independence.* NY, NY: Literary Classics.

Howard, H. (2012). *Mr. and Mrs. Madison's War: America's First Couple and the Second War of Independence.* NY, NY: Bloomsbury Press.

James, W. (1818). *A Full and Correct Account of the Military Occurrences of the Late War Between Great Britain and the United States of America. Volume II.* London: Published for the Author

Langguth, A. (2006). *Union 1812: The Americans Who Fought the Second War of Independence.* NY, NY: Simon & Schuster.

Mahan, A. (1905). *Sea Power in Its Relations to the War of 1812*. NY, NY.

Perkins, B. (Editor) (1962). *The Causes of the War of 1812*. Hinsdale, IL: The Dryden Press.

Pratt, J. (1925). *The Expansionists of the War of 1812*. NY, NY.

Taylor, A. (2010). *The Civil War of 1812: American Citizens, British Subjects, Irish Rebels, and Indian Allies*. NY, NY: Alfred Knopf Publishers.

Utt, R. (2012). *Ships of Oak, Guns of Iron: The War of 1812 and the Forging of the American Navy*. Washington, DC: Regnery Publishing.

2. Sam Smith

Cassell, F. (1971). *Merchant Congressman in the Young Republic: Sam Smith of Maryland, 1752-1839*. Madison, WI: University of Wisconsin Press.

MacDonald, J. (1997). *Tale of Two Soldiers: JE Howard, Samuel Smith and the New Nation*. Thesis for Masters Degree. Maryland Historical Society MF 179.H848 M135.

Pancake, J.(1972). *Samuel Smith and the Politics of Business*. University of Alabama Press.

3. Battle of Baltimore

Lord, W. (1994). *The Dawn's Early Light.* Baltimore, MD: Johns Hopkins University Press.

Marine, W. (1901). *The Battle of North Point.* Baltimore, MD: Hanzsche and Co. Printers.

Sheads, S. (1995). *Fort McHenry.* Baltimore, MD: The Nautical and Aviation Publishing Company of America.

Sheads, S. (1999). *Guardian of the Star Spangled Banner: Lt. Colonel George Armistead and the Fort McHenry Flag.* Baltimore, MD: Toomey Press.

Vogel, S. (2013). *Through the Perilous Fight: Six Weeks That Saved the Nation.* NY, NY: Random House.

Whitehorne, J. (1997). *The Battle for Baltimore 1814.* Baltimore, MD: The Nautical and Aviation Publishing Company of America.

4. Napoleonic Wars

Bell, D. (2007). *The First Total War: Napoleon's Europe and the Birth of Warfare as We Know It.* NY, NY: Houghton Mifflin Company.

Harvey, R. (2007). *The War of Wars: The Epic Struggle Between Britain and France 1789 to 1815.* NY, NY: Carroll & Graf Publishers.

Rothenberg, G. (1999). *The Napoleonic Wars.* NY, NY: Harper Collins Publishers.

5. French and Indian War

Borneman, W. (2006). *The French and Indian War: Deciding the Fate of North America.* NY, NY: Harper Collins.

Fowler, W. (2005). *Empires at War: The French and Indian War and the Struggle for North America, 1754 to 1763.* Ny, NY: Walker & Company.

6. American Revolution

Jackson, J. (1986). *Fort Mifflin, Valiant Defender of the Delaware.* James & Sons: Norristown, PA.

Johnston, H. (1878). *The Campaign of 1776 Around New York and Brooklyn.* Brooklyn, NY: The Long Island Historical Society.

McCulough, D. (2005). *1776.* NY, NY: Simon & Schuster.

Piecuch, J. and Beakes, J. (2009). *John Eager Howard in the American Revolution.* Nautical & Aviation Press: Charleston, NC.

7. George Washington

Aikman, L. (1983). *Rider With Destiny: George Washington.* McLean, VA: Link Press.

Ellis, J. (2004). *His Excellency: George Washington.* NY, NY: First Vintage Books.

Flexner, J. (1974). *Washington: The Indispensable Man.* NY, NY: A Bay Back Book.

Newcomb, J. and Lillback, P. (2006). *George Washington's Sacred Fire.* West Conshohocken, PA: Providence Forum Press.

8. Washington DC

De Angelis, G. (2004). *It Happened In Washington DC.* Guilford, CT: The Globe Pequot Press.

Hunt, G. editor (1906). *The First Forty Years of Washington Society* (from the writings of Margret Bayard Smith) . NY, NY.

Kelly, C. (2005). *Best Little Stories from the White House.* Naperville, IL: Cumberland House.

Mann, N. (2006). *The Sacred Geometry of Washington DC: The Integrity and Power of the Original Design.* NY, NY: Barnes & Noble.

Pitch, A. (1998). *The Burning of Washington: The British Invasion of 1812.* Annapolis, MD: Naval Institute Press.

Standiford, L. (2008). *Washington Burning: How A Frenchman's Vision for Our Nation's Capital Survived*

Congress, the Founding Fathers, and the Invading British Army. NY, NY: Crown Publishing.

9. James and Dolley Madison

Allgore, C. (2006). *A Perfect Union: Dolley Madison and the Creation of the American Nation*. NY, NY: Henry Holt & Company.

Peterson, M. (Editor) (1974). *The Founding Fathers: James Madison, A Biography in His Own Words, Vol. 1 and 2*. NY, NY: Newsweek.

Rutland, R. (1981). *James Madison and the Search for Nationhood*. Washington DC: US Government Printing Office.

10. Masonry in Early America

Bullock, S. (1996). *Revolutionary Brotherhood: Freemasonry and the Transformation of the American Social Order, 1730 to 1840*. Chapel Hill, NC: University of North Carolina.

Hagger, N. (2007). *The Secret Founding of America: The Real Story of Freemasons, Puritans and the Battle for the New World*. NY, NY: Sterling Publishing.

Hall, M. (2008). *The Secret Destiny of America*. NY, NY: Penguin Group.

Morse, S. (1924). *Freemasonry In The American Revolution.* NY, NY: Kessinger Publishing.

Sora, S. (2003). *Secret Societies of America's Elite: From the Knights Templar to Skull and Bones.* Rochester, VT: Destiny Books.

Tabbert, M. (2005). *American Freemasons: Three Centuries of Building Communities.* NY, NY: New York University Press.

Wasserman, J. (2008). *The Secrets of Masonic Washington: A Guidebook to Signs, Symbols, and Ceremonies at the Origin of America's Capital.* Rochester, VT: Destiny Books.

11. Leadership

Antal, J. (2013). *7 Leadership Lessons of the American Revolution: The Founding Fathers, Liberty and the Struggle for Independence.* Havertown, PA: Casemate Publishers.

Barber, B. (2004). *No Excuse Leadership: Lessons from the US Army's Elite Rangers.* Hoboken, NJ: Wiley & Sons.

Blanchard and Miller (2012). *Great Leaders Grow: Becoming A Leader for Life.* San Francisco, CA: Berrett-Koehler Publishing.

Blanchard, K. (2013). *The Servant Leader*. Nashville, TN: Thomas Nelson Publishing.

Blanchard, K. et. al. (2013). *Trust Works: 4 Keys to Building Lasting Relationships*. NY, NY: Harper Collins.

Cameron, K. (2012). *Positive Leadership: Strategies for Extraordinary Performance*. San Francisco, CA: Berrett-Koehler Publishing.

Cannon, J. (2004). *Leadership Lessons of the Navy Seals*. NY, NY: McGraw-Hill.

Cashman, K. (2008). *Leadership from the Inside Out: Becoming A Leader for Life*. San Francisco, CA: Berrett-Koehler Publishing.

Cohen, E. (2002). *Supreme Command: Soldiers, Statesmen and Leadership in Wartime*. NY, NY: The Free Press.

Cohen, W. (2001). *The Stuff of Heroes: The Eight Universal Laws of Leadership*. Longstreet Press.

Covey (1992). *Principle Centered Leadership*. NY, NY: Simon & Schuster.

Crandall and Collins (2007). *Leadership Lessons from WestPoint*. San Francisco, CA: Jossey-Bass.

Creveld, M. (1977). *Supplying War: Logistics*. NY, NY: Cambridge University Press.

Department of the Army (2011). *The US Army Leadership Field Manual*. Pacific Publishing Studio.

Dobelli, R. (2013). *The Art of Thinking Clearly*. NY, NY: Harper Collins.

Dotlitch et. al. (2004). *Leadership Passages: The Personal and Professional Transitions That Make or Break a Leader*. San Francisco, CA: Jossey-Bass.

Fox, W. (2011). *Six Essential Elements of Leadership: Marine Corps Wisdom from a Medal of Honor Recipient*. Annapolis, MD: Naval Institute Press.

Galford and Maruca (2006). *Your Leadership Legacy: Why Looking Toward the Future Will Make You a Better Leader Today*. Boston, MA: Harvard Business School Press.

George et. al. (2007). *True North: Discover Your Authentic Leadership*. San Francisco, CA: Jossey-Bass.

Gilbert, R. (2006*). Extraordinary Leadership: Thinking Systems, Making A Difference*. Falls Church, VA: Leading Systems Press.

Gladwell, M. (2013). *David and Goliath: Underdogs, Misfits and the Art of Battling Giants*. Little Brown & Company.

Glaser, J. (2013). *Conversational Intelligence: How Great Leaders Build Trust and Get Extraordinary Results*. Brookline, MA: Bibliomotion.

Goleman, D. (2013). *Focus: The Hidden Driver of Excellence*. NY, NY: Harper Collins.

Goleman, G. (2011). *Leadership: The Power of Emotional Intelligence*. Northampton, MA: More Than Sound.

Goman, C. (2011). *The Silent Language of Leaders: How Body Language Can Help or Hurt How You Lead*. San Francisco, CA: Jossey-Bass.

Handel, M. (2001). *Masters of War: Classical Strategic Thought*. Portland, OR: Frank Cass Publishers.

Hansen, M. (2010). *Collaboration: How Leaders Avoid the Traps, Build Common Ground, and Reap Big Results*. Boston, MA: Harvard Business School Publishing.

Heath, C. and D (2013). *Decisive: How to Make Better Choices in Life and Work.* NY, NY: Crown Publishing.

Heifetz, R. (2009). *The Practice of Adaptive Leadership*. Boston, MA: Harvard Business School Publishing.

Hybels, B. (2012) *Courageous Leadership*. Grand Rapids, MI: Zondervan Press.

Irwin, T. (2014). *Impact: Great Leadership Changes Everything*. Dallas, TX: BenBella Books.

Kaipa and Radjou (2013). *From Smart to Wise: Acting and Leading With Wisdom*. San Francisco, CA: Jossey-Bass.

Kaplan, R. (2013). *What You're Really Meant to Do: A Road Map for Reaching Your Unique Potential*. Boston, MA: Harvard Business School Publishing.

Klein, G. (2014). *Seeing What Others Don't: The Remarkable Ways We Gain Insights*. NY, NY: Public Affairs.

Kolenda, C. (2001*). Leadership: The Warrior's Art*. Carlisle, PA: The Army War College Foundation Press.

Lafley and Martin (2013). *Playing to Win: How Strategy Really Works*. Boston, MA: Harvard University Press.

Leavitt, M. and McKeown, R. (2013). *Finding Allies, Building Alliances: 8 Elements that Bring and Keep People Together*. San Francisco, CA: Jossey-Bass Publishing.

Lencioni, P. (2006). *Silos, Politics and Turf Wars*. San Francisco, CA: Jossey-Bass.

Linsky and Heifetz (2002). *Leadership on the Line: Staying Alive through the Dangers of Leading*. Boston, MA: Harvard Business School Publishing.

Mahler, M. (2011). *Live Life Aggressively*.

Maxwell and Covey (2007). *The 21 Irrefutable Laws of Leadership: Follow Them and People will Follow You.* Nashville, TN: Thomas Nelson Publishing.

Maxwell, J. (2007). *Be A People Person: Effective Leadership Through Effective Relationships.* Colorado springs, CO: David C. Cook Publishers.

McCoy, B. (2006). *Passion of Command: The Moral Imperative of Leadership.* Marine Corps Association Bookstore.

McIntosh and Rima (2007). *Overcoming the Dark Side of Leadership.* Grand Rapids, MI: Baker Books.

Miller and Blanchard (2011). *The Secret of Teams: What Great Teams Know and Do.* San Francisco, CA: Berrett-Koehler Publishing.

Miller, M. and Lencioni, P. (2013). *The Heart of Leadership: Becoming a Leader People Want to Follow.* San Francisco, CA: Berrett-Koehler Publishers.

Neustadt and May (1988). *Thinking In-Time: The Uses of History for Decision Makers.* NY, NY: A Free Press.

Nye, R. (2001). *The Challenge of Command.* NY, NY: Berkley Publishing group.

Parks, S. (2005). *Leadership Can Be Taught: A Bold Approach for a Complex World.* Boston, MA: Harvard Business School Publishing.

Phillips, D. (1997). *The Founding Fathers On Leadership.* NY, NY: Warner Books.

Price, T. (2008). *Leadership Ethics: An Introduction.* NY, NY: Cambridge University Press.

Puryear, E. (2000). *American Generalship: Character is Everything: The Art of Command.* Presidio Press.

Rath and Conchie (2009). *Strengths Based Leadership: Great Leaders, Teams, and Why People Follow.* NY, NY: Gallup Press.

Rice et. al. (2013). *WestPoint Leadership: Profiles in Courage*

Schein, E. (2010). *Organizational Culture and Leadership.* San Francisco, CA: John Wiley & Sons.

Schwartz, P. (1996). *The Art of the Long View: Planning for the Future in An Uncertain World.* NY, NY: Doubleday Press.

Schwartz, R. (2013). *Smart Leaders, Smarter Teams.* San Francisco, CA: Jossey-Bass Publishing.

Sinek, S. (2011). *Start With Why: How Great Leaders Inspire Everyone to Take Action.* NY, NY: Penguin Group.

Snyder, S. and George, B. (2013). *Leadership and the Art of Struggle: How Great Leaders Grow Through Challenge and Adversity.* San Francisco, CA: Berrett-Koehler Publishers.

Taylor et. al (Editors) (2008). *Military Leadership: In Pursuit of Excellence.* Westview Press.

Thomas, J. (2013) *Leadership Embodied: The Secrets to Success of the Most Effective Navy and Marines Corps Leaders.* Annapolis, MD: Naval Institute Press.

Useem and Bennis (1999). *The Leadership Moment.* NY, NY: Random House.

Von Schell, A. et. al. (2013). *Battle Leadership.* Echo Point Books.

Williams, D. (2005). *Real Leadership: Helping People and Organizations Face Their Toughest Challenges.* San Francisco, CA: Berrett-Koehler Publishing.

Wills, G. (1994). *Certain Trumpets: The Nature of Leadership.* NY, NY: Touchstone.

12. Other

Adams, H. (1877). *Documents Relating to New-England Federalism.* Boston, MA: Brown & Company.

Ammon, H. (1990). *James Monroe: The Quest for National Identity.* Charlottesville, VA: The University Press of Virginia.

Bladensburg Races, A Poem: First printed in 1816, reprinted in 1865

Boorstein, D. (1958). *The Americans: The Colonial Experience.* NY, NY: Vintage Books.

Bowers, C. (1936). *Jefferson in Power: The Death Struggle of the Federalists.* Cambridge, MA: Riverside Press.

Browne, G. (1980). *Baltimore in the New Nation 1789-1861. Chapel Hill, NC:* UNC Press.

Carson, B. (1990). *Ambitious Appetites: Dining, Behavior and Patterns of Consumption in Federal Washington.* Washington DC: American Institute of Architects Press.

Dwight, T. (1833). *History of the Hartford Convention: with a Review of the Policy of the United States Government which Led to the War of 1812.* NY, NY: N. & J. White.

Fields, Barbara J. (1985). *Slavery and Freedom on the Middle Ground: Maryland During the Nineteenth Century.* New Haven, CT: Yale University Press.

Footner, H. (1940). *Sailor of Fortune: The Life and Adventures of Commodore Joshua Barney, USN.* NY, NY.

Garitee, J. (1977). *The Republic's Private Navy: The American Privateering Business as Practiced by Baltimore during the War of 1812.* Middletown: Wesleyan University Press.

Hagger, N. (2005). *The Secret History of the West: The Influence of Secret Organizations on Western History from the Renaissance to the 20th Century.* NY, NY: O Books.

Harding and Harding (1999). *Seapower and Naval Warfare, 1650 to 1830.* London, UK: UCL Press.

Howe, D. (2007). *What Hath God Wrought: The Transformation of America, 1815 - 1848.* NY, NY: Oxford University Press.

Hunt, G. (1906). *The First Forty Years of Washington Society.* NY, NY: Charles Scribner's Sons.

McCutcheon, M. (1993). *Everyday Life in the 1800's: A Guide for Writers, Students and Historians.* Cincinnati, OH: Writers Digest Books.

Meacham, J. (2008). *American Lion: Andrew Jackson in the White House.* NY, NY: Random House.

Myers, J. (2010). *Liberty Without Anarchy: A History of the Society of the Cincinnati.* Charlottesville, VA: University of Virginia Press.

Norton, L. (2000). *Joshua Barney: Hero of the Revolution and 1812.* Annapolis, MD: Naval Institute Press.

Nugent, W. (2008). *Habits of Empire: A History of American Expansion.* NY, NY: Vintage Books.

Paullin, C. (1910). *Commodore John Rodgers.* Cleveland, OH: The Arthur H. Clark Company.

Robbins, K. (2013). *James McHenry: Forgotten Federalist.* Atlanta, GA: University of Georgia Press.

Ryerson, E. (1970). *The Loyalists of America and Their Times: From 1620 to 1816.* NY, NY: Haskell House Publishers.

Schroeder, J. (2006). *Commodore John Rodgers: Paragon of the Early American Navy.* University Press of Florida.

Toll, I. (2006). *Six Frigates: The Epic History of the Founding of the U.S. Navy.* NY, NY: W.W. Norton.

Wood, G. (2009). *Empire of Liberty: A History of the Early Republic, 1789 - 1815.* NY, NY: Oxford University Press.

Yarema, A. (2006). *American Colonization Society: An Avenue to Freedom?* University Press of America.

Zinn, H. (2006). *A People's History of the United States: 1492 to Present.* NY, NY: Harper Press.

Other References and Web Sites

Biographical Directory of the United States Congress

Senate Historical Office: Donald A. Ritchie, Historian

Senate Historical Office at 202-224-6900, 201 Hart Senate Office Building, Washington, DC, 20510-7108.

see The Patriotic Marylander 1914 Edition

Papers of James Madison: See the Online Digital Edition